O.P.

1000

From Whole Log To No Log

From Whole Log To No Log

A History of the Indians Where the
Mississippi and the Minnesota Rivers Meet

By
Edward J. Lettermann

Dillon Press, Inc., Minneapolis, Minnesota 55401

Copyright© 1969 by Dillon Press, Inc.
Minneapolis, Minnesota. All rights reserved.
Printed in the United States of America
Library of Congress Number 79-91356
SBN Number 87518-012-4

To my wife Aldine
For her patience and assistance

Table of Contents

Prologue: The Tale of the Logs i

The Whole Log

The First Inhabitants 7
The Mantanton Dakota *1680-1740* 17
Wabasha I and his People *1740-1775* 29
Old Enemies and New Enemies *1775-1803* 40
American Foothold *1803-1812* 56
White Conflict *1812-1820* 66

The Shared Log

Arrival of the Military *1820-1825* 77
Setting the Bounds *1825-1830* 87
Penasha's Village and Black Dog's Village *1815-1833* 94
Cloudman and the Village on Lake Calhoun *1828-1839* 100
The Mission at Lake Harriet *1835-1839* 116
Kaposia under Big Thunder *1834-1845* 124

No Log At All

"Move Over" *1837-1838* 139
The End of a Dream *1838-1840* 145
Kaposia and Neighboring St. Paul *1846-1851* 165
The Last Years on the Lower Minnesota *1847-1851* 184
The Great Treaty *1851-1852* 198
New Cities and New Settlers *1852 On* 216

Epilogue 231

Appendices
  Major Chiefs 243
  Chronology 243
  Map 249

Footnotes 250

Bibliography 261

Index 269

List of Illustrations

Frontispiece
Unidentified Sioux

The Whole Log
Indian Mounds in St. Paul ... 8
Little Crow III (Walks Pursuing a Hawk) ... 54
Map of Pike's Explorations ... 62

The Shared Log
Cloudman's Village ... 102
Layout of Cloudman's Village ... 114
Attack on Lake Pokegama ... 130

No Log at All
Medicine Bottle's Village ... 162
Little Crow V (His Red Nation) ... 168
Kaposia ... 174
St. Paul in 1851 ... 178
Black Dog's Village ... 190
Mendota ... 200
Big Eagle II ... 212
Teepees in Minneapolis ... 218
St. Anthony and Minneapolis in 1857 ... 220
Sioux in St. Paul ... 226

Epilogue
Camp at Fort Snelling, 1862 ... 236

Prologue: The Tale of the Logs

SOME HISTORIANS WOULD give us the impression that in the year 1835 there was only a military fort on the bluff where the Mississippi and Minnesota Rivers meet—that there were neither settlers nor towns in that large area where the cities of Minneapolis and St. Paul now stand.

But they are not quite correct. In 1835 there were a number of villages — villages with musical names like Kaposia (light footed), Oanoska (Long Avenue), and Reyataotonwe (Inland Village) — and there were settlers, whose ancestors had migrated from the north some one hundred years earlier. These people were the Mdewakanton Dakota or Sioux and they numbered perhaps one thousand, scattered in a number of villages over the region where the Twin Cities now stand.

Then, in the year 1834 the first missionaries arrived from the East. The following year the Rev. Stevens came from New York to minister to the residents of the Inland Village. With him he brought his family which included a little foster daughter, Jane DeBow, and for them he built a Mission House at nearby Lake Harriet. Jane was about six years old when she arrived at Lake Harriet and it seems appropriate that we be introduced to the Mdewakanton Dakota first through her eyes.

Jane's first acquaintance among the natives surrounding her new home was an Indian boy of her own age who stood on the shore of the lake beckoning to her. She joined him and together they had a feast of wild strawberries, the fruit being abundant, and the size and quality now rarely seen out of the gardens.

Her acquaintance thus begun, extended among the Indian children; she romped and played with them, waded and swam in the waters of the lake in their company; learned the Dakota language; which later she spoke like one of themselves, and the comradeship lasted all the years of her association with the Sioux Indians.[1]

By the time Jane DeBow had grown to womanhood, the bustling towns of St. Paul and Minneapolis had replaced the modest Indian villages. Thousands of settlers were pouring into these new towns and carving farms out of the surrounding land. Jane herself married a Mr. Gibbs and with him built a house northwest of St. Paul.*

But Jane's friendship with her childhood playmates survived the changed conditions. The pressures of the newer immigrants had compelled the Indians to move from their earlier villages; yet each year Little Beckoning Boy and the other childhood playmates, now grown, visited Jane at the Gibbs farm house. On one such occasion Little Beckoning Boy lamented the plight of his people and put it to his friend this way: Once the Indian had the whole log. But when the white man came, the Indian moved over and let him sit down. Then the white man began to push and crowd, until the Indian had almost no place on the log.

---

*This pioneer farm home of Heman Rice Gibbs has been preserved as a museum by the Ramsey County Historical Society. It is part of the Gibbs Farm Museum and is located in Rose Township, now Falcon Heights.

Many years later Abbie Gibbs Fischer, Jane's daughter, recalled the final sad visit of these Dakota to the Gibbs home:

> The last time these good friends came was in May, 1862. A large body of them on horseback camped on the little knoll across from our house where the dead tree now is. They were sullen and despondent. Well do I remember the dramatic gestures of their chief as he eloquently related their grievances. My mother followed every word he said for she knew how differently they were situated from their former condition. When she first knew them, they owned all the country—the whites nothing. In these few years, the tables had been turned. Her heart bled for them, her childhood companions.
>
> They slept that night in our kitchen, Little Beckoning Boy and the other playmates. I can still see the sad look on my mother's face as she went from one to the other giving each a big, hot breakfast and trying to cheer them. She could see how they had been wronged. She stood and watched them sadly as they mounted their ponies and vanished down the old trail.[2]

By 1863 the Mdewakanton Dakota had been driven completely from Minnesota. Had Little Beckoning Boy returned, he might have concluded his allegory by saying that in the end the Indian had no log at all.

ately at the top in a pot of water. Next the water was changed to a 5 per cent salt solution in one case, and a 10 per cent solution in the other. After a few hours the wilted leaves of the cabbage had completely recovered, while the turnip had only partially recovered. A day or so later the salt solution was changed to ordinary water, and in a few hours the cabbage and turnip were once more wilted. On placing the plants in salt solution again the leaves resumed their turgid condition. Whenever the plant was placed in fresh water the leaves wilted, and when the plant was placed in the salt solution the leaves became turgid. The old explanation that the cells can stand only pure water, and that salts of any kind tend to plasmolyze them and destroy the turgor, has to be abandoned. The results above described prove that certain plants and probably all are capable of putting forth the required amount of energy to overcome the osmotic resistance of a 10 per cent solution of salt.

As the experiment stands the results might be explained by assuming that the cell secreted salt in sufficient amount to overcome the osmotic resistance of the solution. This can not be the case, however, since the above-named plants thrive equally well when placed in a 10 per cent solution of sugar. Recent experiments of Livingston[1] make it extremely probable that such plants can absorb water from solutions having as high osmotic pressures as 50 atmospheres. Among the fungi there are species that can absorb water from substrata containing as much as 80 per cent of sugar, which is equivalent to about 200 atmospheres of osmotic pressure.

These experiments, together with the early theoretical considerations of Pfeffer, make it highly improbable that the osmotic activity of the cell is to be explained by assuming that only pure water can enter. Moreover, water is given off to the transpiration current and used in the metabolism of the cell. A continuous loss of water, then, is inevitable, and the supply must be kept up by the activity of the cell in obtaining water either from ordinary water or from solutions. This process requires energy, and the amount must often be large. Where does this energy come from?

It will be shown later that the energy used in absorption comes from the respiration of the cell, and that this energy is exerted directly against the osmotic pressure of the surrounding solution. If the cell is capable of using the energy

[1] Livingston, B. E., "Relation of Soil Moisture to Desert Vegetation," *Bot. Gaz.*, 50 (1910) 241.

The First Inhabitants

ONE HUNDRED YEARS AGO, the missionary Samuel Pond wrote of the difficulties inherent in any history of the Indians.

> They had no way of preserving dates farther back than three or four generations. Of all more ancient events they could only say, "That happened long ago." The time which had elapsed since the occurrence of more recent events they measured not by years but by generations. So they would say of an event that it happened in the time of their father, grandfather, or great grandfather, but did not go back more than three or four generations.[1]

This difficulty certainly arises as one begins a history of the Indians who lived in the valley where the Mississippi and Minnesota Rivers meet. Today it is difficult to determine with any degree of certainty precisely when Indians first began living there. Mounds, excavated village sites, and burial pits all indicate the presence of inhabitants and intrigue modern investigators, but they are slow to yield their secrets.

The missionaries who came here in the 1830's asked the Indians about the mounds, but the Indians either said they had no idea who built the mounds or they attri-

Old photograph of the Indian Mounds in St. Paul.
Minneapolis Public Library Bromley Collection.

buted them to the Indians whom their forefathers had driven away generations before. The Dakota remembered that when their fathers had come to the banks of the Minnesota River, they had found Iowa Indians living there in earthen homes. The Chippewa at Mille Lacs said that when they drove the Dakota away from those shores, they had to drop sacks of gunpowder into the chimney holes of the Dakota earthen lodges to extricate the inhabitants. The Indians and the missionaries, it seems, were inclined to believe that the low, nearly flat mounds such as those found along the banks of the Minnesota were in truth the remains of earthen homes, but they believed that conicle mounds such as those which can be seen to this day in St. Paul's Indian Mounds Park were burial mounds. However, there have been various and contradictory theories. In 1876 a St. Paul historian wrote:

> Who and what the Mound Builders were, whence they came, their history and ultimate fate are wrapped in an impenetrable mystery that will perhaps baffle the most industrious student.
> It is agreed that they were a simple and somewhat ingenious race who subsisted partly by cultivating the earth and partly by the chase, and were more civilized than the Red Race who subsequently occupied this region. By what means they disappeared will never be known, but it is beyond doubt that they vanished centuries ago.
> The only memorials of their existence that have survived are the mounds that lie scattered about, generally but erroneously called Indian Mounds. The Indians deny that their race built them, asserting that their fathers "found them here when they first possessed the land."[2]

Yet in 1908 another could write: "From the testimony of Captain Jonathan Carver, it seems to me well nigh certain that some or all of the mounds on Dayton's bluff in St. Paul were built for sepulture [burial] by the Sioux. It was their custom to enwrap the body after death and to expose it in the open air on a scaffold of poles. Later, in many cases, the relatives kept some of the bones and carried them in their journeys, and Carver saw such bundles of bones brought there by the Sioux for interment."[3]

Present-day scholars attribute the mounds to Indians who lived here during the Woodland cultural era, which dates from about 1000 B.C.; but they do not directly connect the ancestors of the Dakota who occupied Minnesota in the 19th century to the Indians who built the mounds. The mounds have contained ancient artifacts as well as man-made trade goods. Because of this scholars seem to feel the mounds were added to, both in numbers and in size, until late in the Woodland era, even as recently as the period of French exploration.

Be that as it may, there were thousands of mounds to be found in the early days in the southeastern part of the state as well as in the Twin Cities area. Of the more than thirty which were once found on the bluffs above St. Paul, only six have been preserved in Indian Mounds Park.

Although the first recorded visits of white men to this area were made nearly a century before, Jonathan Carver in 1766 was the first explorer to mention "the burying place of several bands of the Naudowessie (Sioux or Dakota) Indians," adding that "they always bring the bones of their dead to this place." It is generally accepted that he is referring to the mounds area and that the Indians with him buried their ancestor's bones in or near the existing mounds, perhaps even adding to the mounds.

Systematic excavation of these burial mounds was begun in 1856 by the Rev. Edward D. Neill, Minnesota's first historian. At that time there were eighteen mounds. In the largest of these he found some broken pottery and fragments of a human skeleton. Other diggings about a decade later unearthed additional human bones as well as more pottery fragments, a broken earthen pipe, charcoal and ashes, and a large number of sea shell beads.

The most extensive investigation of the site was made between 1879 and 1883 by Theodore H. Lewis and William H. Gross. At that time sixteen mounds remained. In addition to finding more bones, shells, ornaments and arrowheads, they discovered under one mound eight stone cists or box-like compartments, each about one by two feet and about seven inches deep. These were formed by setting flat pieces of limestone on edge and covering them with stone slabs and boulders, making a heap of stones nine feet in diameter and nearly two feet high. Over this heap of stone, dirt was piled to make the mound about fifty feet in diameter and nine feet high. In these cists there were human bones, but no complete skeletons. Another of these mounds yielded a hearth or fireplace, causing some to interpret the mounds as religious or sacrificial altars as well as memorials to the dead.

Probably more fruitful sources of information concerning the prehistoric inhabitants of the present Twin Cities area were ancient village sites. We know the Dakota Indians who lived here in the eighteen thirties were afraid to build their villages away from the rivers or upstream from St. Anthony Falls; yet during the latter part of the nineteenth century many Indian village sites were found in the area between here and Mille Lacs, an area not occupied by either the Chippewa or the Dakota during the era of settlement by the whites. Both nations considered this region a "road of war" and too dangerous for occupancy.

Lewis reported no less than ten sites "known by frequent stone implements and their fragments scattered in the soil," within the city limits of St. Paul. More recently, as excavations have been made for highways and other improvements, excellent finds have been made along the bluffs of the lower Minnesota River and in other areas.

Writing in the 1850's, Dr. Thomas Williamson, missionary to Little Crow's Band at Kaposia village in present South St. Paul, stated:

> The situation of many mounds indicate that they had their origin as burying places of the dead. But by far the most numerous class appear from their size and situation to be what Dakota tradition says they are, the remains of houses, made of poles and bark, covered with earth.
>
> Mounds of this class are found in clusters of from less than a dozen to upwards of fifty, arranged irregularly as we find the bark houses of the Indians at present. Their base usually approaches to an oval form. Their length is from ten to forty feet, and a few exceed this, with a height of from one to two feet, to three or four. Very few of this class exceed four feet . . . .
>
> Back of them we find the land level, or nearly so, dry and fertile. In front, it descends towards some water, and almost always there is a lake or morass in sight, indicating that the inhabitants depended for subsistence partly on cultivating the earth and partly on water fowl or roots which they obtained from wet, swampy land.[4]

Whether or not most of the mounds were the remains of earthen habitations is now purely a matter of speculation since none of this type seems to have remained. Early farmers plowed right over them and, their contents scattered forever, they soon lost their distinctive characteristics.

It has really not been demonstrated that the prehistoric Indians of the area were significantly different from the later inhabitants of this region, nor that they were more, or less, "civilized." It is evident that they did not have iron tools and implements, but that they did use copper, not smelted or cast, but beaten and shaped in the cold state. They also formed implements of stone, fired pottery and used bone for awls, needles, and fish hooks.

The first white man whom we know to have written specifically of the area we now call the Twin Cities was Father Louis Hennepin, who passed here in the spring of 1680. In his *Description de la Louisiane* (1683) he makes no mention of Indian villages being situated in the immediate vicinity of the present Twin Cities, but within the decade, in 1689, a Frenchman by the name of Nicolas Perrot, who had established a trading post at the foot of Lake Pepin, did comment specifically:

> We did transport ourselves to the country of the Nadouessioux (the Dakota) on the border of the River Saint Croix and at the mouth of the River Saint Peter (Minnesota River), on the bank of which were the Mantantans, and farther up into the interior to the north east of the Mississippi as far as the Menchokatonx (the Mdewakanton), with whom dwell the majority of the other Nadouessioux who are at the north east of the Mississippi.[5]

And in 1700, Pierre Charles LeSueur, who had built Fort L'Huillier near present Mankato, found that the "Scioux of the East" were dissatisfied with his establishing a post so far west, having informed him

> . . . that this river (the Blue Earth River) was the country of the Scioux of the West, of the Ayavois (Iowa) and the Otoctatas (Oto) a little further; that it was not their custom to hunt on the grounds of others without being invited by those to whom they belonged; that when they should wish to come to the fort to get supplies, they would

be exposed to be cut off by their enemies coming up or going down these rivers (the Blue Earth and the Minnesota), which are narrow; and that if he wished to take pity on them, he must settle on the Mississippi in the neighborhood of the mouth of St. Peter's river, where the Ayavois, the Otoctatas, and the Scioux could come as well as they.⁶

So we see that this region at the confluence of the Mississippi and the Minnesota Rivers and the present Twin Cities area was occupied by the Dakota Indians when the first explorers and fur traders came here.

For the sake of convenience, the Indian nations have been divided or classified according to their language characteristics. In 1929, the linguist Edward Sapir arranged the languages of North American Indians into six major groups, and these have become generally accepted as a method of classification, although there are differences of opinion among experts with respect to many of the details of these groupings. Two of these linguistic groups, the Algonkin-Wakashan Stock and the Hokan-Siouan Stock, come into consideration when any study of Minnesota Indians is attempted. To the former belong the Chippewa. The latter is divided into three families, the Iroquois Family, the Caddo Family, and the Siouan Family. The Indian tribes making up the Siouan Family include the Dakota, the Iowa, the Oto mentioned by LeSueur, and a host of other tribes, some of which, it is interesting to note, built earthen homes well into the historic period.

There were a few Siouan tribes on the Atlantic coast in Virginia and the Carolinas. It may be that the family originally inhabited the Ohio River valley and that sometime in the dim past it was split in two parts. Possibly a small portion was forced eastward, while the major portion migrated down the Ohio River valley and into the valley of the Mississippi, some going north on that river, others northwest on the Missouri. At any rate, when the first Frenchmen entered the upper Mississippi, the Siouan tribes occupied much of the area west of the river, the region we call the Great Plains. The Dakota occupied nearly all of present Minnesota, including the region east of the Mississippi. How far west their lands extended is difficult to determine, but it is believed that until the middle of the eighteenth century the Dakota were pretty well confined to Minnesota and eastern South Dakota.

Today we think of the Sioux as the dashing buffalo hunters of the prairies who confronted the U. S. Cavalry during the Indian war era. The term Sioux has become practically synonymous with the branch of the Siouan tribes called the Teton Dakota, or, more correctly, the Lakota. The French explorers first saw the Dakota, as it were, through the eyes of the Ojibway or Chippewa with whom they traded. Thus to the Chippewa word *Na-dou-esse* meaning *snakes* or *enemies,* the French added the plural *x* and gave it a French spelling — Nadouesioux — which was later shortened to Sioux or Scioux.

The Dakota, which word in their own language means an alliance of friends, traditionally believed that at one time they had all lived in the woodland area of central Minnesota with Mille Lacs as the very center of their Dakota world. The Dakota gave to Lake Mille Lacs the name Mdewakan, meaning Mystery Lake. Thus those Dakota who lived there were the Mdewakanton, or People of the Mystery Lake. There were seven tribes: the Yankton, the Yanktonai, the Teton, and the four tribes later to be known as the Santee: the Mdewakanton, the Wahpeton, the Wahpekute, and the Sisseton. In the 1670's the Santee lived near Mille Lacs. North of them, probably at Red

Lake, lived the Yankton and the Yanktonai. The Teton seem to have already moved out of the woodlands and were generally located somewhere between present Willmar and Big Stone Lake. This westward movement was due to the pressure on the Dakota by Algonquin tribes, notably the Ojibway or Chippewa, and the availability of larger herds of buffalo on the prairie. In time, the Yankton and the Yanktonai followed the Teton, and by 1730 the Santee tribes alone remained in present Minnesota. By this time, however, they too were being pushed from their woodland home. The Mdewakanton seem to have been the last Dakota tribe to live in the Mille Lacs area.

When they left their ancestral homes, however, they did not follow their brethren out onto the prairie, but rather chose to migrate southward and eastward down the Mississippi, finally setting up more or less permanent villages on that river below the Falls of St. Anthony, and on the banks of the lower Minnesota. Access to French trade goods doubtless played an important role in this migration.

The Mantanton Dakota
1680-1740

THE FIRST HISTORIC glimpses of the red men inhabiting the vicinity now occupied by the Twin Cities are gleaned from reports written during the fur trade era.

Trade had begun at Mille Lacs as early as the 1670's under two Frenchmen, Pierre Esprit Radisson and his brother-in-law Medard Chouart, the Sieur des Groseilliers. In 1679 and '80, Daniel Greysolon, the Sieur du Luth, showed the traders how to reach the Dakota and opened the area to a host of illegal traders, the "courers de bois" or "rangers of the woods." It was not until a half century later that legal trading posts were established.

The Mantanton "at the mouth, and on the banks" of the Minnesota River traded not only with their brethren of Mille Lacs but also with their eastern neighbors. They benefited from this trade and earnestly desired that permanent French posts be established near them too. Their desire seemed to be nearing fulfillment in 1686 when Nicolas Perrot built a post on the east shore of Mississippi's Lake Pepin and traded with them, but Iroquois trouble in the East called him back there for a time. In 1688 and '89 he again appeared on Lake Pepin and traded with the Dakota, but shortly after he returned to Montreal.

Another voyageur, Pierre Charles Le Sueur, who had accompanied Perrot in 1689, built a temporary post on the island now called Prairie Island in the spring of 1694 or '95, but this endeavor, too, was short lived.

The avowed major purpose of both Perrot's and Le Sueur's attempts to establish posts in this area was to prevent the Ojibway in the northern part of Wisconsin and the Dakota on the upper Mississippi from continuing or renewing their hereditary warfare. The Ojibway, or Saulteur, as the French called them had originally resided on the St. Lawrence River, but had been driven from their ancestral homes by the powerful Iroquois about the middle of the seventeenth century, and had early established villages around the Sault Ste. Marie. Part of the tribe then moved around the north shore of Lake Superior, but the larger division came south and moved into northern Wisconsin. As they became stronger and pressure increased on them from behind, they spread out across central Minnesota, pushing the Dakota before them, in spite of the many attempts made by the French to effect permanent peace between the warring tribes. Groseilliers and Radisson, Du Luth, Perrot, and Le Sueur all labored for peace, and all succeeded to some extent, but only temporarily. As soon as they left the country, hostilities would be renewed —sometimes immediately, more often after a period of a few years.

The French, during the course of the bloody warfare between these two powerful tribes, while traveling through their country on their trading, had often suffered death indiscriminately with Dakota or Ojibway at the hands of their blood-seeking war parties. The interests of the fur trade had also severely suffered, for the warriors of either tribe neglected their hunts to join in the more favorite pastime of war and bloodshed, and their continually prowling war parties prevented the more peaceful-minded and sedate hunters from seeking the beaver in the regions where they abounded in greatest plenty.[7]

In the summer of 1695 Le Sueur took with him to Montreal a number of Ojibway and Dakota tribesmen, including a Mantanton chief by the name of Tioscaté. On the eighteenth of July the French governor, Count Frontenac, held an audience with these visitors.

Tioscaté's part in this meeting is especially interesting. He spread a beaver robe upon the ground before the assembly, then placed upon it twenty-two arrows, each arrow signifying a Dakota village that desired French trade. When this ceremony was completed, he made the following plea:

> It is not on account of what I bring that I hope he who rules this earth will have pity on me. I learned from the Saulteurs (Ojibway) that he wanted for nothing, that he was the master of the Iron, that he had a big heart, into which he could receive all nations. This has induced me to abandon my people to come to seek his protection, and to beseech him to reject me not, though I appear poor in your eyes. All the nations here present know that I am rich and the little they offer here is taken from my lands.[8]

Though the governor told Tioscaté that he would send Le Sueur back to them the following season, events transpired which further delayed the establishment of a permanent trading post among the Mantanton and Mdewakanton on the upper Mississippi.

Tioscaté died in Montreal. An old ecclesiastical register reads: "Sioux, age forty years, deputy of that nation, who had the happiness to be baptized and died at M. Le Sueur's, the interpreter of this Indian. Buried 3 Feb. 1696 at Montreal."

Le Sueur was in France at the time seeking from the king a permanent command over the land of the eastern Sioux, a ten-year monopoly on its fur trade, and the right to mine copper in this region. Only the last request was granted. The decision was made to abandon all trade with the Sioux because of the over abundance of furs on the French market and also because of the enmity of the Ojibway and other tribes. All official or legal fur trade was to be concentrated at Montreal until further notice.

In about the same year that Tioscaté was in Montreal pleading for permanent trading posts for his people, nearly the entire Mantanton division of the Mdewakanton Dakota was destroyed by the Ojibway at the Battle of Point Prescott, as the disaster is now called.

William Warren graphically recounts the Ojibway version of this momentous struggle in his *History of the Ojibways*. He calls it one of the most successful actions in their history: "One of their story tellers, who in his youth had long remained a captive among the Dakotas states explicitly that on this occasion the Ojibways secured three hundred and thirty scalps, and many more (Dakota) than this were thought to have perished in the water."

The massacre ended a peace which had lasted several years. On the St. Croix the two tribes had intermingled freely and some intermarriage had taken place between them, "but the love of war and bloodshed was so inherent in their nature, and the sense of injuries inflicted on one another for centuries rankled so deep in the breast of so many in each tribe that even these ties could not secure a long continuance of this happy state of peace and quiet."[9]

It seems that during a Dakota war dance, a Dakota brave shot an arrow into a part-Ojibway "to let out the hated Ojibway blood which flowed in his veins." The wound was not fatal, but the Ojibway could not forget the incident and for months silently brooded over it. Finally, he left the Dakotas to visit his Ojibway relatives on Lake Superior. Being kindly received by them, he related his tale of injustice and persuaded them to raise a war party and avenge the deed.

Returning to the Dakota, he told them that a large party of his people would soon arrive to smoke the pipe of peace with them.

> Fully believing these tales, the Dakota collected their scattered hunters and sent runners to their different villages to invite all their people to come and camp with them, in order to receive the expected peace party of the Ojibways, and join in the amusements which generally ensued whenever they thus met in considerable numbers. The tribe (it being the season of the year which they generally passed in leisure and recreation) gathered in large numbers and pitched their camp on the south side of Lake St. Croix, near its outlet into the Mississippi.[10]

The Ojibway arrived at this large encampment without discovery and during the night sent five young men into the Dakota camp to spy and count the enemy. Returning to the camp and making their report, they reflected that there were so many that they "became confused and could count no more." At earliest dawn, the Ojibway attacked. The Dakota were taken completely by surprise;

> their women and children ran shrieking to the water's side, and hastily jumping into their wooden canoes, they attempted to cross to the opposite shores of the lake. The wind, however, had increased in force, and sweeping down

the lake in fearful gales, it caused the waves to run high and in many instances the crowded canoes filled with water or upset, launching the fleeing women and children into a watery grave.[11]

In 1700 Le Sueur returned to America, this time by way of the Gulf of Mexico and the Mississippi instead of the Great Lakes. He proceeded up the Mississippi River, through the Twin Cities area, ascended the Minnesota River to the Mankato region, and built a post on the Blue Earth River, which he called Fort L'Huillier.

While he was stationed there, the remnants of the Mantanton visited him and invited him to a great banquet at which were assembled about a hundred warriors. After they had finished eating and had smoked a pipe, Ouacantapai (Wakantape), their chief, pointed to the assembled people, and said to the Frenchmen:

> Behold the remnants of that great village which thou didst formerly behold so numerous; all the others have been slain in war, and the few that thou seest in this cabin accept the present that thou makest them, and are resolved to obey that great chief of all nations, of whom thou hast spoken to us. Thou must no longer regard us as Sioux, but as Frenchmen, and instead of saying that the Sioux are wretches who have no sense, and fit only to plunder and rob the French, thou wilt say: My brothers are unhappy men who have no sense, we must try and get them some; they rob us, but to prevent them I will take care that they do not lack iron, that is to say, all kinds of goods. If thou dost this, I assure thee that in a short time, the Mantantons will become French, and will no longer have the vices with which thou reproachest them.[12]

Le Sueur left in the spring of 1701 to return to France and about a year later the soldiers he had left behind decided to abandon the post because of harassment by the enemies of the Sioux.

For a quarter of a century after the abandonment of Ft. L'Huillier, no official efforts were made to establish a French post near the remaining Mantanton and the Mdewakanton. But this doesn't mean that all contact with Europeans ceased during these years. The unlicensed traders, the hardy *courers de bois,* had been trading among them, and continued doing so. After 1720 their visits were fairly regular, but even before that date they were no uncommon sight, ranging the valleys and canoeing the streams. For obvious reasons, they did not publish reports of their travels or make attempts to interest more traders to come here. Nor did they make any effort to limit the distribution of firearms, lead and powder to the Indians. In 1720, the Canadian governor complained of them to the king: "This (the influx of illegal traders) contributes more than anything else to foster the haughtiness of the Sioux and the Foxes."

In the fall the traders would come, their canoes laden with bundles of bright cloth, knives, beads, and other trinkets. Above all, they brought the weapons on which the red men were becoming increasingly dependent — game was becoming harder to procure by the ancient methods and the tribes were more and more cramped as the unclaimed hunting areas between them grew ever narrower. As competition increased among the traders, they brought with them more and more hard liquor, which was fast becoming the red man's favorite trade article.

The Indian would give anything he had to procure these coveted trade goods, even the robe off his back. And, strangely enough, this is what the trader wanted most. The furs of worn robes were ranked at the top of the six grades of beaver. The traders called it winter-greased beaver and it "was greased by the Indian's own bodies, having been worn by them until the long hair fell out and the skin was soft and supple." Besides the six grades of beaver, the cheapest grade being dry summer beaver, many other pelts were prized by the traders and could be exchanged for the white man's goods—among them mink, otter, and marten.

Inter-tribal trade flourished between the red nations in close contact with the whites and those more remote tribes such as the Dakota. This inter-tribal trade brought English goods to the Twin Cities, not only from the Hudson Bay area, but also from the English settlements along the East coast. The red men to the southeast of the Dakota, the Fox and others, benefited from this trade activity and in periods of peace carried on a lively trade with them.

Eventually historical events did bring about the establishment of a more or less permanent French post near the Twin Cities Area. In the middle 1720's the French observed that the English were acquiring a great influence over these "distant nations." A dispatch of the period read:

> It is more and more obvious that the English are endeavoring to interlope among all the Indian nations, and to attach themselves. They entertain constantly the idea of becoming masters of North America, pursuaded that the European nation which will be possessor of that section will, in the course of time, be master of all America.[13]

In order to counteract this English influence and to bring under control the Indians in central and southern Wisconsin, who had nearly always hated the Canadians preferring to trade generally with the English or the Louisiana Frenchmen, a post was established on Lake Pepin. It was intended to be permanent and was named Fort Beauharnois after the governor of Canada. The "Company of the Sioux" was granted the exclusive right of trading in the country of the Dakota and wherever they went in their hunting expeditions. It was found that the fort or post was on too low ground and a few years later it was moved to higher ground. At this time, we are told, a large number of Dakota established a village in the immediate vicinity of the fort.

This Dakota village very likely consisted of Mdewakanton from Mille Lacs and the remaining Mantanton. From the frequent references to the Wapeton in Le Sueur's Journal we may assume that many of them, too, were drawn to this post and lived in the village nearby. We have no indication that this village was permanent, nor that these Dakota returned here summer after summer as they did to the village sites later, in the days when Minnesota was being settled by the pioneers. In fact, we can be reasonably certain that the village was not permanent, but we see here a beginning of the migration of the Mdewakanton from the Mille Lacs region and the upper Rum River area southward through the Twin Cities area and southeastward down the Mississippi.

During the period when the Company of the Sioux and its successor, the Second Company of the Sioux, had a monopoly on the Dakota trade, enmity between the Dakota and the Ojibway not only continued, but actually seems to have increased. This period has been called the fiercest and most sanguinary in the history of these tribes.

It was during this time, in the early 1740's, that the Mdewakanton who still lived at Mille Lacs were finally driven from their ancient homes never to return except as small marauding war parties seeking vengeance upon the Ojibway who took up residence there soon after.

Warren believed that the Battle of Mille Lacs occurred

in the seventeenth century even before the Battle of Point Prescott, as Folwell notes on page 81, Volume I, *History of Minnesota*. Warren relates that under attack from the Ojibway "the Dakotas took refuge in their earthen lodges." To harass the Dakota and dislodge them from these retreats, the Ojibway threw small bundles of gunpowder into the smoke holes of the lodges.

> Not having as yet, like the more fortunate Ojibways, been blessed with the presence of white traders, the Dakotas were still ignorant of the nature of gunpowder, and the idea possessing their minds that their enemies were aided by spirits, the Dakota were easily dispatched.[14]

Under cover of night, the Dakota fled and Ojibway tradition recalls "that the former dwellers of Mille Lacs became, by this three day's struggle, swept away forever from their favorite village sites."

That "the Dakota were still ignorant of the nature of gunpowder" certainly could not be true in 1740, after their many years of acquaintance with the French and at least two decades of very active trade with them. One is forced to conclude that the momentous "three day's struggle" which the old Chippewa told of was merely the first or, possibly, the greatest in a series of conflicts which culminated in the 1740's in a final unrecorded battle that "swept the former dwellers of Mille Lacs away forever from their favorite village sites." It seems highly unlikely that a single battle would be sufficient cause for the Dakota to completely evacuate "such a desirable point," as Warren himself characterizes it, "a spot covered with their permanent earthen wigwams and the resting place of their forefathers."

Jacob Brower observes the following concerning the date

of the Battle of Kathio, as he calls this encounter related by Warren:

> Unfortunately there has not come into notice any definite information concerning the correct date when the Isanti people were forced to retire from Mille Lac, and it must be arbitrarily determined as having occurred between the time when the Dakotas were last observed by Le Sueur (1700) and 1766 when Carver drew on his map the western boundary line of the Chippewa territories from the St. Croix to Mille Lac, when the Sioux were also marked on the same map as having a village on the east side of the lower portion of Rum River. Such considerations can be safely appealed to in fixing the date of the battle after Le Sueur's explorations and not a long period of time before Carver's advent into the Sioux country at the mouth of the Rum River; hence error of date cannot be materially damaging if we believe it to have been not long before 1750.[15]

In the 1957 edition of Warren's *History of the Ojibway* published by Ross and Haines, Inc. there is a map of "Important Sioux-Chippewa Battle Grounds." Here the date of the Battle of Kathio is given as 1740.

Theodore C. Blegen in his *Minnesota, A History of the State* (1963) informs us: "Decisive were battles fought in the 1740's when the invading Chippewa drove the Sioux out of their northern villages, including the strategic Dakota center at Mille Lacs."

It is unfortunate that we must rely only on Ojibway tradition for narratives of these important happenings in the history of the Dakota. Although the Dakota who lived here in the days of the early missionaries carefully preserved accounts and related them to their children just as they received them from their fathers, few of these traditions have come down to us. "I have heard all the vicissitudes of a battle with the names and exploits of the chief actors minutely and graphically described," S. W. Pond writes, and again: "I have heard many of these legends," yet "failed to make a record of them, thinking it could be done anytime." With the Sioux Outbreak, all possibility of obtaining these legends and traditions was lost. "The young men," he wrote in the late 1860's or early 70's "have had their minds occupied with things new and strange, and the old men who had treasured in their memories things of the past are all gone."[16]

Prior to the Sioux Outbreak a man by the name of James W. Lynd had nearly finished a history of the Dakota similar to Warren's *History of the Ojibway,* but in that holocaust most of his manuscript was destroyed by the Indians and soldiers.

Wabasha I and His People
1740-1775

WHILE WE HAVE no Dakota traditions or legends concerning the battle or battles which displaced the Mdewakanton from the Mille Lacs area, we do have tradition on the period that followed in their history.

One of their most popular recollections was that at one time all the Mdewakanton were united in one band and had their village on the bank of the Minnesota near Nine Mile Creek, the area we know as Bloomington. It was also said that Wabasha was then the chief, and that before Wabasha their people had no chiefs. Presumably, by this last remark, they meant that there was neither before nor after him a greater chief than the mighty Wabasha, the first of a series of hereditary head men of the Mdewakanton branch of the Dakota Nation or confederacy.

It is a reasonable assumption that either Tioscaté, who died in Montreal in 1696, or Wakentape, who followed Tioscaté as the chief of the Mantanton as reported by LeSueur, was the father of the legendary figure known as Wabasha I, who had in his veins both Dakota and Ojibway blood.

Schoolcraft gives this account of the first Wabasha's lineage and birth:

While the Sioux and Ojibway were living in amity near each other and frequently met and feasted each other on their hunting grounds and at their villages, a Sioux chief of distinction admired and married an Ojibway girl by whom he had two sons.

When the war broke out, those persons of the hostile tribes who had married Ojibway wives and were living in the Ojibway country withdrew, some taking their wives along, and others separating from them. Among the latter was the Sioux chief. He remained a short time after the hostilities commenced, but finding his position demanded it, he was compelled with great reluctance to leave his wife behind, as she could not with safety have accompanied him into the Sioux territories.

As the blood of the Sioux flowed in the veins of her two sons, neither was it safe for her to leave them among the Ojibways. They were, however, by mutual agreement, allowed to return with their father.[17]

It would seem from his later adventures that Wabasha I was born about the end of the second decade of the eighteenth century. Doane Robinson places his birth at about 1718, but produces no evidence which justifies so explicit a statement.[18] If the assumption is correct that either Tioscaté or Wakentape was the father of Wabasha I, it would seem more probable that Wakentape was the chief described by Schoolcraft who married a Chippewa maiden during a period of amity between the tribes, or as some would have it, "took prisoner a Chippewa woman and made her his wife."[19] This was not an uncommon practice, even in the days of the early missionaries to our area.

While still a very young man, Wabasha I exhibited a heroism which endeared him to his people forever. One tradition has it that in 1736, a war party of the Mille Lac Dakota had killed and scalped two French voyageurs near the Illinois River. In reprisal, two Dakota and an Ottawa were taken as prisoners to Montreal.

It seems there was some delay in the return of the Dakota, and the tribe was apprehensive for their safety, and that a number of them had been waiting for them at the portage of the Wisconsin. When they were informed by some Ottawa, just landing from a canoe, in answer to their anxious questions that their hostages sent the year before had been burned at Montreal, in anger and ill-directed resentment, they had tomahawked the Ottawa.[20]

On the ninth of March in 1740, Wabasha and nine other Dakota gave themselves up to the French in expiation for this slaughter. After reciting the facts Wabasha concluded: "We have not come here with the idea of hiding anything from you, nor of excusing our people. We have come to deliver up our bodies. We are ready to receive the punishment we deserve." Wabasha was said to have survived this crisis to become a great chief, one of whom Neill could write: "Tradition has preserved the name of no greater nor better man than Wabasha."

By this time the decline of French power in North America was well advanced. Since the eighteenth century, France had been almost continually engaged in wars with the English. In time this struggle manifested itself in colonial conflict on American shores also. The French and Indian War is dated from 1756 to 1763, but fighting had ceased already in September of 1760. During the next two years, French forts were turned over to the English. Most of the trading posts had already been abandoned by 1756, as was the Joseph Marin Sioux post on Lake Pepin.

According to another widely held tradition it was in 1760, when Wabasha was forty years old, that he performed the feat which most endeared him to his people. Previously, when the French had been in complete control of the Great Lakes and the fur trade, Wabasha and his people had generally sided with them against the English. This tradition holds that about this time, Ixatapa, one of Wabasha's braves, quarreled with a trader at Mendota named Pagonta—Mallard Duck as the Indians called him—and shot him as he sat smoking in his cabin. The incident so alarmed the traders that they quit the Dakota country immediately. The Indians suffered much from lack of goods during the winter that followed, and in the spring they held a council and decided to surrender Ixatapa to justice and implore the traders to return to the region. A hundred braves were selected to accompany the prisoner on the journey to Quebec, now under English control, and Wabasha became the leader of the group. As they proceeded farther from home, many deserted the band including the prisoner himself; thus by the time the delegation reached Quebec, only five members remained.

Upon receiving audience with the authorities, Chief Wabasha presented himself to the authorities in Ixatapa's place to be executed for the murder of the trader, but the British, caring little about the death of a trader in the wilds of Minnesota, forgave him and promised that traders would be sent the next season. They gave him presents, among them a number of chief's medals which he was to distribute among the headmen of the Dakota, keeping one for himself.

Before they could return home, smallpox broke out among the small band and all the Dakota are said to have succumbed to it but Wabasha. The next spring he returned to his people and was ever after remembered in story and legend as the chief who brought the traders to the nation when starvation and destitution threatened it.

The Whole Log 33

After Wabasha's journey to Quebec about 1760, if it really occurred then, the Mdewakanton Dakota came in contact with the English at Green Bay, which had been occupied by them since October of 1761. Extracts from the journal[21] of Lt. James Gorrell, an English officer at Green Bay, read:

> On March 1, 1763, twelve warriors of the Sous came here. It is certainly the greatest nation of Indians ever yet found.
>
> I told them I was glad to see them, and hoped to have a lasting peace with them. They then gave me a letter wrote in French, and two belts of wampum from their king, in which he expressed great joy on hearing of there being English at this post. The letter was written by a French trader whom I had allowed to go among them last fall with a promise of his behaving well, which he did, better than any Canadian I ever knew.

A few months later:

> On the nineteenth of June, 1763, a deputation of Winnebagoes, Sacs, Foxes, and Menominees arrived with a Frenchman named Penasha. This Penasha is the same man who wrote the letter the Sous brought with them in French, and at the same time held council with that great nation in favor of the English by which he much promoted the interest of the latter, as appeared by the behavior of the Sous. He brought with him a pipe from the Sous, desiring that as the road is now clear, they would by no means allow the Chippewas to obstruct it, or give the English any disturbance, or prevent the traders from coming up to them. If they did so, they would send all their warriors and cut them off.

This Penasha* mentioned by Lt. Gorell in his journal

---
*Pinchow or Pinichon in French. See footnote on p. 63.

was the renowned Penasha of whom William Joseph Snelling also wrote.[22] According to Snelling, Penasha and another Frenchman were engaged by a trader on the banks of the Minnesota near Wabasha's band. They suspected that the trader was not going to pay them for their services, and by holding a pistol to the trader's breast, the two French adventurers compelled him to write a certificate recommending them as deserving confidence of all persons engaged in the fur trade and competent to take charge of a trading post.

> Armed with these papers, abandoning their concubines, and stealing a canoe, they hurried to Mackinac and showed the superintendent of the fur trade their recommendation. This led to Penasha's employment as a trader, and his companion's engagement as an interpreter, at a good salary.[23]

While trading in the area of the Minnesota-Mississippi, Penasha took as his wife a Sioux maiden, probably a member of Wabasha's band and fathered a son by her, who was also known as Penasha (II). However, the elder Penasha did not remain long at the mouth of the Minnesota.

> Quarrelling with a Sioux, Penasha killed him, took his scalp and fled to the Ojibway, where he was received as a friend. But in time he was captured by the Sioux, who, full of revenge, prepared to burn him. Realizing his dangerous position, he asked as a favor that they would allow him the distance of an arrow as shot, and then be chased by all the young men on horseback. The proposition was accepted, as it would increase their pleasure, as well as justify their revenge. But he ran as men only run when life is in danger, and escaped. He never came back to the Sioux country.[24]

Wabasha eventually moved further down the Mississippi

to the Upper Iowa River with most of his band. Penasha II was chosen chief of the remaining band[25] and it is he who later signed the grant for the land at Fort Snelling with Zebulon Pike. It might also be noted here that Penasha II was the grandfather of Good Road. As nearly as can be determined, it was Good Road and his father Penasha III who signed the 1830 Treaty at Prairie du Chien.

Jonathan Carver visited the Dakota in the fall and winter of 1766-1767. The purpose of his visit was to make preparations for an extended expedition to the Pacific Coast. His difficulties in acquiring the needed supplies brought the venture to an abrupt halt, but of interest here is his stay with the Dakota and his observations concerning the area and the inhabitants:

> In November, 1766, while Carver was making the canoe journey up the Mississippi, with a French Canadian and a Mohawk Indian as his companions, he stopped to spend a day or two with a band of Sioux somewhere between Lake Pepin and the mouth of the St. Croix. These were the first Sioux to whom he came in his journey, and he won their admiration and gratitude by his cool and intrepid conduct in meeting a large number of hostile Ojibways who were approaching to attack the Sioux. In a long parley with several of the chiefs of the Ojibways, interpreted by the Frenchman of his party, Carver persuaded them to desist from the intended attack.[26]

On a map accompanying Carver's own narration of his journey, *Travels Through the Interior Parts of North America*, published in 1778, the country of the Sioux is shown to be west of the Mississippi except for a relatively small area on its eastern side, extending from the St. Croix northwesterly to the Elk River which was called—"River St. Francis."

Proceeding onward, he examined the cave formerly existing in the base of the river bluff near the east edge of the present city of St. Paul. It was long known as Carver's Cave and was much visited, but in 1872 and later, it was partly dug away in the construction of railways along the base of the bluff.

When Carver arrived at the mouth of the Minnesota river, the first severe cold of the coming winter had formed ice on the Mississippi that obliged him to leave the canoe, but he went forward afoot, with a young Winnebago chief, past the falls of St. Anthony, where he arrived November 17th, to the mouth of Elk River, which he called the St. Francis. There he turned back November 21st . . .

Returning to the Minnesota River and finding it not yet frozen, Carver ascended it with his canoe to the neighborhood of the present city of New Ulm, or farther, and wintered in that region with Sioux tribes of the prairies. He continued with them until late in April, and somewhat fully (he claimed) learned their language.[27]

Folwell, commenting on this claim, writes that it is "a statement which may be considerably discounted. If he learned the name 'Dakota' by which those Indians called themselves, he did not note it in his journal."

From Carver's *Travels* . . . we learn that "Near the river St. Croix reside three bands of the Naudowessie Indians called the River Bands. This nation is composed at present of eleven bands. Those I met here are termed the River bands because they chiefly dwell near the banks of this river; the other eight are generally distinguished by the title of Nadowessies of the Plains and inhabit a country more to the westward. The names of the former are Nehogatowonas, the Mawtawbauntowahs and **Shashweentowahs**."

It is not clear whether these are names of individual

bands (or villages). Winchell felt that Carver's Mawtawbaun were the Mantanton, but we have no explanation of what sub-divisions of the Dakota nation the Nehogatowanas and the Shashaweentowahs were thought to be.

If Carver's names for the "three river bands" were the old names of villages or bands of the area, namely Red Wing's, Little Crow's, and Wabasha's, then Carver must have considered Shakopee's band a part of the Prairie Dakota. This might be true if Shakopee's village was then situated at the same place it later was, near present Shakopee, nearer the later Wapeton village at Little Rapids, than to the Mdewakanton villages on the Minnesota.

Although he was writing of the names Indians gave to themselves and each other, Carver himself admits that "there is some difficulty attending an explanation of the manner in which the Indians distinguish themselves from each other," and it is safe to assume, especially in the light of Folwell's statement concerning Carver's ability in handling the Dakota language, that even in his own mind, he was not too clear on the divisions of the Dakota nation.

It is clear now that he was not the great explorer he made himself out to be in his book and that this fact was evident even to his contemporaries.[28] However, Carver did leave us a record of the cave which bears his name and of the red man's life here in the region of the Greater Twin Cities.

> About thirty miles below the Falls of St. Anthony, at which I arrived the tenth day after I left Lake Pepin, is a remarkable cave of an amazing depth. The Indians term it Wakonteebe (Wakan-tepee—Mysterious Dwelling Place). The entrance into it is about ten feet wide and the height of it five feet. The arch within is near fifteen feet high and about thirty feet broad. The bottom consists of fine clear

sand. About twenty feet from the entrance begins a lake, the water of which is transparent and extends to an unsearchable distance, for the darkness of the cave prevents all attempts to acquire a knowledge of it. I threw a small pebble towards the interior parts of it with my utmost strength; I could hear that it fell into the water, and, notwithstanding it was of a small size, it caused an astonishing and horrible noise that reverberated through all those gloomy regions.

I found in this cave, many Indian hieroglyphics which appeared very ancient, for time had nearly covered them with moss, so that it was with difficulty I could trace them. They were cut in a rude manner upon the inside of the wall, which was composed of a stone so extremely soft that it might be easily penetrated with a knife; a stone everywhere to be found near the Mississippi.

At a little distance from this dreary cavern is the burying place of several bands of the Naudowessie Indians. Though these people have no fixed residence, living in tents and abiding but a few months in one spot, yet they always bring the bones of the dead to this place.[29]

Returning from his winter's stay with the Sioux of the West, Carver "left the habitations of the hospitable Indians the latter end of April 1767, accompanied on my journey by nearly three hundred of them to the mouth of the river St. Pierre (Minnesota). At this season these bands annually go to the great cave before mentioned."

When he had arrived at the great cave, and the Indians had deposited the remains of their deceased friends in the burial place adjacent to it, they held their great council, "wherein they settle their operations for the ensuing year."[30]

A later edition of Carver's *Travels* . . . included the description of a vast grant of lands alleged to have been made to Carver by the Dakota at the spring conference in

1767, but Carver's claim and all the legal action attending it for many decades in the nineteenth century have little to do with this resumé. It suffices to record that the lands did include the Twin Cities area.[31]

The reader may be interested in one historical footnote to Carver's claim. In 1824 a group of Mdewakanton Dakota, including Little Crow III, traveled to Washington to meet President Monroe:

> Little Crow brought home with him a fine, new double-barreled gun, which, he said, a white medicine man had given him for signing a certain paper. Moreover the sacred personage had promised to send a keel-boat full of goods to the Kaposia band. The "medicine man," or holy person was Rev. Samuel Peters, an Episcopal clergyman, who had been a noted Tory during the War of the Revolution. He asserted that in 1806 he had purchased from the heirs of Captain Jonathan Carver the right to the "Carver tract." His present and the somewhat munificent one promised Little Crow were doubtless intended to suborn the chieftain in the clergyman's interest.[32]

Old Enemies and New Enemies
1775-1803

THE ERA BETWEEN Carver's visit and that of Lieutenant Zebulon M. Pike of the United States Army in 1805 was a period of almost continuous warfare for the Dakota at the mouth of the Minnesota River and in the regions of the upper Mississippi. Until about 1775, the Mdewakanton Dakota and the Ojibway were engaged in very intensive conflict, at least by Indian standards. Though driven from their former haunts in the Mille Lacs region, the Mdewakanton were not willing to give up all their rights to the territory that lies between Lake Mille Lacs and the Minnesota River, nor were they willing to be pushed farther to the south. After 1775, the warfare took the form rather of Indian assistance, if it may be so termed, in the wars between the whites. The red men, traditionally at enmity with each other, often ended up on the same side of the conflict, on the side of the British against the Americans.

The end of the eighteenth century also saw the gradual settling down of the Indians of the Twin Cities area into a number of semi-permanent summer villages of comparatively fixed location.

In 1768, a major battle occurred between the Dakota and the Ojibway which has become known as the Battle of Crow Wing. More than five hundred Mdewakanton warriors, it is said, set out to seek vengeance on the villages of the Ojibway in the Mille Lacs region. Knowing the entire country well, having recently held it as their own, the older warriors were determined to lead the force around the north of the Mille Lacs area, then down the Mississippi River, to destroy the Ojibway villages, one by one. They did succeed in reaching the upper reaches of the river by a circuitous route through Gull, Leech, Cass, and Winnibigoshish Lakes, and ambushed about thirty young women who were out berry picking, taking a number of them prisoner. They also fell upon a number of isolated families of the Ojibway and obtained a few scalps. With this they were content and decided to return to their homes, passing down the Mississippi in their fleet canoes. Their seeming success, however, was soon turned into bitter defeat.

Some time earlier a party of about sixty Ojibway warriors had left their village at Sandy Lake, gone south and scoured the Dakota country for scalps. Finding none, they started for home. At Crow Wing they discovered the encampment of the large Dakota party which had recently passed through on its way north. The Ojibway party decided to await the anticipated return of the Dakota and give them battle. As Warren reports:

> About half a mile below the main mouth of the Crow Wing, on the east side of the Mississippi the river makes a curve, and the whole force of the current is thrown against the banks in the bend, which rise almost perpendicular from the waters edge, fifty feet high. Boats or canoes passing down the river are naturally drawn by the current immediately under this bank, and with an eye to this advantage, the Ojibway warriors determined to post themselves here in ambuscade. They dug several holes

along this bank, for two or three hundred feet, capable of holding eight or ten men each, in rows, from which perfectly invisible to their passing enemy and sheltered from their missiles, they intended to commence the attack.[33]

The Ojibway perceived that the number of the enemy was extremely large and made their preparations accordingly. They even sent out a hunting party to procure meat to be dried against the time of waiting. Scouts were sent up river to watch for the approach of the Dakota and eventually the enemy canoes came into view:

> Still moving in a compact flotilla, the current at length brought them immediately under the deadly ambuscade. At the sound of their leader's war whistle the Chippewas suddenly let fly a flight of bullets and barbed arrows into the ranks of the enemies, picking out for death the most prominent and full plumed figures among them.
>
> The confusion amongst the Dakotas at this sudden and unexpected attack was immense. The captives overturned the canoes they were in, and the rest, running against one another and those in the water struggling to re-embark, and the sudden jumps of those who were wounded caused many of them to overturn, leaving their owners struggling in the deep current. Many were thus drowned, and as long as they remained in range of their enemies' weapons, the Dakotas suffered severely.[34]

Robinson informs us that the women and children of the Dakotas assembled at the falls of St. Anthony, as was the custom, to await the arrival of the first advance runners. These runners usually preceded a party returning from war, to cry the deeds of valor performed and the losses incurred. On this occasion, however, news of this terrible catastrophe was brought rather by the river itself: with the current came the debris, containing many articles of tribal and individual property and occasionally even "the mutilated body of some of their relatives." The stories of grief which this advance notice brought to the women and children and to other Dakota of this area formed some of "the most pathetic tales which history has preserved us," Robinson concludes.[35]

About a year after the battle of Crow Wing, the Chippewa, under the leadership of an old chief named Noka, pressed farther into the Dakota country than had any previous Ojibway war party and the inevitable encounter took place near the site of present Shakopee. Robinson summarizes this action for his readers thus: "They (the Ojibway under Noka) descended the Mississippi to the mouth of the Crow River, thirty miles above the falls (of St. Anthony), where they hid their canoes and struck across country to the Minnesota at the village of old Shakopee, the father of the Shakopee of 1812. The attack resulted in a drawn battle, both parties taking scalps and both claiming the victory. The Chippewas were, however, compelled to withdraw to their own country without inflicting especial damage."

The campaigns of the next three or four years have not been recorded, but it is probable that each spring both tribes had war parties on the move. In 1772, as nearly as can be determined, an Ojibway chief by the name of Big Marten gathered together a force of about one hundred and twenty men and led them south into the Mdewakanton country. Just north of the mouth of Elk River, on the banks of the Mississippi, they happened upon a Dakota party of about equal strength led by Little Crow (II).

> The Chippewas were first to discover the presence of the enemy and were the stronger party, so that in every

way they possessed the advantage. The Dakotas were on an open plain below a heavily wooded bottom, from which the Chippewa attacked them. They returned the fire, both parties being well armed with muskets. The warriors of both parties jumped continually from side to side to prevent their enemies from taking sure aim, and as they stood confronting one another for a few moments on the open prairie, exchanging quick successive volleys, their bodies in continual motion, the plumes on their heads waving to and fro, and uttering their fierce quick sharp battle cries, they must have created a singular wild appearance.

For a time, the Dakota held their own, but eventually they were compelled to retreat. A running battle continued for about three miles down the bank of the Mississippi; then, to the great relief of Little Crow's men, a large party of Mdewakanton from Shakopee's village came across from the Minnesota River and put the Ojibway to flight. Big Marten and his men started up the Elk River bank, found a grove of oak where they chose to make their stand, and quickly dug in. For several hours the struggle continued, neither side gaining, until nature turned the tide in favor of the Dakota forces:

> It was early spring, just as the grass was starting, and the prairie in the vicinity was covered with a heavy coat of last year's grass, to which the Dakotas set fire. A high wind was blowing and the Chippewas were soon seeking safety in flight. The best runners among them could only keep away from the flames, while the old and the weak and the wounded were soon overcome. Such Chippewas as escaped, reached the Mississippi and took refuge upon an island. The Dakotas followed them to the water's edge, but did not care to attack them upon the island retreat, and both parties returned to their respective countries.

Big Marten was among the few who escaped and, seeking revenge for the losses he and his men had sustained, he attempted a rerun of the excursion the next spring. He could muster but sixty warriors this time. Once again, "as if by prearranged signal," the opposing forces met on the battlefield of the previous year. Very probably the Dakota received advance word that Big Marten was approaching and decided to wait for the Ojibway at the mouth of Elk River. At any rate, about four hundred Mdewakanton were assembled under the command of Wabasha, Little Crow, Shakopee, and Red Wing. Even so, the Ojibway sneaked up on them so stealthily that they had the initial advantage over the Dakota. As soon as the Dakota realized that the Ojibway were upon them, they took cover and for nearly the whole day the opposing forces could do little but watch each other, occasionally one side or the other succeeding in picking off an individual who dared to show his head. Finally, Big Marten was killed by a Dakota bullet, and under cover of darkness, his warriors deserted the field, returning to their villages up the Mississippi.[36]

This flurry of Sioux-Chippewa warfare in the early 1770's somewhat discouraged trading activity with the Dakota, but in 1773 Peter Pond and a partner established themselves with nine clerks at Prairie du Chien. The Sioux of the River, as Carver called the Mdewakanton, doubtless contributed most of the profits which Pond and his partner reaped that season. Pond himself set up shop on the Minnesota River near the present town of St. Peter and traded with the Wapeton.

During the summer of 1774, the British commander at Fort Detroit asked Pond to call a meeting of the chiefs of the Dakota at his post on the Minnesota the following winter and invite them to a great peace council to be held at Mackinac the following summer. Pond's mission must have been successful as he informs us:

> The Spring is now advancing fast. The Chefes coming with a Number of Natives to go with me to Mackinac to Sea and Hear What thare farther (their father) Had to say.[37]

The Proclamation of 1763 by King George III had provided that the Indians of the Northwest should be under the protection of the king and that no one was allowed to buy land from them or make settlements on their land. Traders could get licenses from the colonial governors to trade with the Indians, but were not supposed to found permanent settlements.

Louise Phelps Kellogg tells us in her *The British Regime in Wisconsin and the Northwest* that as early as 1763 there had appeared a series of plans for interior colonies, some of them backed by the most influential men of the seaboard and settled colonies. In his *Travels* Jonathan Carver had advocated the division of western lands into eleven "plantations or subordinate colonies, chusing such lands only for this purpose as being contiguous to some river."

In 1774, the Quebec Act set aside the Proclamation of 1763 and extended the limits of the province of Quebec westward to the Mississippi and southward to the Ohio, virtually closing this area forever to settlement and exploitation from the eastern thirteen "American" colonies. This included western Wisconsin and eastern Minnesota as we know them, the area in which the Mdewakanton lived and roamed. As events were taking shape in 1775, the Dakota believed that their best chance of keeping the status quo lay with the British and their local representatives, the traders, rather than with the dissatisfied American colonists.

This decision was not made on the basis of any lofty thoughts concerning freedom or justice, but on the basis of very practical, down-to-earth principles: From the British came their trade goods, their arms and ammunition, their blankets and beads, their beloved "Miniwakan" or mystery water. From the British they received the assurance that the Indian's situation would remain the same as it had been; that each year they would receive their "presents" so that they could hunt and trap, keeping their wives and little ones sheltered, fed, and clothed. "Taxation without representation" meant nothing to them, but the full pot and the warm blanket did. Certainly, too, the easier course was to follow the British, whom they knew, rather than to risk the Americans, whom they did not.

In 1775 traders in Wisconsin were requested to round up their Indians to be used as troops around Montreal in 1776. About two hundred Chippewa and Ottawa traveled to Montreal only to learn they were not needed. "After giving them suitable presents, the Governor dismissed them with orders to return the next year."[38]

Two years later the Dakota were approached to serve as "frontier raiders," to harass the Americans in outlying areas. We are told that in February of 1778 Charles Gautier appeared on the St. Croix, searching for Sioux and Winnebago who were hunting in that region. Learning that Wabasha, the principal Sioux chief, was then hunting around the Falls of St. Anthony, Gautier proceeded to the St. Peter River (the Minnesota) where "he stopped a hostile demonstration of Sioux and Winnebago against the Chippewa."[39]

At that time, Wabasha was living on the lower Minnesota near its mouth, probably in the present area of Bloomington. This was Spanish territory, but the Spanish had never attempted to push their occupation this far north and the British treated it as though it were just as much their territory as the land lying east of the Mississippi. Wabasha, hearing that Gautier was in the area, went to him and invited him to come and visit his village.

Accepting his invitation, Gautier spent two weeks with Wabasha's band. From then on Wabasha espoused the British cause and was willing to help them any way he could. The rest of the Mdewakanton bands, though at first inclined toward the British, were drawn from them to the Spanish at St. Louis.

In the spring of 1779, Wabasha and his warriors went to Prairie du Chien and awaited orders from the British. The noted chief sent some of his young men, with an interpreter, to Mackinac and expressed his wish to attack the Sauks and Foxes who had been friendly to the Americans. The commander at Quebec wrote to Colonel Arent Schuyler De Peyster, commandant at Mackinac, on the third day of July, 1779: "Wabasha's proposal is a very uncommon one from an Indian, though it would be very imprudent to adopt it, yet the zeal he has manifested merits our attention."

The American Revolution was now well under way. France had formally entered the conflict on the American side in June, 1778, and in 1779, the Spanish became allies of the French though they did not make a treaty of alliance with the United States. The British, therefore, undertook to capture Spanish Louisiana before it could be organized for defense. Orders for an attack on the Spanish were received at Detroit the end of January, 1780, and were immediately forwarded to Mackinac whence the expedition was to start. The Lieutenant Governor sent the trader Cadotte to Wabasha, who was prevailed upon to lead his warriors in this British expedition down the Mississippi.

In the meantime, Matchekewis, a well-known Chippewa chief, and his band were also mobilized, and numerous Winnebago, Menominee, Sauk and Foxes, Ottawa, and other tribes assembled at Prairie du Chien. Altogether there was "a force of about twelve hundred—a motley army of traders and their engagees, Indians of all the upper river tribes composing the main body, led by Generals Wabasha and Matchekewis, proudly arrayed in the scarlet coats of British officers."[40]

The British had great plans for Wabasha. They were so certain of the success of their plans to capture St. Louis that they "had made arrangements for occupying all of the Illinois region after its conquest. Hesse (a Prairie du Chien trader turned soldier) was to remain in command at St. Louis, whence all the traders (about 40) who accompanied the expedition were to have free access to the rich fur trade of the upper Missouri. Wabasha was to sweep south and take Spanish Ste. Genevieve and American Kaskaskia, and the rest of the Indians under Matchekewis were to return to Mackinac."[41]

But all of these great plans came to naught. The Spanish had heard of the intended attack and accordingly prepared their fortifications.

> A block house was built and small cannon placed therein. The assault on this defensive work took place about noonday (the twenty-sixth of May, 1780); the Winnebago Indians led the van and were repulsed with the loss of a chief and four warriors killed and several wounded. The Indians were immediately discouraged and refused to go against artillery and block houses. They scattered throughout the country, cutting off peasants working in their fields who had unguardedly left the fort . . .
> The entire body of the Indian forces at once began a

retreat. Wabasha and his braves, accompanied by most of the traders, pushed back up the river to Prairie du Chien. Matchekewis took his people along the Illinois river to Mackinac by way of Chicago.[42]

About two hundred and fifty French and American troops with about a hundred Spanish subjects from St. Louis and about fifty friendly Indians from that area then came north and attacked the Sauk Indians. The Spanish division of the expedition proceeded as far as Prairie du Chien and plundered the traders' post.

Meanwhile, Wabasha and thirty-five warriors, most of whom were Dakota of his own band, had been sent to Prairie du Chien to keep the traders' store of furs from falling into the enemy's hands.

> Arriving at Prairie du Chien, the pelts were found in a log house. After resting a short period, the canoes were filled with three hundred packs of the best skins, and the balance, sixty-five packs, were burned to keep them from the Americans.[43]

Five days later, the "Spanish division" arrived at the post, but because of Wabasha's efforts the furs did not fall into its hands.

At the end of the war, a government trader was sent by the British commandant at Mackinac to Prairie du Chien to hold council with the Dakota and other tribes, and, in view of the peace with the United States, to urge the cessation of hostilities. On this occasion, the twenty-fourth of May, 1783, the speaker for the Dakotas, probably Wabasha, is reported to have said:

> My father, I am content that the great chiefs on the other side of the greatest lake are for making peace. My English father, you give us pleasure to have come upon

our ground; our heart is joyful and content. It is you who give us light. We will be quiet.[44]

Returning from his part in the Revolutionary War, Wabasha and most of his band left the present Twin Cities area and took up residence lower down the Mississippi almost as far as Prairie du Chien, that is, at the mouth of the Upper Iowa River. Finally, his village, Keoka, became more or less permanently established at the site of present Winona. He and his successors still had their troubles, not only with the Chippewa but also the Sacs and Foxes. Red Wing, whose village was at the head of Lake Pepin, and the Wabashas, carried on almost continuous warfare with the Chippewa of Wisconsin. Since both of these villages were outside of the greater Twin Cities area, a more detailed description of these forays need not be pursued.

However, farther north, the other Mdewakanton also resumed their age old enmity with the Chippewa. The most notable of these encounters is called The Battle of St. Croix Falls, and it probably took place in 1783. White Fisher, a famous war chief of the Lake Superior Ojibway gathered together about three hundred warriors to march into the Dakota country. He arranged to meet a band of Sandy Lake Ojibway numbering about sixty warriors at the confluence of the Snake River and the St. Croix. On arriving there, however, White Fisher was disappointed to find that the Sandy Lake party was nowhere in sight. Nevertheless, confident that his contingent was large enough to inflict some damage on the Dakota, he proceeded down the St. Croix. While preparing to make the portage at the Falls, the Ojibway perceived a large group of Foxes and Mdewakanton at the other end of the portage. Neill, in his *History of Minnesota,* reports the outcome:

The Ojibway instantly prepared for battle, and the

scouts of the enemy having discovered them, the hostile parties met as if by mutual agreement in the middle of the portage. The Foxes, after seeing the comparatively small number of the Ojibways, and over-confident in their own superior numbers and prowess, requested the Dakota not to join in the fight, but to sit by and see how quickly they could rout the Ojibways. This request was granted. The fight between the contending warriors is said to have been fiercely contested, and embellished with many acts of personal valor. About noon the Foxes commenced yielding ground, and at last were forced to flee in confusion.

At this point, the Dakota, who had been quietly smoking their pipes and calmly viewing the fight from a distance, came to the aid of their distressed allies and soon routed the Ojibway, inflicting great losses.

Even though this type of feuding between the tribes on the Upper Mississippi did not take a great toll in lives, it nevertheless was a disrupting influence on the fur trade in the area. Repeated attempts were made to pacify the various tribes.

In 1786, the Indian agent at Montreal sent his deputy West to try and arrange a peace. The deputy employed Joseph Ainse to visit the upper Mississippi. He gathered at Prairie du Chien a large delegation of Sioux, Chippewa, Menominee, Sauk, and Foxes. Perrault describes the ceremonies by which each group massed in columns and moved across the prairies, forming into three large triangles, each with its orator in the center, holding the pipe of peace. Then to the sound of a chant, the Chippewa leader presented the pipe to the Sioux, all of whom accepted it except one young chief. After he had been pacified, the ceremony continued and they completed the peace pact. The chiefs accompanied Ainse and the traders to Mackinac where in July, 1786, the delegations from the

Mississippi and Wisconsin met the Chippewa from Lake Superior.

Notwithstanding all the ceremonies and the large amount of presents given by the British officers, the peace was not lasting, the Sioux of Wabasha's Band were attacking a Chippewa party on St. Croix River while the treaty was being drawn at Mackinac.[45]

At the Prairie du Chien council there were five bands of the Dakota represented, Little Crow's, Wabasha's, Red Wing's, Shakopee's and Penasha's, this last presumably being the "one young chief" who had to be pacified at the ceremony.

Long, who visited this area in 1817 and again in 1823, asserted that the Little Crow he met, Chetanwakamani, was called Little Crow because his father and grandfather before him had been. Perhaps the first chief Little Crow carried this as his personal name. Chippewa tradition states that a chief who came against them had as his totem a crow, and they thus named him Little Crow. At the rendezvous in the spring of 1660 Radisson had noted that the Dakota warriors "had the skin of a crow hanging at their girdles," but these may have been medicine bags rather than totems.

Dr. Asa W. Daniels in his "Reminiscences of Little Crow," wrote:

> His (Little Crow V) totem, or sacred animal, was a crow, the skin of which was carefully prepared to represent the bird in repose, and was worn back of and below the right shoulder. It was in some mysterious sense regarded as the ancestral spirit or soul of the family. He led his soldiers in the attack upon New Ulm in August, 1862, and during that long, all-day fight ten of the defenders were killed and among them was Jerry Quane,

Little Crow III (Walks Pursuing a Hawk).
McKinney & Hall, *History of the Indian Tribes of North America*, Biddle, 1836.

who fell far out toward the enemy's line. On gathering up the dead the following morning, the totem of Little Crow was found attached to his breast, a silent but significant message.[46]

It seems clear that this was no medicine bag, for no Dakota admitted into the sacred "medicine-lodge" would part with his medicine bag, even to show that he had slain another. The Mdewakanton did not make use of the totem-system as the Chippewa and other tribes did to reckon and signify kinship, but it may be, as Daniels states, that the Little Crow succession of chiefs did regard the bird as the "ancestral spirit or soul of their family."

Little Crow III (Chetanwakamani or Walks Pursuing a Hawk) was born in 1769, according to Doane Robinson, and became chief probably about 1795. Under Little Crow III the Kaposia band, which had heretofore been migratory, took up residence within the Twin Cities area, near and for a time in present St. Paul.

After 1775 all of the Mdewakanton bands founded more or less permanent summer villages; and in general these locations did not change much in the ensuing years—not until 1853 and 1854. In these years, as we shall learn later, they removed to the reservation at the Redwood Agency on the Minnesota River between Rock Creek* and Yellow Medicine River.

---

*Rock Creek is not generally shown on modern road maps; it was four miles below Fort Ridgely and was also called Little Rock Creek and Mud Creek.

American Foothold
1803-1812

AFTER THE REVOLUTIONARY WAR, Wabasha was established with his summer village on the Mississippi below the widening of that river called Lake Pepin; Red Wing dwelt near the top of Lake Pepin; and Little Crow III by 1805 had moved from the area of the mouth of the St. Croix to Pig's Eye about four miles below the confluence of the Mississippi and Minnesota Rivers. Penasha was living with his band on the Minnesota River near the mouth of Nine Mile Creek, and Shakopee was farther up that river near the present town which bears his name. Doane Robinson also mentions as chiefs of this period White Bustard who lived near Penasha and Killiew, the Eagle, who lived upstream on the Minnesota. Little else is known of these two chiefs who probably were not hereditary head men, but chosen leaders for parts of existing bands. Later more is heard of the White Bustard, or Outard Blanche, from Zebulon Pike and it is a possibility that Killiew, the Eagle, was the chief also known as Great War Eagle I or Black Dog, the father of Grey Iron, who had his village closest to the newly established Fort Snelling in the 1820's.

The villages of these bands are called permanent villages

even though, strictly speaking, the Dakota did not live in their villages year-round. There were several months of each year when the villages were completely abandoned; only in the summer months were they really alive and active. September took the families from their villages. The women, children, and older men travelled north to the rice lakes to gather that important part of their winter diet, while the young and middle aged men went on the fall fur hunt. Early winter found the hunters in the woods pursuing the deer to feed and clothe themselves; as the winter hunting season closed about the end of January, the men and their families usually returned to the vicinity of their villages. But instead of occupying their bark huts or pitching their tepees within the village area, they found shelter from the winter blasts among the thickets and evergreen woods adjacent to their village sites. In the spring they would be off again; the women, children, and old men to the sugar bush, the younger men scouring the country for muskrat and other fur bearers. Generally they returned from these activities in May, finally occupying their villages, re-working their bark huts, or pitching their tepees within the village area. If the village was to be relocated, as often happened in the early years of this period, then the relocation was made in the spring, before planting time. The Mdewakanton Dakota raised some corn, though they often consumed it before it had ripened, and also generally a few pumpkins.

The Rev. Gideon Pond, an observer in the area a few years later, was convinced that the presence of the traders was more significant in the migration of the Mdewakanton Dakota from Mille Lacs and the upper Rum River to the Twin Cities area than was the advance of the Chippewa across central Minnesota. Pond stated:

The Indians would hunt in the direction where the interest of the trade required, and their home would be in the vicinity of the trade, where they learned to depend for a thousand little articles which gratified their desires, if they did not add to their comfort. When to this we add the fact that the traders taught them to plant corn, which actually took place of wild rice, nothing was wanting to bring the Mdewakanton south to the Minnesota River.[47]

The traders on whom the Indians now depended were generally English even though on paper the land east of the Mississippi belonged to the United States, and the area of Minnesota west of the Mississippi was held by the Spanish. These British traders held great influence over the Dakota until after the War of 1812. Folwell observed that "for all practical purposes the whole territory might as well have remained a part of Canada."

In the early 1780's a number of traders had joined together and formed the Northwest Company. By 1795 this company had set up numerous posts in the West and was carrying on a very lucrative trade in Wisconsin and Minnesota, perhaps more with the Chippewa, but also with the Dakota.

Primary among these British traders was one Robert Dickson, who during this period of history began to acquire much influence over the Mdewakanton, influence which did not decline until 1815. In 1788 this red-headed Scotchman took out his first trading license, although he had already been engaged in the field for a number of years. On August 19th, 1794, along with other Canadians at Prairie du Chien, he received his American commission and became one of the two justices of the peace for the area, although he apparently did not renounce his British allegiance. Later Dickson organized a British fur trading company in which many of the prominent British traders of the area participated. This company covered the entire trade south and west of the upper lakes—all the region not under the direct control of the Northwest Company.

The treaty of 1783 had obligated the British to withdraw all troops south of the Canadian border, but the new American government under the Articles of Confederation was not able to enforce this phase of the treaty. The British were slow to remove their soldiers, and it was not until 1794 that a time limit was set for their removal—June 1, 1796.

On March 10, 1804, the Americans became the possessors of the Louisiana Territory. This area had been given to the Spanish by the French in 1762 to prevent the English from claiming it after the French and Indian war. In 1800, by secret treaty Spain returned it to France, and it was bought by the United States from Napoleon. This purchase put all of Minnesota under American jurisdiction.

Having purchased the Louisiana Territory, the United States government became increasingly interested in winning the favor of the northwestern Indians and the control of their fur trade. Clashes between the British traders on the upper Mississippi and the Spanish traders of the Missouri region had become more common over the years. Furthermore, American traders were trying to enter the region.

In 1805, the year following the Louisiana Purchase, General James Wilkinson, commandant at St. Louis, issued a proclamation forbidding the subjects of any foreign power to enter the fur trade of northern Louisiana. All traders were required to apply to St. Louis authorities for a license and to subscribe to an oath of fidelity to the United States. They were forbidden to carry to the Indians of that region uniforms, medals, or any ornaments bearing devices or emblems of a foreign power; no goods could be used for trade that had not been manufactured in the United States or imported by its citizens.

As a further effort to break the monopoly of the British traders on the upper Mississippi, the commandant also sent Lieutenant Zebulon M. Pike north on his important exploratory mission in the same year. He was instructed to record his topographical observations, to note the "population and residence" of the Indians, to conciliate them, to look for positions suitable for military posts, and to ascend the main branch of the Mississippi to its source. "In addition to the preceding orders," he was told, "you will be pleased to obtain permission from the Indians who claim the ground, for the erection of military posts and trading houses at the mouth of the river St. Pierre (the Minnesota River), the Falls of St. Anthony and every other critical point which may fall under your observation."

Pike travelled north to accomplish his assignment. He noted that the Mdewakanton

> Extend from Prairie Des Chiens to La Prairie du Francois (Shakopee), thirty-five miles up St. Peter's (Minnesota River). This band is sub-divided into four divisions under different chiefs.*

As ordered, Pike set out north to undertake the task of negotiating with the Mdewakanton for the desired land.

---

*Coues, Elliott, The Expeditions of Zebulon Montgomery Pike, Vol. I, p. 342. This author finds it almost certain that Pike did not mean individual bands here, although some commentators have taken it that way. His conjecture is that these "four divisions" were:
    I: Wabasha (at Upper Iowa River);
   II: Red Wing (near the mouth of the Cannon River);
  III: Little Crow (at Pig's Eye) and Black Soldier (at Phalen Creek), or Outard Blanche if Black Soldier was not a headman;
  IV: Penasha (at Nine Mile Creek), possibly Black Dog (Killiew, the Eagle) and Shakopee (at present Shakopee).

He arrived at the confluence of the Minnesota and Mississippi Rivers on September 21, 1805; and his party encamped on the island now bearing his name. On the following day, September 22, 1805, Little Crow III came with one hundred and fifty warriors, and preliminary arrangements were made for the council to be held the next day. Under the entry for September 23, Pike indicates who was present at the council:

> Le Petit Corbeau, he signed the grant; Le Fils de Pinichon, he also signed; Le Grand Partisan, L'Original Leve, La Demi Douzain, Le Boucasse, and Le Boef-qui-Marche.*

L'Original Leve or Rising Moose was a head man of Wabasha's band and probably represented him. The *Journal* for September 23 continues:

> Prepared for the council, which we commenced about twelve o'clock. I had a bower or shade, made of my sails, on the beach, into which only my gentlemen (the traders) and the chiefs entered. I then addressed them in a speech, which, though long, and touching on many points, its principal object was the granting of land at this place, falls of St. Anthony, and St. Croix river, and making peace with the Chipeways. I was replied to by Le Fils de Pinchow (Son of the Pinchow, or Penasha II), Le Petit Corbeau (Little Crow III) and l'Original Leve (Rising Moose, a head man of Wabasha's band).

---

*These were identified by Dr. Thomas Foster in the **St. Paul Democrat** May 4, 1854, as follows:
  Le Petit Corbeau: Little Crow
  Le Fils de Pinichon: the son of Penasha
  Le Grand Partisan: a principal soldier
  L'Original Leve: Tamaha
  Le Demi Douzen: Shakopee
  Le Boucasse: Wahkantahpay, a Wapekute chief
  Le Boef-qui-March: Red Wing

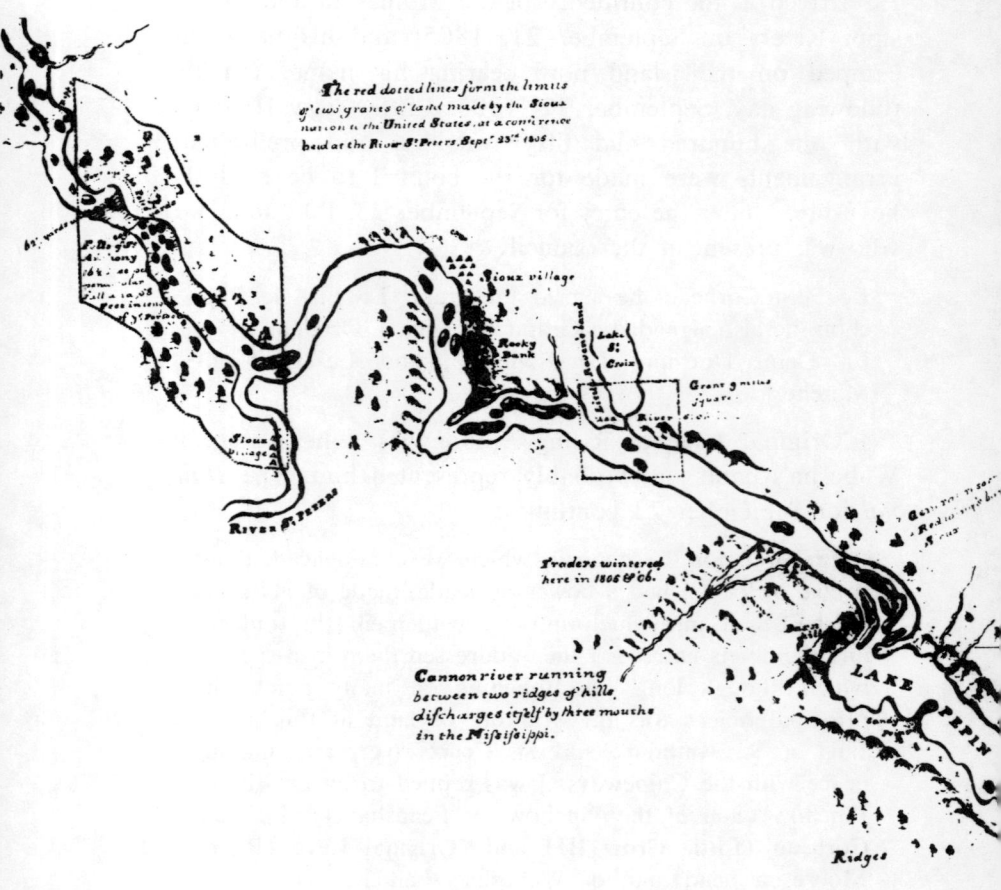

From the map compiled in 1805 by Anthony Nau showing Zebulon Pike's explorations of the Mississippi River Valley. This section includes the two grants of land made by the Sioux to the United States at the conference on the River St. Peters (Minnesota River).

National Archives, Chief of Engineers map M34.

They gave me the land required, about 100,000 acres and promised me a safe passport for myself and any Ojibway chiefs I might bring down, but spoke doubtfully with respect to the peace. I gave them presents to the amount of about two hundred dollars, and as soon as the council was over, I allowed the traders to present them with some liquor which, with what I myself gave, was equal to sixty gallons. In one half hour, they were all embarked for their respective villages.[48]

Penasha II* signed the treaty with his mark and Pike added the chief's personal name "Wayagoenagee" (He Sees Standing Up) nearby.

Apparently the Indian representatives felt it was sufficient to have Little Crow and Penasha sign the grant "since their bands claimed exclusive possession and were conceded by the others to have the immediate right to dispose of the lands embraced by the military reserve."[49]

Thus the Dakota gave to the United States two tracts of land; one, nine miles square at the mouth of the St. Croix, and the other, "from below the confluence of the Mississippi and the St. Peter's (Minnesota) up the Mississippi to include the falls of St. Anthony, extending nine miles on each side of the river."[50]

For these grants they received two hundred dollars worth of trade goods, sixty gallons of whiskey, and the promise of more cash or presents, to be given them before the

---

*His son, Penasha III, was known as Panishihowa by Beltrami; Takopepeshene by Major Long; as "Tay-Koo-Ke-Paysh-Nee" or "What is He Afraid Of" by the Indians; as Pinnichonon or Pinchon by the French; and as Pinneshaw by the English. In later years the Indians adopted this word "pinneshaw" to signify a very brave and fearless man.

It is interesting to note that Sibley was given the name "Walker-in-the-Pines" by a nephew of Penasha's. This nephew had performed some extraordinary feat in battle and acquired thereby the name Penasha. Therefore he no longer needed his former name, "Walker-in-the-Pines."

government took possession of the grants. The Senate later fixed this amount at two thousand dollars.

On his return in spring Pike spoke well of Penasha, who had spent the preceding winter near his post and had gotten along so well with his men. At this time, Penasha was instrumental in making the arrangements for a council of Dakota and Chippewa representatives whom Pike called together for the purpose of ending the inter-tribal warring. Represented bands of the Dakota were the Sisseton (Siessitongs), the Wapeton (Gens des Feuilles) and the Mdewakanton (Gens du Lac). Under the date of April 11 Pike describes the Council:

> There were about one hundred lodges, or six hundred people. The council house was two large lodges, capable of containing three hundred men. In the upper were forty chiefs and as many pipes set against the poles, along side of which I had the Sauteur's (Chippewa's) pipes arranged. The interpreter informed the Dakota that I wanted some of their principal chiefs to go to St. Louis, and that those who thought proper might descend to the prairie (Prairie du Chien) where we would give them more explicit information. They all smoked out of the Sauteur's pipes excepting three.[51]

It appears that the goal of the council was not entirely achieved, for on the following day Pike's *Journal* recorded:

> April 12, 1806, Saturday: At an Indian village a few miles below the St. Peter's, we were about to pass a few lodges, but on receiving a very particular invitation to come on shore, we landed, and were received in a lodge kindly; they presented us sugar, etc. I gave the proprietor a dram and was about to depart, when he demanded a kettle of liquor; on being refused, and after I had left the shore, he told me that he did not like the arrangements

(for a permanent peace between the Dakota and the Chippewa) and that he would go to war this summer. I directed the interpreter to tell him that if I returned to the St. Peter's with the troops I would settle that affair with him.*

On his journey north Pike had observed the competition among the traders. Probably as a result of his observations, late in 1806 a new trading company was formed at Montreal—the Michilimackinac Company. All of the traders operating from Mackinac were invited to join, including the partners of Robert Dickson and Company. Early in 1807, this new company came to an agreement with the Northwest Company, dividing the trade in the Northwest between them. The Northwest Company gave to the Michilimackinac Company virtually complete control over the Sioux trade, while retaining the trade of the northern tribes.

---

*This village was probably the same "camp of four lodges" located at the site of downtown St. Paul, which Pike had visited the previous autumn (September 21, 1805). At that time he had met a brave by the name of Black Soldier. It is possible that Black Soldier was a warrior under chief Outard Blanche (White Bustard or White Turkey). White Turkey is also mentioned by Forsyth (Minn. Hist. Coll. Vol. III, pp 139-167) in 1823. At this later time White Turkey's band was located on the Minnesota River four miles above its mouth, two miles below Penasha's. It may be that the village of "four lodges" which Pike found at the mouth of Phalen Creek was White Turkey's and that in time it removed from there up the Minnesota to the vicinity of Penasha's where Forsyth found it.

White Conflict
1812-1820

THE DAKOTA PROMISED Pike fidelity to the Americans and peace with the Chippewa. The British traders promised that they would quit using liquor in their trade with the red men; and after exploring the north country, Pike returned to St. Louis with the treaty in his pocket, confident that he had performed the arduous task which had been set up for him.

But neither the Indians nor the traders kept their promises to him. The British traders, Cameron and Dickson, "utterly disregarded the rules established by Pike for the government of trade and conducted affairs to their own pleasure, particularly in the matter of dispensing liquor and their liberality in this behalf was (to the Indians) a strong point in their favor, and an influence against the Americans. The Dakota Indian loved his toddy and freely gave his affections to the men who catered to his appetite."[52] Dickson had little difficulty enlisting Little Crow III and Penasha with their bands on the side of the English in the western campaigns in the War of 1812. In fact, with the exception of a part of Wabasha's band, all of the Mdewakanton bands cooperated with the British.

The winter of 1811-12 had been especially severe in the area, and many of the Dakota were on the point of starvation. Robert Dickson, along with some of his partners in the South West Company,* was obliged to furnish provisions and ammunition to the customers to keep them alive. Dickson was said to have used fifteen hundred dollars worth of goods in this humane effort.

The following summer, with the knowledge that a state of war existed between the United States and Great Britain, Dickson began immediately enrolling Indians as auxiliary troops. He was present with "over fifty Sioux, two score Winnebago, and as many Menominee" on the seventeenth of July, 1812, when the American troops at Mackinac were obliged to capitulate without firing a shot.[53]

An American taken prisoner at this capitulation later wrote:

> Those who commanded the Canadians were traders, some of whom were lately concerned in smuggling British goods into the Indian country, and in conjunction with others, have been using their utmost efforts several months before the declaration of war to excite the Indians to take up arms. The least resistance from the fort would have been attended with the destruction of all the persons who fell into the hands of the British, as I have been assured by some of the British traders.[54]

After the fall of Mackinac, Dickson was appointed deputy superintendent for all Indians in "Michigan and the conquered territory." He thus set out on an ambitious tour to visit the various tribes in the Northwest. On his arrival at Prairie du Chien in April, 1813, he found that the events had excited the Sioux with an eagerness to go to war.

---

*The South West Company was formed by John Jacob Astor in 1810. It included most of the members of the old Michilimackinac Company.

They were ready to invade American territory by way of the Mississippi, but Dickson told them there were no armies in that direction and their war would (in that direction) be waged upon helpless thousands of women and children. Instead, he designed to lead his Indian warriors to the front where the Americans were assembling, prepared to avenge the defeats of the last summer and early winter.[55]

At Prairie du Chien, Dickson spent six weeks organizing his expedition and returned to Mackinac with over six hundred Indian warriors, including nearly a hundred Dakota from the valleys of the upper Mississippi and Minnesota. In July Dickson's warriors took part in the Siege of Ft. Meigs, on the western edge of Lake Erie near the present city of Toledo, Ohio. This small American post was garrisoned by only one hundred and sixty regulars with but one cannon and a small six pounder. But with brave determination the American commander and his small band repulsed the British force of six hundred British regulars and eight hundred Indians. The Indians deserted at once in large numbers. Dickson sent the remaining Dakota back home by way of Mackinac and instructed his subordinates to furnish clothing for the returning chiefs, and to forward ammunition for their winter hunt.

When the siege at Ft. Meigs was lifted, Dickson decided to attack Fort Stephenson, located southeast of Meigs. Most of the Dakota with him refused to follow him. Only Little Crow III and sixteen of his warriors remained with Dickson, who then decided nothing more could be accomplished because of the lateness of the season and the lack of followers. Thus these warriors too were sent back to their homes in time to pursue their winter activities.

After the winter deer hunt, Little Crow III and Wabasha

traveled to Mackinac with two hundred other braves, pleading for soldiers and ammunition to protect them from the Americans who, they feared, would come up the Mississippi to attack them. In early May after they had returned to their villages, Dickson again gathered together about eighty Winnebago, one hundred and twenty Menominee and one hundred Dakota, including Little Crow III and his braves, and once again traveled to Mackinac, arriving the first of June, 1814. They "found that the garrison at this place had been reinforced by British soldiers, and that a Colonel Robert McDouall was in command. On the fifth of June, the new commandant held a council with the western tribesmen, when the Sioux chiefs, Wabasha and Little Crow III, Tomah of the Menominee and Caramaunee of the Winnebago band were the orators. McDouall gave them news of British successes and commended the tribesmen to the care of Dickson."[56]

In the meantime Prairie du Chien had been taken by the Americans and a trader's post was fortified and named Ft. Shelby. News of the arrival of the Americans at Prairie du Chien reached Mackinac June 21. The commander there realized that if the Americans should retain their hold on Prairie du Chien, the British influence with the Indians throughout the Northwest would be greatly impaired. "A greater part of my Indian force," he wrote, "was from the countries adjoining La prairie des Chiens, they felt themselves not a little uneasy at the proximity of the enemy to their defenseless families."[57]

He consulted with Dickson and decided that the Dakota and the Winnebago could best be spared from Mackinac. Dickson remained and a force of seventy-five white volunteers and one hundred and thirty-six Indians, with an old Northwest trader Wm. McKay in command, was sent to assault Ft. Shelby. The Americans sent out the flag of truce on July the nineteenth and Colonel McKay accepted it. "With great difficulty, McKay controlled his fierce Indian allies, the villagers supposed to be their friends suffered more at their hands than the American garrison,"[58] which was later allowed to return to St. Louis.

On the first of September, McKay returned to Mackinac and an interpreter, Francis Freniere, received the following order from Captain Thomas Anderson, at Prairie du Chien, "Proceed with all haste up the Mississippi till you fall in with the Little Corbeau. You will tell him that the enemy are on the way up here. That Robert Dickson will be here in a very short time." Freniere returned from his mission on the fifteenth, reporting that Little Crow III was eager to go against the Americans. Renville, arriving two weeks later, told the commander that Little Crow III and a hundred of his warriors would soon be down.

At eleven o'clock on the twenty-eighth they arrived, Little Crow expressing their desire "to strike everything American in their way." He had been called to Prairie du Chien because Captain Anderson had received word that Major Zachary Taylor was ascending the Mississippi from St. Louis with a large force to retake the fort. Little Crow III and some of his braves remained at the fort while Wabasha and about fifty of the other Dakota joined a band of nearly eight hundred warriors, mostly Sauk, who hastened downstream to intercept Taylor, and if possible, to delay his ascent.

At Rock Rapids, Taylor perceived that the water was too low and also that a wind storm was brewing. He therefore anchored his eight barges containing three hundred troops. The British attacked and wounded eleven men, three of whom died. Believing that Prairie du Chien was not worth the price, Taylor returned downstream and the Indians returned home. Prairie du Chien was guarded by the British garrison until May, 1815. It was not until then that news finally reached them of the peace that had been declared between Great Britain and the United States on December 24, 1814.

In June 1816, Little Crow III and Wabasha were invited to the British post at Drummond's Island to be thanked by the English for their services during the war. According to the minutes of the council held at this time, which are in the possession of the South Dakota Historical Society, Little Crow III said (among other things of like tenor):

"The Big Knives (Americans) addressed us by the left hand, and holding in their right a switch which implies that the Big Knives intend to deprive us of our traders and build forts on our lands without permission. Your children are not afraid of them. No, they believe themselves strong enough to resist them with your consent and determination."[59]

Soon thereafter, American dominance was completely assured in the west and the old chiefs (Little Crow III and Wabasha), like the consummate politicians which they were readily fell in with the new order of things.

Then they remembered what had occurred down at Drummond Island after this manner: They recalled that they made the weary tramp of eight hundred or a thousand miles through the wilderness, not to implore aid from the British, but to show their contempt for them. They related how Colonel McDonell had profusely thanked them for their service to the king and had pointed to small pile of presents he had offered them.[60]

Wabasha refused the presents, saying: "I have lived long

and always found the means of subsistence, and I can do so still."

They then recalled that Little Crow was even more defiant and vehement in his reply:

> After we have fought for you, endured many hardships, lost some of our people and awakened the vengeance of our powerful neighbors, you make a peace for yourselves and leave us these goods to pay us for having deserted us. But no! We will not take them; we hold them and yourselves in contempt.

So saying, Little Crow III was said to have kicked the goods right and left and withdrawn from the council.
After all the Dakota Indian of 1815 was very human.[61]

Much mention has been made of the contribution of Little Crow III and his braves to the British cause in the War of 1812. However, no mention is made of Penasha II, the other hereditary chief of the area, or of White Bustard and the Eagle, the two mentioned by Pike as living on the lower Minnesota, or of Black Soldier, on the Mississippi above Little Crow's village.

Although the majority of the Mdewakanton co-operated with the British, some of the chiefs may have been cool toward the thought of whole-hearted conflict. It is said that Wabasha refused to go with Dickson on the excursion which preceded the seige of Ft. Meigs, but that he sent his nephew and other braves to represent him. Perhaps at this time Penasha and his subchiefs also felt cool toward the British, as did Red Wing who, when offered a British medal, is reported to have said:

> You tell me that the lion on this medal is the most powerful of all animals. I have never seen one, but I

believe what you say. The lion, like our tiger (wild cat) sleeps all day, but the eagle, who is the most powerful of all birds sleeps only at night, in the daytime he flies about everywhere and sees all on the ground. He will perch on a tree over the lion and they will scold at each other for a while, but they will finally make up and be friends and smoke the pipe of peace. The lion will then go home and leave us Indians with our foes. That is the reason for not taking up my war club.[62]

In July, 1815, representatives of the United States government had called the chiefs and head warriors to a council or conference at Portage des Sioux; a point near the confluence of the Mississippi and the Missouri rivers. At this time, the Mdewakanton signed treaties placing them "in all things and in every respect, on the same footing upon which they stood before the late war."[63] Perpetual peace was promised and it was agreed that "every injury or act of hostility committed by one or either of the contracting parties against the other shall be mutually forgiven and forgotten."[64]

The Shared Log

Arrival of the Military
1820-1825

THE ENGLISH TRADERS were quick to realize the error made by their government in neglecting the Dakota at the close of the War of 1812 and strenuous efforts were made to draw them away from American centers of trade to Canadian posts.

In April of 1816, the United States Congress decided that "licenses to trade with the Indians within the territorial limits of the United States shall not be granted to any but citizens of the United States," and the president was given authorization to call upon military force to carry out this order.

The trade with the Dakota which had been carried on by the British traders was now to be transferred to government owned trading houses or "factories." At these posts, Indians could exchange their furs for goods at cost, eliminating the cheating by the traders and the whiskey traffic, though the Indians, it seems, were often willing to submit to the one for the sake of the other.

In 1818, the Superintendent of Indian Trade recommended the establishment of such a government factory to be located "on the river St. Peter's (Minnesota) at or about its junction with the Mississippi," but by the time the military post was established here, the factory plan was practically dead, and trade with the Mdewakanton was carried on much as it had been before the war, except that the local traders "speedily obtained naturalization papers and, as American citizens, continued in business."[1]

During the summer of 1817, Major Stephen H. Long was sent to the Upper Mississippi region to study existing military establishments and to examine the sites which Pike had acquired from the Mdewakanton in 1805. Major Long's journal of his 1817 expedition identifies Penasha's village and places the village of Black Dog or Big Eagle I a number of miles upstream on the Minnesota, probably above Shakopee's.

As a result of Long's findings, the war department determined to establish a military post on the more northern of the two tracts acquired by Pike, namely the area "from below the confluence of the Mississippi and St. Peters, up the Mississippi to include the Falls of St. Anthony, extending nine miles on each side of the river." Lieutenant-Colonel Henry Leavenworth was' selected to carry out this difficult project.

Leavenworth and his men arrived at the mouth of the Minnesota on August 24, 1819, accompanied by Major Thomas Forsyth, who had joined them at Prairie du Chien. With them they brought to the Dakota "a quantity of goods, say $2,000 worth," in payment for the lands ceded by them to the United States under the Pike treaty.

In a letter to Governor William Clark at St. Louis, reviewing his journey and his dealings with Little Crow III, Major Forsyth reported:

> Little Crow's village is at a place called the Grand Marais being twenty-three leagues above Red Wing's

village and within five leagues of the mouth of the St. Peter's (Minnesota) River. Here I found the Little Crow, a steady, generous and independent Indian; he acknowledged the sale of the land at the mouth of the St. Peter's River to the United States, and said he had been looking each year, since the sale, for the troops to build a fort, and was now happy to see us all, as the Sioux would now have a father with them.

I gave him a better present than to any other village below, as he lived immediately in the vicinity of the troops. The day after my arrival at the mouth of the St. Peter's, Penasha and the White Bustard with their bands came down from their villages to visit me. To these chiefs I was equally as liberal as I was to Little Crow, and for the same reason, and they returned home contented.

On the following day Shakopee and two other chiefs from farther up the Minnesota arrived and to them Forsyth gave the remainder of the goods.

In the daily journal[2] which Major Forsyth kept he wrote of Little Crow: "His independent manner I like. I made him a very handsome present, for which he was very thankful, and said it was more than he expected."

Forsyth assured each of the chiefs "that the President of the United States had sent me to acquaint the Sioux that the troops were sent to build a fort at the mouth of the St. Peter's; that they must not think that anything bad was intended; that the fort would be a place where any little thing they wanted repaired by the blacksmith would be attended to and it would also be a place of trade; that their enemies would not be allowed to injure any of the Sioux at or near the fort, but, at the same time, the Sioux must not injure any of the Chippewas that might visit it." He also "took especial pains to impress upon them that the

Americans were very numerous and powerful and must not be trifled with."[3]

At this point, it would be well to consider more fully the geography of the area we now know as St. Paul, specifically with respect to the location of Kaposia* prior to its removal from the east bank of the Mississippi to its later site in South St. Paul on the western bank of that stream. Reference has been made to the Grand Marais, linking it with Pig's Eye Lake, across the River from South St. Paul.

Pig's Eye Lake and marsh, on the alluvial bottomland of the Mississippi about two miles southeast from Dayton's Bluff and the Indian Mounds, were named in allusion to Pierre Parrant, a whiskey dealer, who about the year 1842 removed to the vicinity of that lake. He had a defective eye, whence he received this nickname, applied also to the village of St. Paul at its beginning.[4]

It is evident that this area has undergone changes in its physical characteristics during the last century and a half. In fact, in an atlas published in 1874, a map of St. Paul shows no body of water where Pig's Eye Lake is now situated, but calls it "the hay meadows," indicating that if there was water there at all, it was so shallow that marsh hay could grow there.

It is probable that at Pike's time, the water was higher and the land between Pig's Eye Lake and the Mississippi formed an "island," as Pike called it, about two miles long and a half to one mile wide. This "island" seems to have been the location of Kaposia until the early 1820's. As

---

*"Kapozha" the original form of this name has been translated as "Light," "Light-Footed," and "not encumbered with much baggage." Perhaps the name was given very early to this band of Mdewakanton Dakota because of the fleetness exhibited by them in la crosse, the Indians' favorite game of ball.

we have seen, Major Forsyth in 1819 still located Kaposia "at a place called the Grand Marais." Sometime between 1819 and 1823, probably in 1822, Little Crow III and his people moved their village to present downtown St. Paul, near the mouth of Phalen Creek where Pike had found the "camp of four lodges" in 1805.

On our present maps of St. Paul, Phalen Creek is not marked, but upon inspection of the land between Lake Phalen and the Mississippi, it will be noted that the railroad lines leading from the east side of that lake southward, form a backward "S" as they enter downtown St. Paul and pass under East Seventh Street and Kellogg Boulevard, to meet the Mississippi and turn east and west. This course is the valley of old Phalen Creek. Just east of this railroad junction, between there and the most western tip of Indian Mounds Park, was the site of Kaposia after it had been removed from the Grand Marais. The date of its removal from the mouth of Phalen Creek is as uncertain as its establishment there but it seems to have been about 1833. Forsyth located the other villages in the area also:

> I this day (Aug. 29, 1819) accompanied Col. Leavenworth in his barge up the St. Peter's river to the White Bustard and Pinichon's villages—a distance to the first village of four miles and to the second village two miles higher.

Above these two were Shakopee's, thirty miles up the Minnesota River from its mouth; the Arrow's, twenty-four miles above Shakopee's; and Red Eagle's, six miles yet above the Arrow's. In 1805 Pike had not mentioned the location of Shakopee's village, although Shakopee was present at the council held on Pike Island.

Colonel Leavenworth was too busy readying his establishment for the coming winter to give much attention to his Indian neighbors the fall of 1819, but the next spring he induced the local bands to seek means for establishing a permanent peace with their age old enemies, the Chippewa. He sent a large delegation of them into the Chippewa country to negotiate a treaty, but they turned back after making twenty-three camps and not finding any Chippewa. Before turning back, they wrote a letter to the Chippewa and left it on a high pole in the vicinity of their last camp. This letter consisted of a piece of birch bark on which were marked, with the point of a knife, the Mississippi and Minnesota rivers, the American camp, the journey of the Dakotas, and a few Chippewa and Dakota whose leaders were shaking hands.

It so happened that a few days after the Dakota had posted this note, it was discovered by a party of thirty-eight, which included Governor Lewis Cass of Michigan Territory,* Henry R. Schoolcraft, some soldiers and traders, and ten Chippewa, all of whom were returning from an exploration of the Upper Mississippi. The note was shown to the Chippewa and they immediately understood its meaning.

Cass' party reached Leavenworth's camp on the thirtieth of July. The next day about three hundred Dakota gathered around the camp and concluded a peace treaty with the Chippewa. Little Crow III was present on this occasion and was dramatically described by Schoolcraft:

> Le Petit Corbeau was among the first to greet us. He is a man below the common size, but brawny and well proportioned; and although rising of fifty years of age, retains the looks and vigor of forty. There is a great deal

*At this time the area of Minnesota was a part of the Michigan territory.

of fire in his eyes, which are black and piercing. His nose is prominent and has the aquiline curve, his forehead falling a little from the facial angle, and his whole countenance animated, and expressive of a shrewd mind.[5]

Although a treaty of peace was made, we are told that "the Dakotas were very indifferent about the proceeding and some of them refused to smoke the peace pipe after the treaty was signed."[6]

Little Crow III very clearly explained to Major Forsyth the rationale of his people:

> I mentioned to Little Crow the barbarous war that existed between them and the Chippewa, and if there was not a possibility of bringing about a peace between the two nations. He observed that a peace could easily be made, but said "it is better for us to carry on the war in the way we do than to make peace, because," he added, "we lose a man or two every year, but we kill as many of the enemy during the same time. If we make peace the Chippewa will overrun all the country between the Mississippi and Lake Superior and have their villages on the banks of the Mississippi itself. In this case the Dakotas will lose all of their hunting grounds on the northeast side of the river. Why then should we give up such an extensive country to save the life of a man or two annually? I know it is not good to go to war, or to make too much war, or against too many people; but this is war for land which must always exist if the Dakota Indians remain in the same opinion which now guides them."
>
> I found the Indian's reason so good that I said no more upon the subject.[7]

The Dakota of the area had to establish and maintain their right to hunt in the regions which were near them. Their livelihood depended upon it. As the Chippewa were pushed westward by the advance of white settlement, it became ever more important that constant efforts be made to save what hunting territory remained to them. The alternative was to gather together their baggage and their people and move westward out of their beloved lake-studded woodlands and to change their way of life completely in joining their brethren on the plains. This they were unwilling to do.

In 1823, Major Stephen Long returned to Minnesota with orders from the war department to conduct an expedition of exploration up the Minnesota and down the Red River to the forty-ninth degree of north latitude and thence eastward along the Canadian boundary. The object of the expedition was to make a general survey "of the country on the route pointed out." Major Long was accompanied by several scientists and an artist. William H. Keating, his mineralogist, also wrote the journal of the expedition. He described the Kaposia village and burying ground as follows:

> The party landed at a short distance above (the Red Rock), to visit the cemetery of an Indian village then in sight. The cemetery is on the banks of the river, but elevated above the water's level, it exhibits several scaffolds, supporting coffins of the rudest form; sometimes a trunk (purchased from a trader), at other times a blanket, or a roll of bark conceals the body of the deceased. There were also several graves, in which are probably deposited the bones, after all the softer parts have been resolved into the elements by long exposure to the atmosphere.
>
> Returning to the boat, the party ascended and passed an Indian village consisting of ten or twelve huts, situated at a handsome turn on the river, about ten miles below the mouth of the St. Peter; the village is generally known by the name of the Petit Corbeau or Little Raven, which

was the appellation of the father and grandfather of the present chief. He is called Chetan-wakoamane (the good sparrow-hunter).

The Indians designate this band by the name of Kapoja, which implies that they are deemed lighter and more active than the rest of the nation. As the village was abandoned for the season, we proceeded without stopping.

The houses which we saw here were differently constructed from those which we had previously observed. They are formed by upright flattened posts, implanted in the ground without any interval, except here and there some small loopholes for defence; these posts support the roof, which presents a surface of bark. Before and behind each hut there is a scaffold used for the purpose of drying maize, pumpkin, etc.[8]

The "handsome turn on the river" is northwest of Dayton's Bluff, or above it; the cemetery "on the banks of the river, but elevated above the water's level" must have lain between the village and the high bluffs. (Indian Mounds Park).

Warren Upham states:

Apparently the burial place of the Sioux here described was on the lower northwestern part of Dayton's bluff, above Carver's Cave, where these Indians fifty-seven years before in Carver's time, were accustomed to bring their dead. A group or series of many small artificial mounds marked the place within the memory of the first white settlers. It is about a third of a mile northwest from the large mounds preserved in the Indian Mounds Park at the highest part of this bluff.[9]

It is reasonable then to conclude that in 1823 Kaposia was located on the north side of the Mississippi, near the top of the curve it makes in flowing from a northeast to a southeastward course. Phalen's Creek, as it was later called, entered the Mississippi here and it is probable that Kaposia was established at this point because it was a good place to beach canoes and because it was closer to the center of trade, which was shifting from Prairie du Chien to Mendota.

Long, incidentally, in 1823, located the village of Big Eagle (Black Dog) upstream from Shakopee's band on the Minnesota. In 1805 Pike failed to mention Black Dog. It may be that Black Dog's band was still a part of Penasha's band on the lower Minnesota in Pike's time, or it may be that Black Dog's village was distinct but simply unknown to Pike, who never actually ascended the Minnesota River above Penasha's village.

Setting the Bounds
1825-1830

WE HAVE ALREADY discussed the failure of the treaty between the Chippewa and Dakota, which Colonel Leavenworth and Governor Cass negotiated at the fort in 1820. In March, 1819, Major Lawrence Taliaferro had been appointed Indian agent at Fort Snelling. He apparently did not arrive at the fort until the summer of 1820, remaining there until his resignation in 1839.

Filled with the energy and idealism of youth, he set before himself three principal tasks: (1) to establish and maintain peace between the warring Indian nations, (2) to protect the Indians from the white man's lust and greed, and (3) to induce the savages to cultivate the soil as the beginning of their civilization.[10]

In 1823 young Taliaferro brought together once again a number of Dakota and Chippewa chiefs and induced them to make a pledge of "permanent" peace. His efforts produced little success.

> The morning after the council, Flat Mouth, the distinguished Ojibway chief arrived. As he stepped from his canoe, Penasha held out his hand, but was repulsed with

scorn. The Dakota warrior immediately gave the alarm and in a moment, runners were on their way to the neighboring villages to raise a war party.

On the sixth of June, the Dakotas had assembled, stripped for a fight, and surrounded the Ojibways. At the solicitation of the agent and the commander of the fort, the Dakotas desisted from an attack and retired.

On the seventh, the Ojibways left for their homes, but in a few hours, while making a portage at St. Anthony, they were again approached by the Dakotas, who would have attacked them, if a detachment of troops had not arrived from the fort.[11]

In the early months of 1824, Major Taliaferro was instructed by the United States government to arrange a conference between President Monroe and some important Chippewa and Dakota chiefs and braves. Thus, Little Crow III, Wabasha, and others of Mdewakanton Dakota started on a journey to Washington, making the first lap of their trip by keel boat to Prairie du Chien, where they were joined by a number of Chippewa. From there they went by steamboat down the Mississippi and up the Ohio to Pittsburgh. From Pittsburgh to Washington they traveled by rail.

The traders were opposed to this visit and, at Prairie du Chien, had induced Wabasha and some of the other Sioux to return home. Little Crow, however, changed their minds and prevailed upon them to continue the journey with their agent and the Chippewa. Little Crow III told them:

> You can do as you please, but I am no coward nor can my ears be pulled about by evil counsels. We are here and should go on, and do some good for our nation. I have taken our father here (Taliaferro) by the coat tails,

and I will follow him until I take by the hand our great American Father.¹²

In Washington the Indians had a satisfactory interview with the president, but apparently they were even more impressed by a magician whose tricks they saw at a theater. The outcome of the presidential meeting was an agreement "that in the following year there should be a grand conference or convocation of the Northwestern tribes to compose their differences and to establish a permanent peace."¹³

Accordingly, in August of 1825, there assembled at Prairie du Chien two large bodies of the most influential members of the area's natives — one hundred and fifty Chippewa, assembled by their agent, Schoolcraft, and a delegation of the Dakota numbering three hundred and eighty five, led by their agent, Major Taliaferro.

The arrival of the Dakota was positively dramatic. Taliaferro had allowed them to stop along the way to deck themselves out for the arrival.

> They were all in small canoes and when the gorgeous head-dresses had been donned he again embarked them, having in the meantime decorated the canoes, which were dressed up in regular columns, and the grand entry was made with drums beating, many flags flying and with incessant discharges of small arms. It is doubtful if a more picturesque demonstration has been anywhere made than was that brilliant flotilla of nearly two hundred canoes sweeping down the Mississippi.¹⁴

In addition to the Dakota and the Chippewa, there were also present at this congress Sacs and Foxes, Menominies, Iowa, Winnebagoes and Ottawas, some of whom came hundreds of miles. After much bargaining, map studying, and cross-questioning, on August 19 an agreement was drawn up which was acceptable to the tribes involved.

Section one of this treaty provided for a general peace among all the tribes. Section five, which is of chief interest to this study of the Twin Cities Indians, defined the line dividing the territory of the Dakotas and the Chippewa. This line, the Indians promised, would never be crossed except on peaceful missions. It commenced on the east bank of the Mississippi, opposite the mouth of the "Ioway" river, running back to the bluffs and along the bluffs to the Bad Ox river, thence to the mouth of Black River and thence to "half a day's march below the falls of the Chippewa river."

The boundary agreed to in the treaty was indefinite and difficult to draw. It was probably of little beneficial effect, for within a year of the signing of this treaty Chippewa and Dakota were killing one another "within a mile of Agent Taliaferro's door." It was not until ten years after the treaty that any actual marking of the boundary was attempted.

On the twenty-eighth of May in 1827, a party of twenty-four Chippewa arrived at the fort. It included a chief, seven warriors and sixteen women and children. Assured by the officers at the fort that they would be protected, the Chippewa made camp nearby. That afternoon they were visited by some warriors from Shakopee's band whom they received well. Together they feasted on meat, corn and maple sugar, and smoked the pipe of peace. However, as the Dakota departed that evening, several turned around and fired their guns into one of the tepees. The reports vary as to the casualties, but apparently most of the nine occupants of the tent were injured, two of them fatally.

As a result of this slaughter, the Chippewa executed four Dakota from Shakopee's band under the eyes of the soldiers. In the traditional manner, the four men were forced to "run the gauntlet." "Upon the broad prairie the prisoners were given their freedom. They were told to run, and when a few paces away, the Chippewa warriors fired and the Sioux fell dead."

The fact that the Chippewa came to Fort Snelling, and considered Taliaferro their agent, though after 1827 he was not, attests to his stature among them. He did succeed, however, in keeping to a minimum slaughter between the warring tribes in the fort area. Farther away from the fort, clashes between them were more common, and resulted in more scalpings; yet it was in the area of the Twin Cities that the Chippewa and the Dakota repeatedly came into closest contact.

The use of liquor in the fur trade and the sale of liquor to the Indians by those who were not fur traders, were constant sources of difficulty and served to make the Indian agent's task of regulating its introduction and use a burdensome responsibility.

> The eagerness for liquor on the part of the Indians made its introduction all the more easy. For it they were willing to pay much; eight horses were at one time exchanged for eight kegs of whiskey.[15]

Taliaferro was thoroughly hated by the unscrupulous traders and other whites who attempted to take advantage of the Indians. He did not retire from his long service as Indian agent a rich man, as did many who were willing to take bribes and carry on under-handed dealings. He labored long and hard to establish and maintain peace between the Chippewa and Dakota, but pressures beyond Taliaferro's control prevented a peaceful co-existence. In a speech at Fort Snelling, June, 1829, Little Crow III expressed his own high opinion of Major Taliaferro:

My father: we have been a long time acquainted with each other, and you know how the hearts of my children are pleased; for my part I am getting old and the day is at hand when I must follow all the old people in the grave, but after my death my people will speak of me and my counsels, and you well know that they have been good, for since the last war (1812-15) I have listened to the Americans and have no cause to repent having followed their advice.

My father: we never wish to lose you, for no matter what man we get he can never please us as well as you have done. You know us and our ways. We have been left destitute by our trader taking away all our guns which we got on credit from him last winter. But you have given us powder, lead and tobacco with which we are much pleased, as it will enable us to live some time yet.

My father: a few words and I have done. I was the first man to take thirty of my men and visit your people after the war. I returned home, and then made one more trip to visit the British, but have not done so since you came among us ten years ago.[16]

In 1830, a plan was developed which it was hoped would end for all times the continual inter-tribal warfare in the Northwest, especially between the Dakota and the Sacs and Foxes of Wisconsin. It was proposed to secure from each of these warring tribes a strip of land twenty miles wide which would become a neutral area or no-man's land, where neither tribe would hunt. To accomplish this purpose, the tribes were called to Prairie du Chien and after much bickering, the "neutral belt" was formed between the warring Indians.

It is of interest to note that the old chiefs of three bands

—Little Crow III, Black Dog, and Penasha III—were present with their sons who would succeed each of them within the decade. Both fathers and sons affixed their marks to the original treaty. Within a few years of the treaty-signing, probably in the winter of 1833-34, Little Crow III Chetanwakamani (Walks Pursuing a Hawk) died, and his son Wakinyantanka or Big Thunder was acclaimed chief of the Kaposia band, then located on the east side of the Mississippi in present St. Paul. Big Thunder had probably been born around 1790. He was chief of the Kaposia band about fifteen years and was killed when he accidentally shot himself.

Penasha's Village and Black Dog's Village
1815-1833

WILLIAM JOSEPH SNELLING has recorded that in his time the chief of Owaw Hoska or the Long Avenue Village—Penasha's village—was the son of the Penasha who signed Pike's Treaty, that he was the fifth in descent from the old French trader Penasha, and that by this time, the Penasha line had lost all traces of European blood. It is doubtful that such a long line of Penashas had been chiefs of Owaw Hoska or Oanoska. It seems more likely that the Penasha with whom Pike had dealt in 1805 was the son of the trader, and that the chief whom Snelling and Long knew was the grandson of the Frenchman. This Penasha (III) probably was the chief of his band from 1815 until 1833. His village was located on the north side of the Minnesota River at Bloomington.

 The general rendezvous of the Mdewakanton was at no remote period, on the north bank of the Minnesota River, a little below the mouth of the Nine Mile Creek. There they were secure from the attacks of their enemies, being protected on one side by the river and on the other by a lake several miles in length.[17]

Pond's mention of the lake, "several miles in length" is worth noting. In Andreas' *Atlas* of 1874, this lake is shown and called "Long Lake." By 1898 according to Dahl's *Atlas of Hennepin County,* the water was gone from this area and it was known as "Long Meadow." Parts of it were being farmed, and much of it undoubtedly produced marsh hay. Presently, it is still low and marshy, but designated as "Long Meadow Lake." The Long Avenue Village was situated on the higher ground between old Long Lake and the Minnesota River, at times very near to the mouth of Nine Mile Creek and at times nearer the fort.*

The location a few miles up or down the river would not change the significance of the name, which probably derived from the long trail or "avenue" leading from the high "look-out" point where the fort was built, up the north side of the Minnesota River, all the way to Shakopee's village.

In his time, Penasha was already somewhat of a legend.

> There, at Owaw Hoskah, he passes the summer with his band and may be seen weekly and daily, visiting the agency to ask for some of his father's milk; a harmless, worthless, drunken vagabond. Yet he has a fund of humor that frequently amuses the officers of the garrison and procures him a bottle of whiskey.
>
> One day, visiting Fort Snelling with his face blackened, the commanding officer asked him the reason why he had smeared himself in that manner.

---

*In 1834, S. W. Pond located Penasha's village "near the mouth of Nine Mile Creek." In 1835 Taliaferro noted the distance to the village from the fort as seven miles "by water." Earlier, it must have been closer to the fort, perhaps only five and a half miles in 1823, according to the historian of the Long expedition, Professor Keating. In 1819, Major Forsyth located the village six miles up the St. Peter's, but he probably reckoned the distance from Leavenworth's encampment, "on the south bank of the St. Peter's, half a mile from its mouth."

"It is because my brother is dead," was the reply.

"Why then, do you not act as we do? When we lose a relative, we array ourselves in good black broadcloth."

To this Penasha replied: "Father, every nation has its customs, you are rich and we are poor. Therefore, we show our grief by smearing our faces with soot and you attire yourselves in black cloth. But as you do not approve of my following the customs of our ancestors, to please you I am willing to compromise. Give me a black dress for this occasion, and in return, I will give you as much soot as shall serve for the purpose of mourning all the days of your life."[18]

On another occasion when Penasha visited the fort, Colonel Snelling asked him if the Rum River, where Penasha anticipated a journey with his band, was so named "because rum runs there instead of water?" The Dakota chief replied:

No father, it does not. If it did, I would live on its banks till I had drunk it dry. You would never see me here again.[19]

It appears that Penasha's independent spirit was always somewhat of an annoyance to the officers at the fort. Even Major Taliaferro was unable to win Penasha to his way of thinking. Taliaferro's conviction was that the Indians should be taught to raise their own food as the first step toward their "civilization," and he was successful in enlisting the support of the commander at the fort in this venture.

Colonel Snelling once proposed to this chief and his people, in council, to give them potatoes, seed corn, a plough, etc. and to send men to their village to teach them how to use the implements of husbandry, and to raise cattle and swine.

"You see," said the officer, "that the chase is uncertain support, and that you are often obliged to ask us for food to keep you from starving. Work, then, as we do, and you will be above the necessity of begging."

This suggestion appealed no more to Penasha than it did to his son and his people ten or fifteen years later, although it seems they were willing enough to attach themselves to Cloudman's Lake Calhoun Band and reap the benefits of their foresight and industry. Penasha, after filling his pipe, exhausting its contents and deliberately knocking out the ashes, finally replied to the Colonel's proposal:

"Father, I have been reflecting on your proposal, as its importance deserves. What you say is true. You speak with but one tongue. It is certain that we are often without anything to eat. But it strikes me that we have no need to labor to procure corn, or squashes, or potatoes or cattle or pigs, while we have so good a father, who gives us all these things without any trouble on our part."[20]

Taliaferro's diary fixes old Penasha's death somewhere between June of 1832 and August of 1833, at which time Tucanwashtay or Good Road became chief of the band at Long Avenue Village.

Of the three old chiefs who signed the treaty in 1830, the last to die was Black Dog or Wamditanka (Big Eagle). His death occurred in 1838 and his son, Mazarota or Grey Iron,* became chief of Black Dog's band. Black Dog was not a hereditary chief, but "a selfe made"[21] chief, according to Taliaferro, having probably gathered most of his followers from old Penasha's band a number of years earlier, perhaps even as early as 1800. Of old Black Dog

---

*also called Pamayayaw or My Head Aches.

—Big Eagle I—Samuel Pond later wrote: "He was an old man in 1834, and may have appeared to better advantage when younger."[22]

In this history Black Dog's other name—Big Eagle— is suffixed with the Roman numeral I since his grandson, the son of Grey Iron, also took the name Big Eagle when he became chief of the old Black Dog band in 1853. The grandson of Black Dog then is designated as Big Eagle II for the sake of convenience.*

By 1825, when Black Dog signed the Treaty of Prairie du Chien with the other Dakota, it is probable that his village was located closer to the confluence of the Minnesota River and the Mississippi. Long and Keating had found it situated about twelve or thirteen miles from that point. In 1822 the Columbia Fur Company had established its headquarters at Mendota and possibly the presence of this "somewhat elaborate structure" attracted the band and influenced the location of its village—Tetankatane—nearby. During these years, Tetankatane acquired a second name, by which it was known to the early settlers—Magayutashnee or "People who do not eat geese," perhaps "because they found it more profitable to sell game at Fort Snelling."[23] This location near Mendota was near the northeast end of Black Dog Lake, which was in those days about four miles long, an ox-bow lake occupying a deserted path of the Minnesota River on its south shore, about two or three miles from the river's mouth.

This period brought an increase of hostile activity among the Dakota and the Chippewa. The Chippewa threatened the Sioux of the Upper Minnesota, and the Sioux in turn raided the Chippewa camps on Mille Lacs and Sandy Lake.

---

*This designation is not used by historians generally. Big Eagle II is usually just called "Big Eagle, Grey Iron's son."

In August, 1830, Governor Cass instructed Schoolcraft, the Chippewa Agent at Sault Ste. Marie, to proceed into the Indian country and effect a peace. Schoolcraft went the following year, and the success of this trip led to the expedition of 1832, which had as its avowed objective that the party should "visit as many of the Indians as circumstances will permit" but which in fact resulted in the discovery of the source of the Mississippi River.

Schoolcraft visited Chippewa bands in the north, then proceeded to Fort Snelling. He arrived July 24, 1832, and asked the local Dakota chiefs to meet with him.

> After Mr. Schoolcraft had stated to three or four of the principal Sioux chiefs who had been requested to visit him the object of his tour and mentioned the complaints which the Ojibways brought against them for breaking the treaties of Prairie du Chien and Fond du Lac, Little Crow rose and replied that he recollected those treaties when they smoked the pipe and all agreed to eat and drink out of the same dish. He wished the line to be drawn between them and the Ojibways, the sooner it was fixed, the better. Black Dog, and the Man-who-floats-on-water* also spoke in much the same manner.[24]

---

*Man-who-floats-on-the-water is undoubtedly "Drifter," second chief of Cloudman's band.

Cloudman and the Village on Lake Calhoun
1828-1839

MAJOR TALIAFERRO WAS convinced that the only way to "civilize" the Indians was to teach them how to farm, and he early endeavored to induce them to give up the uncertain chase, and to settle permanently on good ground, suitable for cultivation. It is true that the Dakota had, for many years, depended on the soil for part of their subsistence, even planting small gardens of corn and pumpkins, but farming was considered "squaw-work" and few of the mighty Dakota braves were interested in thus belittling themselves in their brethren's eyes. Taliaferro's goal then was to convince the *men* to take up the labor of raising food, instead of considering it a disgrace and leaving all the work of soil preparation, planting, cultivation, and harvesting to the women and children.

Philander Prescott had come to the area in 1819 with the soldiers under Leavenworth when they established the post which in time became known as Fort Snelling. Prescott, just eighteen years of age, was employed as clerk of the sutler's store and shortly after his arrival entered the Indian trade. In the fashion of the times he took as his wife an Indian maiden, the daughter of chief Kee-e-hie.

Old Kee-e-hie or members of his family seem to have owed the young trader a considerable payment for goods received. Kee-e-hie was unable to procure the requisite pelts and offered his daughter in exchange, a not infrequent occurrence in those days. After completion of his service, Prescott chose to remain in the area.

As part of the treaty of 1830, the government promised to station among the Mdewakanton for a period of ten years, a resident blacksmith "together with all necessary tools and agricultural implements, to the amount of four hundred dollars annually."[25] Eventually, a blacksmith's shop was built near the Major's house, just outside the fort. It measured sixteen by eighteen feet. From it the Indians could procure chains, traps, axes, muskrat and fishing spears, hoes and all sorts of other hand-made tools of iron. These tools proved a valuable aid to those who adopted the mode of life which was so strange to them, especially to the hearty braves who always considered the cultivation of crops "woman's work." In 1828 Major Taliaferro had initiated a project which in time drew a large number of Mdewakanton from the local bands, especially Penasha's, and even attracted Wapeton from farther up the Minnesota River. This project developed into a large village on the banks of Lake Calhoun in Minneapolis. He first consulted with Philander Prescott, who has described the beginnings of this agricultural experiment:

> The following spring the Indian agent, Major Taliaferro, tried to induce the Indians to engage in farming at Lake Calhoun, and wanted me to go out with my old father-in-law and another chief, Marpiya-wichasta (Cloudman). My old father-in-law was the first one that would venture out. His name was Kee-e-he-ie, "He That Flies." The agent sent a soldier and a team of two yokes of

Cloudman's Village on Lake Calhoun by George Catlin, 1835.
Smithsonian Institute.

cattle and we two plowed about a month, but there were but few Indians that would venture out the first year as they were afraid of the Chippewas. The next year quite a number came out and we had more applicants than we could supply places for and some went to work with their hoes and dug small patches of ground to commence with.[26]

Other sources confirm that in the first year the community numbered only eight persons—two families—but nevertheless prospered and grew. In 1830, the following year, Taliaferro appointed Cloudman chief of the little village. Cloudman did not sign the treaty at Prairie du Chien that year, probably because the Lake Calhoun band was so small. In 1831 Taliaferro appointed Prescott government farmer to the village and gave the community a name—Eatonville, in honor of Secretary of War John H. Eaton. The Indians themselves named the village Reyataotonwe, or Inland Village, since it was away from the rivers where they had always had their villages before.

"On May 1 (Taliaferro) goes out to find most of the Indians 'at work, cutting down trees, grubbing out the roots, etc. What was more encouraging (says Taliaferro in his journal) some of the men were at this unusual kind of labor for them. They laughed when they saw me. I praised them in every agreeable way that could be conveyed to them in their language.' On August 14, 1833, the journal records: 'Much corn is being raised, from 800 to 1,000 bushels—3rd year of this establishment—advanced from 8 to 125 souls.' "[27]

In the spring of 1834, Samuel and Gideon Pond arrived at Fort Snelling, determined to spend the rest of their lives as missionaries among the Dakotas. In a letter written to a relative back in their home state, Connecticut, Gideon described the site of the Indian village on Lake Calhoun:

I will suppose that you should make us a visit in the summer. Leaving Fort Snelling and traveling northwest, you would cross a green and level prairie three miles wide where you would come to a beautiful stream of water called by the Indians Little River (Minnehaha Creek). It issues out of a lake a short distance from where we cross it and it falls, I think nearly a hundred feet. After crossing the stream and getting out from among the trees which grow on its banks you would enter upon another prairie stretching off to the northwest, you would perceive a hill which would appear to you much higher than any other ground.

As you draw near to the hill (the highest point of Lakewood Cemetery) following an Indian footpath you would see white cloths fixed to the tops of poles. They are waving over graves. The top of that hill is the burying place of the Indians who always bury the dead in high places. If you should go to the top of the hill you would see the hair of their surviving friends, which they have cut off and strewn about the graves. Often they cut themselves very badly with knives when their friends die. Perhaps too, you would see some food which they have laid by the graves for the dead to eat.

After passing a little to the right of the burying place you turn to the left and pass through the cornfields on your way to the village. Here you would see the women dressed in something like a petticoat and a short gown, taking care of their corn. If the corn were ripe enough to eat, the men and boys would be there too. If not, some of the men and boys would be after deer and fish and some would be doing nothing. Some of the men helped their wives raise corn last year and more of them said they should next year.

The village which stands on the southeast side of the

lake (Calhoun) consists of fourteen dwelling houses, besides other small ones. The houses are large and two or three families live in some of them. You would not see our house from the village, but turning to the right along the east bank of the lake and ascending a hill, after walking about a quarter of a mile, you would find our house on the high ground I mentioned before as being covered with timber, between the woods and the lake.[28]

Year by year the village grew so that by 1839, the last year that Cloudman resided on Lake Calhoun, the community numbered 500 persons and was the largest village in the Twin Cities area. It attracted not only would-be farmers, but also many opportunistic relatives and friends who found the labors of their industrious fellows a stable source of supply for their own needs.

It is worth noting that though the Kaposia band numbered 300 in 1823,[29] it had diminished to 183 in 1834 when Little Crow IV, was chief.[30] Whether or not a family or a group of families stayed with a chief often depended upon his popularity and ability in the field of oratory. It is possible that this factor would account for the decline of the Kaposia band since there is no record of an epidemic or great battle which would have depleted the band to such an extent during these years. Penasha's band remained about the same size, 150 members, until the late thirties. It is probable that a major part of this band eventually took up residence at Lake Calhoun, if not to farm, at least to profit from the industry of those who did.

It might be well at this point to digress sufficiently to include a biography of one of the exceptional Indians of the area under discussion, a man of whom much and little is known, Cloudman or Marpiya-wichasta. Cloudman's lineage is somewhat obscure—when signing treaties, he designated his band as Mdewakanton; yet he is more often referred to by others as a Wapeton. Since he was not a hereditary chief, perhaps both are valid. Cloudman's own calculations would place his birth around 1795. However, Thomas Hughes recorded his birth as being around 1780 "at the village of the father of old chief Good Roads up the south side of the Minnesota some eight miles from Mendota."[31]

This village we know as Penasha's village.

John H. Stevens, Minneapolis' first settler, states that both Cloudman and Good Road were born "on the shores of Lake Calhoun." But Stevens knew these chiefs only as old men, heads of bands then located on the north side of the Minnesota at Bloomington (Oak Grove), or some years across the river and he could easily have been mistaken as to such long ago events. It is very well established that there was no Dakota village on the shore of Lake Calhoun when Leavenworth arrived with his men in 1819. It is not unlikely that Cloudman* was of Wapeton stock and born while the Wapeton resided near present Carver and that as a young man he chose to join Penasha's Mdewakanton Band, then located only a short distance below on the Minnesota River banks at Nine Mile Creek. It is also probable that he took a Mdewakanton maiden as his wife.

He was one of five sons of "Old Eve." Her three elder sons were "Cloudman, Eagle Help, and Paul Mazakutamane, all men of mark in their different spheres."[32]

In his youth, Cloudman had been as true a Dakota as any of his brethren, but with the coming of the white soldiers in 1819, his philosophy of life began to change.

---

*He is sometimes called Cloud by Holcombe. The Cloudman who signed the Treaty of 1851 at Traverse des Sioux with the Wapeton and Sisseton as a principal warrior of Chief Running Walker may or may not be the same Lake Calhoun Cloudman.

The Rev. Gideon Pond, who knew him well, relates:

> It was Cloudman's activity and resolution in war that had raised him to the rank of chief. His father and uncle had also been great warriors, the one killing fifteen and the other seventeen of the enemy. The uncle had himself fallen in battle, and this event aroused the fiendish passions of the young man who then determined on revenge or death. He braced himself for murder and savage cruelty, knowing that success would not only gratify his love of revenge but also raise him to honor. He added that he still wished to die in battle.
>
> Cloudman said that one time eleven warriors fought with one hundred Ojibways and killed a number without having one wounded. He laid his hand upon his mouth, a mark of wonder and said:
>
> "There the Great Spirit fought for us."
>
> He spoke of their cruelties and of once bringing home a boy and burning him alive, saying that they felt no pity in time of war.
>
> "Our hearts," he said, "are strong and such things cannot move us."[33]

The winter of 1828-29 had been an especially severe one for the Dakota:

> Many of the Indians died of starvation and cold. They had been out west of Lake Traverse and the Cheyenne River in search of buffalo, but were not successful, and the snow fell very deep and they could not follow the game, and they turned back hoping to reach their old villages where they had some corn cached in holes in the ground. They had eaten all of their dogs and horses and had become so weak they could with difficulty walk and they could not see where to go and there was no timber or wood with which to make a fire and none but the strongest survived.[34]

Cloudman later related to the Rev. S. W. Pond his personal experience in this blizzard and the profound effect it had on his philosophy of life, which Pond recorded in detail:

> . . . this determination to try to obtain at least a part of his support by agriculture was first formed during a winter blizzard, when he lay buried in the snow on the prairie. He, with a party of hunters, was overtaken by a snow storm on the plains near the Missouri, and the storm was so violent that they had no alternative but to lie down and wait for it to pass over. They had a little dried buffalo meat with them, and lay separately in the snow, and each wrapped in his blanket. The chief related how, as the snow drifted around and over him, he pressed it back to gain a little more room, and often made an opening through the drift over his head, hoping to find the tempest abated, but could see only the drifting snow.
>
> In the meantime, he could hold no communication with his buried companions and knew not whether they were dead or alive. During his solitary confinement he had leisure to reflect on the vicissitudes of a hunter's life, and remembering that Major Taliaferro had the year before tried to persuade him to plant at Lake Calhoun, he determined to follow his advice if he lived to reach home again.
>
> He was the first of the party to discover that the storm was over, and, extricating himself from his prison, he called for his comrades. He said he hardly expected to find them all alive, but they all answered to their names, though some of them were unable to crawl out of the snowdrifts or to walk after they were taken out by their companions. They had been lying, without being aware of it, not far from a large camp of Indians, who came to their assistance.
>
> Having reached the conclusion that it would be better

for the Dakotas to turn their attention to agriculture and adopt the customs of civilized people. Marpiya-wichasta tried to pursuade others to adopt his views.[35]

It was the following spring that Cloudman accepted Major Taliaferro's invitation to begin the experiment at Lake Calhoun. Thus Cloudman's resolve a decade earlier to give up war and his conclusion reached during the terrible blizzard the previous winter, together with his innate qualities of leadership, made him the Major's obvious choice for chief of the little band.

His new philosophy brought upon him the derision of his fellow Dakota though many of his relatives and companions were willing enough to join his band and reap the fruits of his labors in the field. "See Cloudman! He hoes corn like a woman!" they would jeer, but he was not turned from his chosen course.

> (Cloudman) maintained that war begot war, that it never settled any dispute but only aggravated the irritation and made the continuation of war more inevitable. He also believed that the agricultural life was preferable for his people to the chase and later he advocated the white man's civilization with its religion and schools as far superior to the red man's savagery with its deprivations and cruelties, and advised his people to follow the white man's trail. But Indian government is purely democratic. No chief can compel obedience to any policy of his own, unless it is in accord with the wishes of his people. Hence the chief could not make his subjects adopt his advanced ideas or program, nor could he stop his band from going on war campaigns against the Chippewas, if they in council chose so to do.[36]

Of his philosophy, S. W. Pond states: It would have been well for the Dakota if they had more chiefs like him, but he was far in advance of his contemporaries and was the only chief who was decidedly in favor of abandoning the chase and cultivating the arts of civilized life. He was a man of superior discernment and of great prudence and foresight. He did not hesitate to tell the Dakota that the time had come when nothing but a change in their mode of life could save them from ruin, yet they were slow to adopt his new notions. He was opposed by many of the other chiefs, and none of them entered heartily into his views.[37]

Unlike the more prominent of his brothers, Little Paul Mazakutamane, he did not become a Christian, unless he was among the many who were converted and baptized while interned at the camp of "friendlies" near Fort Snelling in the winter of 1862-63 just before his death. According to the Rev. Samuel Pond, Cloudman, "a thoughtful man of good judgment, told me that he regarded many of the wakan-men as imposters, but that he thought some of them honest men and their statements concerning supernatural things reliable."[38] Cloudman's other living brother, Eagle Help, was a medicine man of wide renown, and undoubtedly the seemingly miraculous cures which he often produced had an effect on Cloudman's thinking. However, he realized, as did others of the Dakota, that many of the barbaric practices of their forebears would have to be eliminated from their lives before their adjustment to the new mode of living could be effected.

He also was aware of the great damage that liquor was causing among his people, although he was neither a teetotaler nor a prohibitionist. In his journal at a later date, after Cloudman's band moved to Oak Grove, the Rev. Gideon Pond wrote: "This afternoon a neighboring Indian brought a keg of whiskey to our village and invited the chief and the chief soldiers to drink. The invitation was refused and the refusal so angered the Indians that now, about sunset, they are about killing Marpiya wichasta (the chief) and are running about the village in first rate style."[39] Very obviously, Cloudman's efforts in the direction of discouraging the use of liquor among his followers were not especially appreciated by some of his band.

In considering Cloudman's characteristics, perhaps one must endorse Holcombe's description: "Chief Cloudman was a strong and very peculiar character. In some respects he was a thorough Indian, in others he was like a white man."

Cloudman was the father of seven children, all of whom were probably born before Cloudman had moved to the area of Lake Calhoun. One of Cloudman's daughters, "Stands Like a Spirit" became the wife of Captain Seth Eastman, who was stationed at the fort nearby from 1830 to 1836. To this union was born a daughter, who was named Mary Nancy. Eastman, however, forsook "Stands Like a Spirit" and young Mary Nancy, when he was transferred to another station; and they returned to Cloudman's household on Lake Calhoun. By the time the family moved to Oak Grove, Mary Nancy had become a "lovely and talented young woman," much sought after by the young men of the local bands.

> Among her many suitors was a young man whom she looked upon with favor, but he did not possess sufficient of this world's goods to purchase her, as the Indian marriage custom was. The Indian law required the groom to purchase the bride from the parents or relatives.
>
> The mother and the grandmother thought they ought to get a very good price for such a handsome girl, much more than the young man could pay, and one or two rich

old Indians were bidding for her, and the one who paid the most, was sure to get her. The girl, however, did not like any of them, but insisted on her own choice.

So the young couple concluded to elope, and a certain dark night was appointed when the young man was to come at a late hour to the tepee where she slept and give her a certain signal. But the young brave had a very special friend to whom he told the whole plan, and this young friend was secretly very much in love with the same girl but did not have the requisite horses, beaver and buffalo robes to pay for her. This friend was Ite Wahanhdi-Ota, Many Lightnings, a noted warrior of excellent character, descended from a famous Wapeton Chief.

On the night appointed, Many Lightnings got to the girl's tepee an hour or two ahead of his friend and gave the signal she and her lover had agreed upon. She, thinking it was her lover, joined him quickly with her bundle of clothes, and the two hurried from the village, he, with face covered in his blanket (as was the custom), and she following in the trail behind.

After they had gone ten or twelve miles without saying a word, and were nearing the village where Many Lightnings lived, he stopped and drew the blanket from his face and revealed his identity to her. Surprised to stupification, she stood trembling. Then recovering her voice, she said:

"Oh, why have you done me this wrong? Why did you deceive me? Why did you deceive not only me, but your friend, your sworn comrade, your codah? How dared you do such a thing?"

He pleaded his great love for her as his only reason. He was ready to die for her. She stopped him.

"What shall I do? The Great Spirit has punished me for being disobedient to my mother and grandmother. How dare I go back home and bring disgrace on my aged grandmother, for no one will believe my story, for they will say I am your 'castoff.' I will be your wife, since it cannot be helped now. My mother must not be disgraced. Fear not, I will do my duty towards you and be a faithful, obedient wife to you."

To save him from the vengeance of his friend, it was agreed that it be told that she had met her husband at the medicine dance, and became so enamored of him that she discarded her first lover and went with him.

Many Lightnings and his beautiful bride lived happily together many years and, strange as it may appear, she seemed to love him with more than ordinary affection. And he proved himself a man in every respect and a most devoted husband. As a hunter, he was unsurpassed and was looked upon as an oracle and leader in every enterprise among his people.[40]

The youngest of the five children born to Mary Nancy and Many Lightnings was Ohiyesa, Charles A. Eastman, an Indian of great renown who contributed much to the uplifting of his people. His autobiography, contained in *Indian Boyhood* and *From the Deep Woods to Civilization*, was penned for his own son and is especially interesting and informative.

Returning to a consideration of the village on Lake Calhoun, one can refer to the map which Major Taliaferro drew of the Fort Snelling region in 1835. It embraces most of what is now known as the greater Twin Cities area and shows a number of rectangles and trapezoids on the east shore of Lake Calhoun. These undoubtedly represent fields under cultivation by Cloudman's people.

It is by no means to be understood that the five hundred Dakota living on the banks of our Lake Calhoun in 1839 were all diligent farmers. In fact, Samuel Pond goes so far

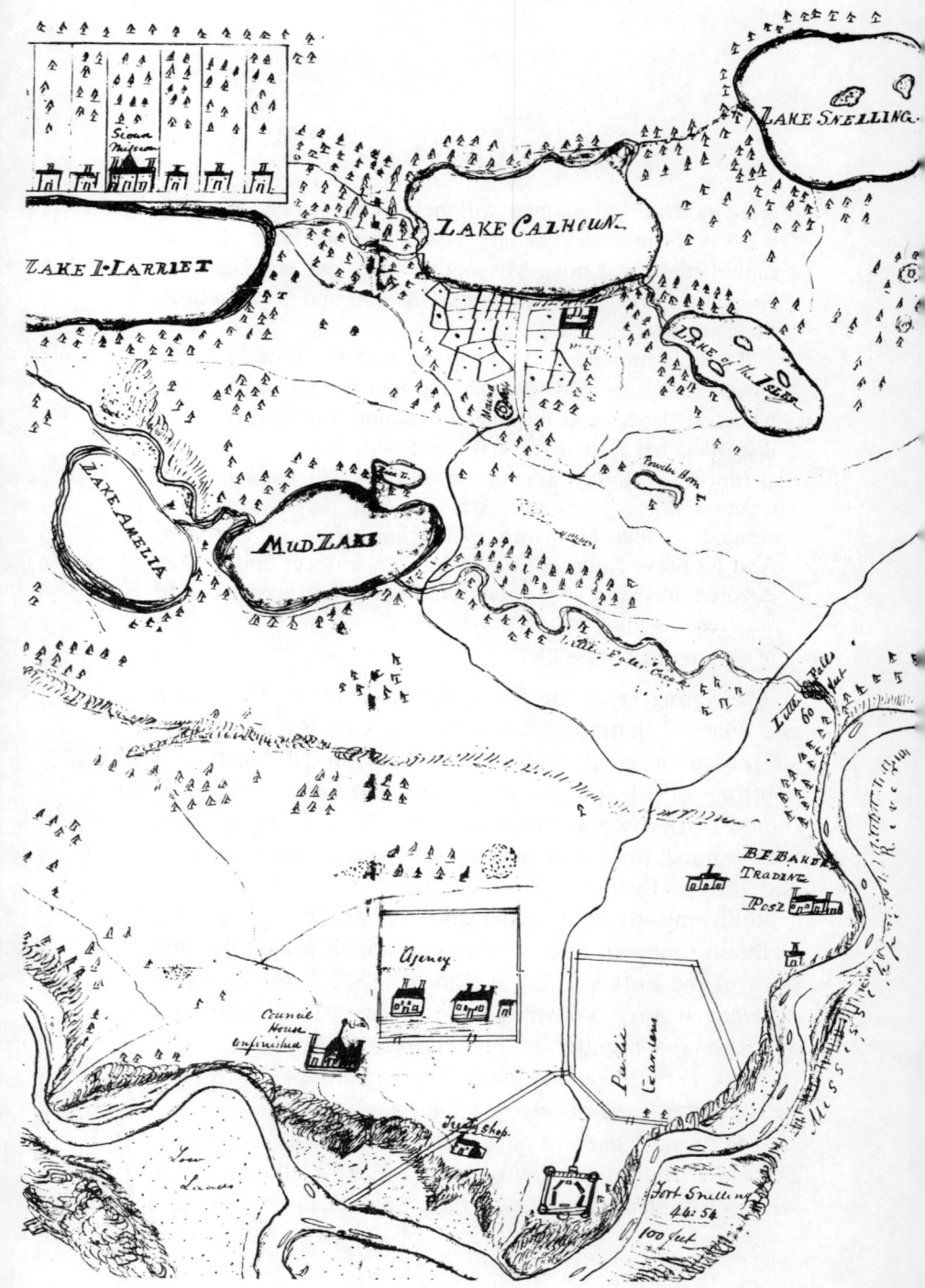

Layout of Cloudman's Village and the Mission at Lake Harriet, taken from Taliaferro's map, 1835.

as to say that Cloudman had "no success" in convincing the other Dakota to follow his example.

Within a few years of Cloudman's settlement on Lake Calhoun a subchief, Kaboka or Drifter, joined the band with his followers and caused friction among the dwellers at Reyatoatonwe. His previous history is a mystery; but he was decidedly anti-missionary and anti-civilization. Red Bird, Cloudman's brother-in-law, a noted Wakan-man or medicine-man, opposed the efforts of Taliaferro and Cloudman toward civilization. He became the chief soldier or war-chief of the band, and always had a following, especially among the younger braves who would not engage in the "squaw-work" of farming nor adopt other civilized habits.

The Mission at Lake Harriet
1835-1839

IN SEPTEMBER OF 1829, the Rev. Jedediah D. Stevens and the Rev. Alvin Coe* visited Fort Snelling. They had been exploring possibilities for mission work among the Chippewa in Wisconsin and had decided to include the side-trip into the Dakota region. These men were kindly received by Major Taliaferro. "The old saw mills and buildings of the government at St. Anthony Falls were placed at their disposal, as was also the Indian farm which had been established at Lake Calhoun by the government authorities and called Eatonville."[41]

In spring Stevens returned to his mission in Wisconsin to continue his work there for several years; but in May, 1835, he returned to Fort Snelling, this time to settle and labor among the Mdewakanton. The Stevens family that arrived consisted of Rev. and Mrs. Stevens, their two sons, Dwight and Evert, Rev. Stevens' niece who had come out with them to be a teacher, and Jane DeBow, their six and a half year old foster daughter.

For three years Jane DeBow lived with the missionary's

---
*They were missionaries under the American Board of Commissioners for Foreign Missions, a Presbyterian-Congregational group.

family near the Lake Calhoun village, and her reminiscences of that period as set down by her daughter are an interesting addition to the history of Cloudman's Band. The title of the booklet of reminiscences is *Little Bird That Was Caught,* referring to the name that the Indians gave her because she was not really a member of the Stevens family, but had been "caught" away from her own family. Writing of this period, Samuel Pond stated:

> In the fall of the year 1835, I sold part of the corn I raised to Mr. Sibley, and though Gideon had worked all summer for Mr. Stevens gratuitously, we had more money than when we landed at Fort Snelling, and if I had sold all I raised it would have amounted to considerably more than the salary that I received from the board for several years after I was married.
>
> We purchased a cow and were about to make some improvements in our house when Mr. Stevens said if we remained at Lake Calhoun, he could do nothing at Lake Harriet, and that might have been true, for he was never popular with the Indians. He also claimed that as we had approved of his building at Lake Harriet we were in some measure responsible for the success of his mission. We learned afterwards that he wrote to Secretary Green (of the Mission Board) that the reason why we joined him was we were so uncomfortably situated at Lake Calhoun, but we did not know it then, or we should have stayed there, so we reluctantly abandoned our house, turned over our cow, corn and potatoes, of which we had a large crop, to Mr. Stevens and Gideon remained with him (at the Mission House) and I went off with the Indians on a hunting expedition. The language, however, was the game I went to hunt, and I was as eager in pursuit of that as the Indians were of deer.[42]

From several accounts the reader might well conclude

that Rev. Stevens' ministry was not entirely successful.

Stevens continued in charge of the mission, obtaining, however but slight influence over the Indians. He either could not or would not acquire the language. He preached frequently in English at the fort or at the mission. He opened two schools; one for the Indian children, taught by his niece who learned Dakota rapidly; the other, a small boarding school for the mixed-blood daughters of traders, army officers, and the Indian agent.[43]

Another missionary of the time, Stephen R. Riggs, spent a short time at the Rev. Stevens mission and his reactions were hardly enthusiastic:

The Dakotas did not yet care to hear the gospel. The Messrs. Pond had succeeded in teaching one young man to read and write, and occasionally a few could be induced to come and listen to the good news. It was seed sowing time. Many seeds fell by the wayside or on the hard path of sin. Most fell among thorns. But some found good ground and lying dormant a full quarter of a century, then sprang up and sprouted in the prison at Mankato. Also of the girls in that first Dakota boarding school quite a good proportion became Christian women and the mothers of Christian families.[44]

In the spring of 1836, Gideon left the Lake Harriet Mission and went up to Lac qui Parle. There he married and remained until April, 1838.

In the meantime, Samuel spent a year in Connecticut studying theology. He was ordained March 4, 1837, and returned to Lake Harriet in May of that year, where he continued to assist Rev. Stevens in his school. That summer he wrote the story of Joseph, the first non-textbook to be printed in the Dakota language.

In order to learn the Dakota language, the Rev. Stephen R. Riggs spent three months at Lake Harriet prior to taking up work at Lac qui Parle. His young wife Mary came with him, and the letters written during this brief period by Mary Riggs to her family in the East include valuable detail of the Indian life at Lake Calhoun and Lake Harriet, which warrant quoting:

> About a mile north of us is Lake Calhoun, on the margin of which is an Indian village of about twenty lodges. Most of these are bark houses, some of which are twenty feet square, and others are tents of skin or cloth. Several days since, I walked over to the village, and called at the house of one of the chiefs. He was not at home, but his daughters smiled very good-naturedly upon us. We seated ourselves on a frame extending on three sides of the house, covered with skins, which was all the bed, sofa, and chairs they had.
>
> Since our visit at the village, two old chiefs have called upon us. One said this was a very bad country—ours was a good country—we had left a good country to live in his bad country and he was glad. The other called on Sabbath evening, when Mr. Riggs was at the Fort, where he preaches occasionally. He inquired politely how I liked the country, and said it was bad. What could a courtier have said more?
>
> The Indians come here at all hours of the day without ceremony, sometimes dressed and painted very fantastically and again with scarcely any clothing. One came in yesterday dressed in a coat, calico shirt, and cloth leggins, the only one I have seen with a coat, excepting two boys who were in the family when we came (Dwight and Evert). The most singular ornament I have seen was a large striped snake, fastened among the painted hair, feathers, and ribbons of an Indian's head-dress, in such manner that it could coil round in front and dart out its

snake head, or creep down upon the back at pleasure. During this, the Indian sat perfectly at ease, apparently much pleased at the astonishment and fear manifested by some of the family.[45]

Mary recounted the hardships suffered by the members of the Lake Calhoun band, even in summer, when life was comparatively easy. It does not require too great a strain on the imagination to bring to mind the even greater sufferings which these people underwent in the winter season.

Some Indian women came in yesterday bringing strawberries, which I purchased with beans. Poor creatures, they have very little food of any kind at this season of the year, and we feel it difficult to know how much it is our duty to give them.[46]

In Jane DeBow Gibbs' reminiscences, we read of the Stevens family's arrival and the first few weeks spent in the officers' quarters at old Fort Snelling while Rev. Stevens and the Pond brothers were building the Mission House. The Rev. Stevens had decided to erect the Mission House on the west side of Lake Harriet, hoping that the Indians would gather there to hear the Word. He and the Pond brothers constructed the building and on completion the family moved in. Thereafter Rev. Stevens established a school for the Indian children and attempted to preach the Gospel to their parents.

School opened during the summer with six Indian children; the number soon increased to twenty-five, and included half-breed children, the dusky progeny of the traders, the children of Mr. Sibley and of Mr. Prescott, the daughter of Indian Agent Taliaferro, and others known to history. The native children were shy as wild birds of adult people, but having made friends of Jane and the Stevens' children, were thus led to listen to the singing and reading which were the first forms of instruction the missionaries undertook.

To interest the Indian mothers in the school, the children were given presents to carry home. The reward of merit and of punctual attendance most frequently took the form of turnips, as much as a bushel of the vegetable being sometimes distributed to the handful of pupils in a day.[47]

Writing of this school in January, 1836, Rev. Stevens recorded: "On the nineteenth instant, we commenced a school with six full blood Indian children, at least so in all their habits, dress, etc; not one could speak any language but Sioux. The school has since grown to the number of twenty-five. I am now collecting and arranging words for a dictionary. Mr. Pond (Gideon) is assiduously employed in preparing a small spelling book, which we may forward next mail for printing."[48]

Though somewhat successful with the Indian children through the help of the Stevens boys and little Jane, the Rev. Stevens does not seem to have been able to interest the adults in religion. Gideon Pond tells us, "Mr. Stevens located himself on the west shore of Lake Harriet, about midway. He labored to draw the Indians to him, but succeeded with only two or three families."

In October of 1837, Samuel again accompanied the Calhoun Indians on their hunting expedition as he had in the fall of 1835.

> I was more comfortable, or rather, less uncomfortable than in the winter of 1835. We were three months without bread and salt, but had plenty of good food. Fortunately for me, the lock of my gun was broken soon after we started, by a boy to whom I lent it, so that I was excused from hunting, and could spend my time more profitably,

for when I accompanied the hunters, I seldom heard a word spoken except while a deer was being dressed, while there was always talking enough at the tents, and if I was tired of listening to the gossip of the Indians, I had with me a pocket testament and lexicon in Greek. The family that I lived with consisted of a middle aged man and his wife and two of his nephews, both old enough to hunt and, as the men were all good hunters, we had always venison enough and a surplus for those who had none. The old man made an estimate of the number of deer that I ate, and I paid him so that he and his wife said it was enough, and, what was unexpected and remarkable, they never afterwards claimed that I was under any obligations to them.[49]

In the spring of 1838, considering "that it did not seem advisable for us to be at Lake Harriet while Mr. Stevens was there," the brothers decided that Samuel should leave Harriet and that Gideon should leave Lac qui Parle in order that they might together start a new mission station, possibly at Traverse des Sioux. However, the Treaty of 1837 changed the situation at Lake Harriet. According to the provisions of the treaty, Major Taliaferro, in the summer of 1838, received instructions to appoint a farmer for each band of the Mdewakanton. Samuel Pond wrote:

"Mr. Stevens, Mr. Prescott, and others applied for the appointment of farmer for the Lake Calhoun band, but the agent refused to give it to them, and offered it to me. I at first told him I could not take it, but he said the Indians would be dissatisfied if he gave it to anyone else, so I consented to hold it until I could ascertain whether Gideon would take it off my hands. This pleased Taliaferro for he was very unwilling to have my brother leave Lake Calhoun (when he had left to go to Lac qui Parle in the spring of 1836)."[50] In January of 1839, Stevens received the appointment of farmer to the Wabasha band, and in July of that year he left for Winona, putting Samuel Pond in charge of the Mission at Lake Harriet.

Gideon decided to accept the position as farmer of the Calhoun band. "In April, 1839, with my wife and eldest daughter, I floated down in a canoe from Lac qui Parle to Mendota, and returned to Lake Harriet, at the earnest solicitation of the Indians of the Lake Calhoun band and their agent, and received the appointment of farmer for that band. I held that appointment until I was satisfied thoroughly that I could turn it to no good account to the Indians and then resigned and put myself under the Dakota Presybytery as a candidate for the ministry. This I had long before been urged to do and I had already made some progress in Latin, Greek, and French. When we returned to Lake Harriet from Lac qui Parle, immediately the Indians sent some of their children to us for instruction."[51]

Again, the brothers were together, laboring in the field they loved the best, and we can easily imagine the zest with which they attacked the task before them, freed of the rather restraining cloud which had existed over them while the seemingly over-bearing Rev. Stevens had been in charge of the Lake Harriet mission. But now, when their paths seemed to become freed of all obstacles, their work was again curtailed—this time by the age old conflict between the Dakota and their neighbors to the north and east, the Chippewa.

Kaposia under Big Thunder
1834-1845

As INDICATED IN an earlier chapter, the village of Kaposia was moved to the east shore of the Mississippi River near downtown St. Paul around 1822 under the leadership of Little Crow III. By 1833, probably, the village had migrated to the opposite side of the river in the vicinity of South St. Paul.

During the winter of 1833-34 Little Crow III died and was succeeded by his son Big Thunder or Little Crow IV. Shortly thereafter several families in the band who were dissatisfied with Big Thunder's leadership left Kaposia and moved about eight miles down the Mississippi on the east side. Medicine Bottle,* a well-known medicine man, was chosen their leader and under him they built their lodges of bark and willow and cultivated their gardens and fields.

Samuel and Gideon Pond arrived in 1834 and both have recorded in detail their first encounter with the Kaposia band and Little Crow IV.

After the arrival of my brother and myself at Fort

---
*Waukan-ojan-jan in Dakota, which translates as Spirit Light or Holy Light; but the pioneers and fur traders used the name Medicine Bottle.

Snelling in May, 1834, we ascertained to our satisfaction that our first move should be to assist the Indians about their cornfields, as by this, we could show our good will, conciliate their favor and the better acquire their language. Invited by the father of the present chief of Kaposia, my brother spent one week at that village helping them plow. The oxen were Indian property, kept at the Fort Snelling agency. At that time, the Indians appeared anxious that we should locate at that place, but afterwards the chief and some of the soldiers treated us coldly. It was not long before the agent, Major Taliaferro, returned from the East, where he had spent the winter.[52]

* * * * *

I stayed last week with a band of Indians nine miles south of this place. I went to help them break up planting ground, and as I had no other shelter, I slept in the house of the chief and ate with him. He had two wives and a house full of children. He appeared to be much pleased with the plowing. They have never had any done before.

When the Indians learned that I would plow for them, they took down the plow in a canoe and I drove down the oxen. At Kaposia the chief was Big Thunder (Little Crow IV) and the chief soldier was Big Iron. These two held the plow alternately while I drove the oxen. I suppose they were the first Dakotas who ever held a plow. The dogs or Indians stole my provisions the first night I was there, and I did not fare sumptuously every day, for food was scarce and not very palatable.[53]

On this first encounter the Pond brothers appear to have been well impressed by Big Thunder or Little Crow IV.

He is a man of fair intelligence, a warm friend of the whites, loved by his people, and not hostile to the approach of civilization.[54]

Henry H. Sibley, who arrived in the fall of 1834 to assume

his duties as head of the Sioux division of the lately reorganized American Fur Company, seems to have formed a similar opinion of Little Crow IV:

> He was highly respected among his people. He was very anxious that they be taught to rely for subsistence upon the products of the soil, rather than upon the precarious fruits of the chase, and he set them a good example by working industriously in his own field.[55]

Apparently longer association with Little Crow IV tempered Samuel Pond's high opinion of him. In his book, written between 1865 and 1875, Samuel Pond recalled:

> His features were repulsive, his manners ungainly and awkward, and his disposition unamiable. His countenance, which could never have been beautiful, had been rendered more disagreeable by a wound received in the mouth. His behavior in his youth had been so unsatisfactory that when his father died in the winter of 1833-34, Major Taliaferro, the Indian agent, did not acknowledge him as chief of the Kaposia band without great reluctance. He had a super abundance of energy and resolution, and quite enough shrewdness and cunning; but he had always an ungovernable temper, and though in some respects superior to his son Little Crow (V), he could never play the hypocrite so well as he.[56]

The Pond brothers' encounter with the village of Kaposia was brief as they then located at Lake Calhoun with Cloudman's band. The first mission actually established at Kaposia was that of the Pittsburgh Conference of the Methodist Episcopal Church. In the spring of 1837, the Rev. Alfred Brunson of the Pittsburgh conference arrived at Kaposia where, after consultation with Major Taliaferro, he intended to establish a mission.

Elder Brunson took with him to Kaposia David King, teacher, and his family; a "farmer" to show the Indians how to cultivate the soil; Jim Thompson, the negro interpreter, and a hired man of all work. Missionary buildings of log were soon erected and the work begun. Big Thunder urged his people to listen to the counsels of their new friends. He sent some of his children to the mission school, but princes and princesses are often impatient of restraint and hard study, and those of Big Thunder made but little progress.

In the fall, Rev. T. W. Pope and Rev. James G. Whitford, with a lay member named Hiram Delap, were added to the force of workers at Kaposia. The winter of 1837-38 was spent comfortably. The school prospered and many of the Indians learned to read and write English, for this school would teach nothing but that language. Other mission schools taught an Indian language, or both Indian and English, but David King said that English would finally become the universal speech of the savages, and might as well be learned first as last, and Superintendent Brunson agreed with him. Chief Big Thunder tried to induce the missionaries to teach his people to read and write their own language, as the Pond brothers were doing, but the "sacred white men" refused.[57]

There is evidence that this mission had mediocre success. There was a school and a teacher named David King but there were few students. Mr. King and his assistant, A. Robertson, also conducted experiments in agriculture and thereby demonstrated the possibilities available for farming in the region.

The Methodist mission at Kaposia was disrupted by the continued hostilities between the Mdewakanton and the Chippewa. The Chippewa were menacing the village and in return Big Thunder (Little Crow IV) frequently sent out war parties. It was his opinion that having the school in session under these circumstances was useless. Though Big Thunder closed the school, he promised that it would reopen when the Chippewa had been driven off. Subsequently the entire mission closed down; there were no missionaries at Kaposia again until after the death of Big Thunder.

Each spring seemed to be the signal for an attack, either by the Dakota or by the Chippewa in retaliation for previous wrongs. In 1841 it was the Chippewa who attacked first, killing a sub-chief Kaboka and his son from Cloudman's band. In retaliation the Dakota organized three war parties to attack the Chippewa village located on an island in Lake Pokegama. The advance party was made up of warriors from Kaposia, including three of Little Crow IV's sons. The party was discovered by the enemy at St. Croix Falls. In the ensuing battle two of Little Crow's sons were killed; but the third survived and succeeded in killing a Chippewa, and later became Little Crow V.

Sibley's account of Big Thunder's reaction to this family tragedy gives a helpful glimpse into the character of the man.

> The old chief evinced, on one occasion, some of the chivalry of the olden time, although in a manner somewhat revolting to the tastes of civilized man. Two of his favorite sons joined a war party which proceeded up the St. Croix River in search of Chippewas, and in a skirmish near the Falls, both of them were killed, but the bodies remained unmutilated, the Chippewas having been driven off with the loss of one man killed and another wounded. The father of the young men, who had remained in the village, was speedily notified of the occurrence, whereupon he gathered all the wampum and silver work belonging to the members of his family, and taking his double

barrel gun, which he highly valued, he made a forced march, with others of his band, to the spot where the action took place.

The bodies remained where they had fallen. Under his direction the blood was washed from their features and replaced by war paint, new clothing put upon the bodies, and the hair was combed, plaited and strung with small silver brooches, silver bands enclosing their arms and wrists, and a large quantity of expensive wampum was hung about the necks.

When these details had been attended to, the corpses were arranged in a sitting posture secured to the trunks of trees, and the old chief deposited his double-barrel gun by their side, took a parting look at his dead children, shook them by the hand and returned to his village. Some of the Chippewas, in two or three days afterwards, came back and appropriated the scalps and the valuables, and left the bodies uncared for.

Having heard of these singular proceedings of the old chief, I asked an explanation of Little Crow when next I saw him and he did not hesitate to give it. He said he had opposed the formation of the war party, but the young men were so bent upon avenging the death of some of their friends who had been killed by the Chippewas, that he finally withdrew his objections.

"My two sons," continued he, "joined the party and were killed. While I grieve deeply at their loss, they fell like brave men in battle, and the enemy was entitled to their scalps. I wished the Chippewa to know by the treasures lavished upon the bodies, that they had slain the sons of a chief."

Some weeks subsequently, he returned in person, collected the bones, and had them properly interred near the village.[58]

The second party, consisting of Black Dog's and Good

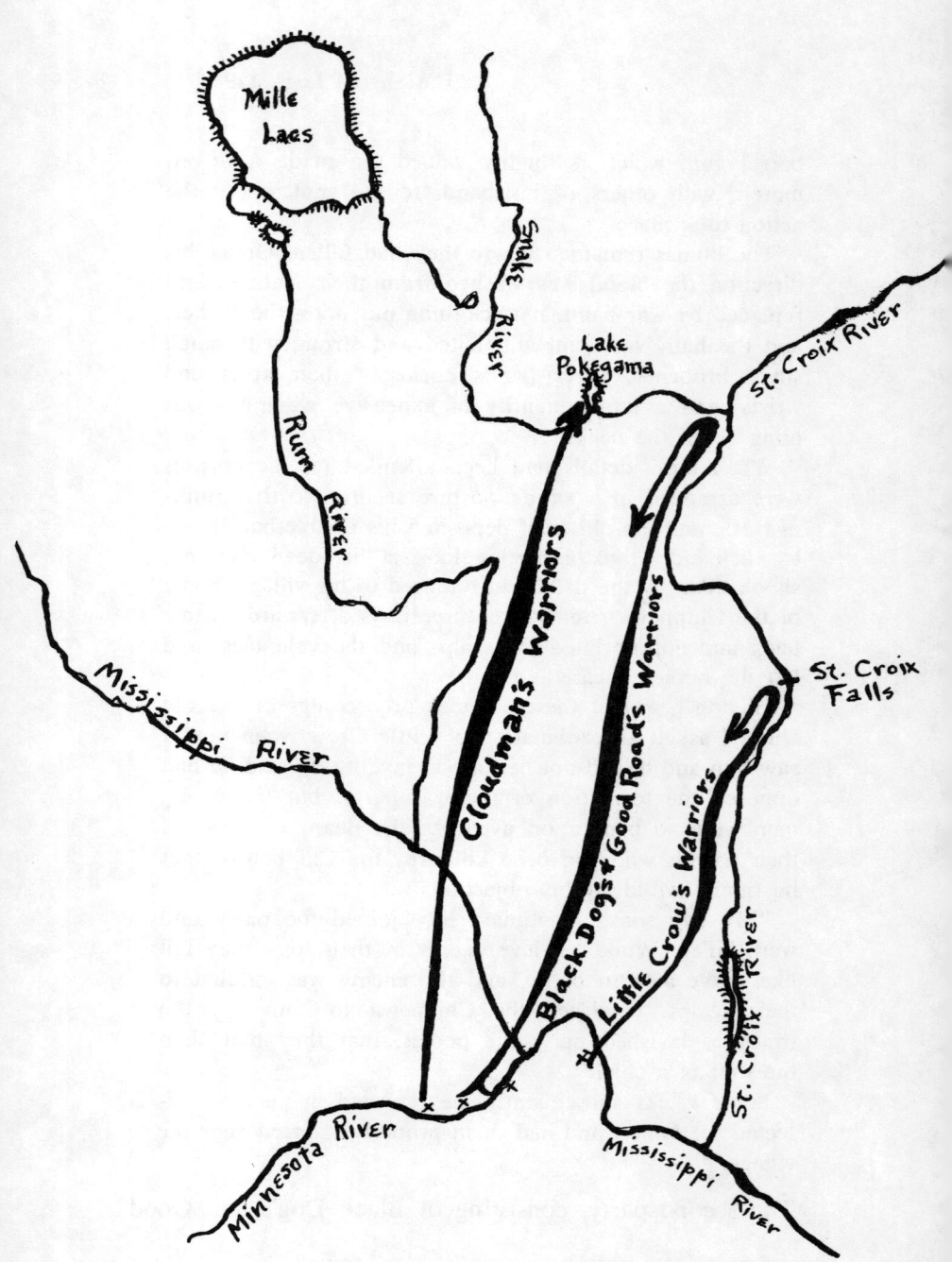

The Attack on Lake Pokegama in May, 1841.

Road's braves proceeded by land in a northeasterly direction (from Minneapolis to Rush City) thence east toward the St. Croix and the mouth of the Snake River. Apparently they intended to wait for Little Crow's contingent to arrive. Somehow, they later learned of the catastrophe at the Falls or they supposed that the Ojibway had discovered them. At any rate, they too returned to their homes, passing by the Falls of the St. Croix, where they learned of the death of Little Crow's sons.

The third party consisted of one hundred and eleven warriors from the Lake Calhoun Band which had in the meantime moved to Oak Grove in present Bloomington on the Minnesota River. Cloudman was not present as he had long since given up war. Possibly this party was led by Traveling Hail, who was a noted warrior. They travelled up the Rum River Valley to the Cambridge area, then proceeded across country to the valley of the Knife River. They arrived at the west side of Pokegama Lake May 23.

The Chippewa village was principally on an island in the lake not far from the eastern shore. Since 1836 there had been a Presbyterian mission on the eastern shore and several Indian families, including that of the chief, had built log houses around the mission.

Two days before the arrival of the Lake Calhoun warriors, the Chippewa had learned of the engagement with Little Crow's braves at St. Croix Falls.

> On May 24th, three young men left in a canoe to go to the west shore of the lake and from thence to Mille Lacs, to give intelligence to the Ojibways there of the skirmish that had already occurred. They took with them two Indian girls, about twelve years of age, who were pupils of the mission school, for the purpose of bringing the canoe back to the island.[59]

As the canoe approached, the Dakota on that side of the lake could no longer contain themselves. Their original plan had been to wait until part of their number had sneaked around the south side of the lake, near the mission and commence the attack. Instead those on the west shore opened fire on the three Chippewa runners. They fled into the woods, leaving the two little girls to suffer the brunt of the attack.

The little girls in their fright, waded into the lake, and as in Indian warfare it is as noble to kill an infant as an adult, a delicate woman as a strong man, the Dakota braves, with their spears and war clubs, rushed into the water after the children and killed them. Their parents upon the island heard the death cries of the children; and for a time the scene was one of wildest confusion. Some of the Indians around the mission house jumped into their canoes and gained the island. Others went into some fortified huts.[60]

The noise from the west shore gave the Chippewa at the mission time to prepare for defense. The Dakota were repulsed, and finally with the loss of two of their number they returned to their homes on the Minnesota River. The Chippewa had lost only the two twelve year old girls.

Retaliation for the Pokegama incident came in the following summer—1842. About a hundred Chippewa warriors descended on Little Crow's village. They had slipped down the St. Croix Valley to the head of Lake St. Croix. From there they marched across country to St. Paul to attack first the few Indians and mixed bloods living on the north side of the Mississippi (Pig's Eye) and then they fell upon any of the Kaposia villagers that might be in the near vicinity.

The Chippewas reached the vicinity of Pig's Eye at the close of a day's march from the St. Croix and went into bivouac for the night. By ten the next morning, they were well concealed among the thick timber and brushwood at about the mouth of the large ravine called Pine Coulie (north end of Pig's Eye Lake). Scouts were sent out to ascertain the exact location of the isolated Sioux.

On Pig's Eye bottom a little distance away from the Pine Coulie, where the Chippewas lay in ambush, were the cabin and little fields of Francois Gammel (or Gamelle), a French-Canadian who had come to Minnesota as a voyager in 1829, and for some years had been in the employ of the American Fur Company at Mendota. He married a Dakota woman and they had one son, David, then a child, and afterwards a Union soldier in the Fifth Minnesota. That morning a Kaposia Indian, named Khadayah, or Rattler, had come over to Gamelle's house with his two wives and little son and daughter to help the Gamelles hoe their corn. Gamelle, his wife and one of the Rattler's wives were in the field at work. The other Mrs. Rattler was taken suddenly ill and she and her husband were in the house. The three children were playing nearby.

A squad of Chippewas that had been sent out to reconnoiter crawled through the bushes outside the field, and seeing the two Sioux women at work fired upon them, killing Mrs. Rattler instantly. Mrs. Gamelle was mortally wounded. Her husband lifted her in his arms and carried her into the cabin. The Chippewas rushed after him, and actually scalped the dying woman in her husband's arms.

Then, not knowing the Rattler and his other wife were hidden in the room, they ran away, giving the scalp halloo, having the scalps of two women at their belts. Gamelle caught up his gun and shot one of them through the leg. His comrades were helping him off the field when they saw Rattler's little boy trying to hide in the brush; his little sister had already hidden herself, along with little David Gamelle. The Chippewas at once seized the little Rattler boy, scalped him and cut off his head, and this gave them another scalp. They now had three scalps of the enemy to dance and gloat over.[61]

The warriors of Kaposia that morning were in no condition to wage a battle for the protection of their village. They had secured a quantity of whiskey and were in the process of consuming it. But when two runners arrived telling of the enemy's approach, a great change came over the village.

The drunken babble was changed to the shrill and inspiring war-whoop. The guns and tomahawks were hunted up, and fifty warriors led by the head soldier of the Kaposia band hurried to their canoes and crossed the river to meet the enemy, regardless of his strength and position. Straggling reinforcements followed as fast as they could. The word went to Fort Snelling and the whiskey seekers returned at once to their village to help defend it. The women and children of the village yelled and screamed constantly, with the idea that the Chippewa would conclude that there was a large force yet to come upon them.

Meanwhile, the Chippewa had advanced from the Pine Coulie to near the bank of the river, above the noted Red Rock, and here, on the flat bottom land back to the foot of the bluff, the fight raged with great spirit for several hours. The Sioux were constantly re-enforced, and about noon the Chippewas began to fall back to the Pine Coulie fighting every foot of the ground.

The Sioux followed them, drove them over the bluff, through the timber, and pursued them well on the way to Stillwater. From first to last these were stirring incidents and hand-to-hand fights were numerous.[62]

Big Thunder had survived many violent encounters. Yet, his death was the result of an accident with his own gun. In October of 1845 Big Thunder and . . .

> a wife and two or three grandsons set out with a cart drawn by his yoke of oxen to gather some newly ripened corn on the crest of the high hill back of Kaposia Village. His loaded gun lay in the cart, the rear end of which was open. As the vehicle ascended the steep, high hill, the weapon was sliding towards the ground and the chief caught it by the muzzle and was drawing it towards him when it was discharged, the load entered his body. He was loaded into the cart and taken back to his lodge and the village medicine man was summoned, and Surgeon George F. Turner of Fort Snelling also came, but the old chief was past all pagan sorcery or Christian surgery. He died and before death directed that his wayward but favorite son Taoyateduta (His Red Nation) should be his successor.[63]

No Log at All

"Move Over"
1837-1838

EXCEPT FOR THE small military reservation at Fort Snelling, which the Indians ceded to the government in 1805, and the strip which they had given the United States as a neutral barrier in 1830, the Mdewakanton Dakota did not actually sell, or part title with, any considerable portion of their land until the Treaty of 1837. During the first quarter of the nineteenth century, in fact even as late as 1830, it was understood by almost everyone of any knowledge or position in the United States that the land in this area would probably never be settled by farmers and business men, but would always remain in the hands of the Indians. This feeling dated from the time of the British occupation and did not easily die.

However, in the thirties, settlements were creeping ever closer to the upper Mississippi and the Minnesota rivers. As forests were depleted and as the tremendous demand for lumber further east steadily increased, the lumbermen agitated for the opening of the magnificent stand of virgin pine along the banks of the Chippewa River in northwestern Wisconsin.

This land was inhabited by the Chippewa, but the Dakota also had an ancient claim to it. In 1837, it seemed expedient to sign treaties with these two tribes and acquire the land for the government, which, in turn, would allow the lumbermen to take the timber from it. The lumbermen argued that since the game in the area was nearly gone, it was no longer of much value as hunting grounds for the Indians.

In July of 1837, about twelve hundred Chippewa assembled at Fort Snelling to negotiate the treaty with Henry Dodge, Governor of the Wisconsin Territory and ex-officio Commissioner of Indian Affairs for the Territory. By this treaty, the Chippewa ceded not only the greater part of northern and western Wisconsin, but also a large part of Minnesota, the southern part of the counties of Crow Wing, Aitkin and Pine and the entire counties of Mille Lacs, Kanabec, Benton, Isanti, Chisago, Sherburne, Anoka, Washington, and Ramsey.

The Mdewakanton Dakota were present at this meeting though they did not participate. Thus they were well prepared to negotiate a similar treaty in September of the same year. Major Taliaferro led the Mdewakanton chiefs and their head men to Washington, D. C. Those residing on the Minnesota River assembled at Fort Snelling and boarded the steamboat *Pavillion*. The *Pavillion* proceeded down the Mississippi River to Kaposia where Big Thunder (Little Crow IV) and his head soldier boarded, then to Red Wing, where Wacoota and his head soldier joined the delegation, and finally to Winona where Wabasha and Thin Face, his head soldier, boarded the steamer. All together the party included twenty-six Indians, the Major, and a number of other white men who were interested in the treaty. Among these were the local traders Sibley, Bailly, and Faribault.

The treaty was negotiated and signed on September 29 in a church in Washington. Little Crow IV, Grey Iron, Good Road and seventeen other chiefs and principal soldiers of the Mdewakanton bands signed the treaty, which was later ratified by the United States.

Actually, the only band which had to move its village from the eastern side of the Mississippi seems to have been the small band headed by Medicine Bottle. It is quite well established that when the treaty of 1837 was signed Little Crow's band had already moved to the west side of the Mississippi at South St. Paul, probably in the spring of 1833. Thus Kaposia lost only some additional hunting area on the east side and was not materially affected by the land provisions of the treaty.

By the treaty of 1837, the Dakota became "annuity Indians"—that is, they were to receive an annual stipulation of cash and goods. Prior to this time, of course, when agents of the government met with the Indians to secure treaties of amity and friendship or to settle boundary disputes, it had been customary to give them presents of blankets, powder, lead, and sometimes small sums of money. Food was always distributed to them, if available, especially in times of poor hunting or severe weather. But to provide a sizeable amount of aid that the Indians could count on receiving yearly "for twenty years," as stated in this treaty, was new. This provision created a condition which contributed greatly to the general debilitation and decline of the Dakota from this period until their expulsion from the state in 1863. Such is the opinion, at least, of many of the responsible men—traders, missionaries, and agents—who were in daily contact with them. According to Sibley, "The decay of the Dakota in our midst may be dated from the time of their treaty in 1837."

Samuel W. Pond has described the Dakota as they were before the annuity system began, then compared those earlier Indians with their offspring who participated in the great Outbreak of 1862;

> The perpetrators of the horrible crimes then committed (1862) had been led onward to them by many years of luxurious idleness and riotous living. Hockakaduta (Red Middle Voice, one of the worst sub-chiefs involved), Little Crow (the fifth, His Red Nation), and their associates had for more than twenty years been fed and clothed by government annuities.
>
> They had been furnished with tobacco to smoke and money to buy whiskey, and all their wants had been so far supplied that they were enabled to spend a great portion of their time in idleness or something worse. The pressure of want being removed, the industrious habits of their ancestors were abandoned. As that restless energy which had characterized them found no legitimate fields of exercise, it sought illegitimate ones, and they were fast losing every redeeming trait of savage character.[1]

Perhaps Rev. Pond was a little too severe, but it may be safely stated that as time went by the Dakota began to depend more and more upon the doles of the whites and less upon their own enterprise for their livelihood. Begging was substituted for hunting and trapping, especially as it became more difficult to procure game.

Undoubtedly, the worst result of the opening of the area east of the Mississippi to white settlement and the factor that had the greatest detrimental effect upon the Indians was the whiskey trade which now could flourish anywhere along the east bank of the Mississippi.

> The sellers lost no time in establishing their "groceries" opposite the Indian villages. They were not breaking the

law forbidding the introduction of whiskey into the Indian country. The Indian came over to the white man's country and bought the coveted fire water. Immediately after the first payment under the treaty in September, 1839, there began a carnival of intoxication which continued for years.[2]

Henry Sibley expressed a similar opinion:

Recourse to liquor and other evil habits are but the natural consequences of that system which drives him (the Indian) from his home, interferes with his habits of life, and regards him as an outcast from the land of his fathers, without holding out to him any promise for the future.[3]

The treaty of 1837 did also provide for a greater amount of agricultural assistance to the Indians than had been forthcoming from the government in previous years. Article II read:

"In order to enable the Indians to break up and improve their lands the United States will supply, as soon as practicable after the ratification of this treaty, agricultural implements, mechanics' tools, cattle, and such other articles as may be useful to them, to the amount not exceeding $10,000." This clause gave Major Taliaferro a chance to expand somewhat his efforts toward the introduction of agricultural pursuits. The following spring he went down the Mississippi and purchased a large number of horses, cows, oxen, and various pieces of farming implements. He also set up a number of blacksmith shops near the Dakota villages so that most of the principal bands had blacksmiths of their own.

One should not fail to note the beneficial effect of these provisions of the treaty to those Indians who realized that their old way of life was passing and who therefore were making a real effort to adjust to the white man's system. The attempts of these Indians to become farmers should not be minimized by over-emphasis upon the indolence and laziness more evident to observers at the time.

The End of a Dream
1838-1840

IT CANNOT BE stated categorically that the treaties of 1837 and the resulting "annuity system" caused an increase of restlessness among the Dakota and Chippewa; but it is true that during the years following 1837 there was a noticeable increase of war-like activity between these tribes.

Though hostility between them had been continuous through the decade following the execution of four Dakota by the Chippewa under the eye of Col. Snelling and his soldiers in 1827, both the Dakota and the Chippewa seem to have considered the immediate area of the fort to be a sort of hallowed place, where no violence was to be done. Indians who would have immediately attacked one another on the hunting ground were outwardly friendly at the fort and usually committed no violence against each other, however hostile were the feelings within their hearts.

However, in the spring of 1838 an event took place which intensified tension between the tribes and caused a peculiarly explosive situation. Gideon Pond happened to be on the scene and described it later to his brother:

In April, 1838, eleven Dakotas were treacherously slain

near the Chippewa River, about thirty miles from Lac qui Parle, by the Chippewas, led by the celebrated Hole-in-the-Day.

The Chippewas pretended to be on a friendly visit to the Dakotas, and lay down with them in their tents, but rose on them in the night and killed them. The next day, my brother, G. H. Pond, aided by an Indian named Tatemine, gathered the scattered fragments of their mutilated bodies and buried them. (He had accompanied the hunting party which had earlier separated into two camps. The members of the lodges with whom he was staying, escaped massacre.)[4]

On August 2 of the same year Hole-in-the-Day visited the fort, bringing with him some of his men from Gull Lake and Swan River. His presence touched off a series of encounters which resulted in many deaths among the bands dwelling within the vicinity of the fort. Actually this visit to the fort was not necessary. Hole-in-the-Day knew that he and his men were unwelcome. Since 1832 their agent had been Schoolcraft and their agency at Michilimackinac. But with the permission of Taliaferro and Major Plympton, the commandant, the Chippewa were allowed to remain at the fort until the evening of August 6th. This visit caused much consternation among the Dakota, and on August 3rd they reacted accordingly.

About three months after the massacre, Hole-in-the-Day, with two or three others, made a visit to Fort Snelling. He went first to Patrick Quinn's (Government farmer for the Penasha Band), who lived by the Mississippi about a mile above Fort Snelling, and whose wife was a half breed Chippewa. The Dakotas of the Lake Calhoun Band heard of his arrival and started out in a body to kill him, but the agent, Mr. Taliaferro, persuaded them to turn back, giving them leave to kill him if they could, on his way home.

The Dakotas seemed disposed to take the agent's advice, and started for home, but two of them whose relatives had been shot a short time before near Lac qui Parle, hid themselves near Quinns and in the evening, as Hole-in-the-Day's party was passing from Quinn's house to another nearby, they killed one of them and wounded another, but the chief escaped, having exchanged some of his clothes or ornaments with another of his party who was mistaken for him. One of the Dakotas was badly wounded. They were both confined in the fort a while, but were finally released on the condition that their friends should chastise them severely in the presence of the garrison.[5]

On August 6th, Major Plympton sent the Chippewa home. He also advised them never to return to the vicinity of the fort, "without previous permission and a full understanding of the matter."

The Indian killed by the Dakota on this occasion was buried in the fort graveyard. A year later toward the end of June, 1839, a much larger band of Chippewa—hundreds, in fact—visited the fort under the false impression that by the Treaty of 1837 they were to receive their annuities there. In addition to Hole-in-the-Day's Band, other Chippewa arrived at the fort. On June 24th Major Taliaferro reported nine hundred Chippewa present, over a hundred from the Crow Wing country, a hundred and fifty from Leech Lake and the remainder from the Upper St. Croix River area.

At the same time, there were more than twelve hundred Dakota assembled around Fort Snelling to receive the annuities due them under the Treaty of 1837.

Taliaferro lamented, "I have my hands full."[6]

The Rev. E. G. Gear, visiting the Fort at this time, recorded this touchy situation first hand:

> The Chippewa remained encamped on the east side of the Mississippi, in the place assigned them, for several days, and the utmost harmony seemed to exist between them and the Sioux. Feasts, dances, games of various kinds, and interchange of visits were constantly kept up during the whole time, and hopes were entertained that a better state of feeling had taken place, and a permanent peace might be arranged.
>
> Nothing occurred of a suspicious or exciting nature until a short time before the Chippewas left, when a Sioux is affirmed to have fired into a canoe of Chippewas nearly or quite under the walls of the Fort. This was not discovered by his people, who would have punished him, had he not immediately escaped up the valley of the St. Peter (Minnesota River), and eluded pursuit.
>
> It is further reported and believed that Strong Ground, a Chippewa chief and brother of Hole-in-the-Day, was watched with evil intentions by a number of Sioux, one evening as he was returning from the Fur Company's store; but, being informed of the fact, he escaped the snare and reached the camp in safety.[7]

In spite of these minor disturbances, the Chippewa and the Dakota met at the agency council house, smoked the pipe together and agreed to remain at peace with each other for another year. The Chippewa then prepared to go home. One group, under Strong Ground, decided to go to La Pointe by way of the St. Croix River valley, while the rest under Hole-in-the-Day began their journey north. They camped at the Falls of St. Anthony overnight.

> Here they were visited by a company of Sioux from the Lake Calhoun Band, who were received and entertained

in the most friendly and hospitable manner. They were feasted, as they had been while the Chippewas were at the Fort, upon dogs, the highest honor, it is said, that the Indians of these tribes can confer upon strangers or friends. And it was during this entertainment probably, that the seeds of the difficulty were first sown, as other matters appear to have occurred.

Some of the Pillagers, a band of the Chippewas who have long been notorious for their infamous conduct, either actuated by the spirit of vengeance and regardless of the late armistice, or jealous of the distinction conferred upon the Sioux, showed a strong disposition to quarrel, if they did not break out in actual violence. This induced Hole-in-the-Day to send his visitors home to their lodges, under a strong escort, and at parting, charged them to beware of the Pillagers, as they were bad people, and that he could not be responsible for their conduct.

The next morning, Hole-in-the-Day broke up his camp and moved up the River, and it appears from circumstances, that during the following day, or the following night, two of the Pillagers fell off from the party and went into the neighborhood of the Calhoun Band; for on the morning of the second, before it was fairly light, they fell upon a respectable Sioux by the name of Badger, murdered and scalped him, and made their escape.[8]

The victim of the ambush, which took place on the pathway from Cloudman's Village to the Mission House on Lake Harriet, was no less than the son-in-law of Chief Cloudman himself, a young man described by Taliaferro as "most respectable and much esteemed." His Indian name was Hupachokanaza or Middle Iron Wing, but he was commonly called Neekah or the Badger. With him was a young boy, Cloudman's son, who hurriedly returned to the village on Lake Calhoun and informed his people of the attack. This young son of Chief Cloudman was still alive in 1906, seventy-eight years of age and living at Flandreau, South Dakota. He had taken the name David Watson after his conversion to Christianity. It is highly possible his reminiscences are the basis of the following description of the event:

> Just after daylight on the morning of July 2, an Indian called the Badger, a son-in-law of sub-chief Cloudman and a nephew of Red Bird, the medicine man, left the Calhoun village to hunt pigeons in the woods south of Lake Harriet. His nephew (David) a lad of ten years was with him. The path ran along the east side of Lake Harriet and thence to the grove. On the southeastern side, in easy range of the path, low in the tall grass and weeds lay the Chippewas in ambush, crouching like tigers in a jungle and every whit as fierce and dangerous. When the Badger came up in the right position, they fired at the same instant and both bullets struck him, killing him instantly. In a few seconds, his scalp was torn off. The boy, who lived to be David Watson, was not harmed, perchance he was so little he was not seen in time, but at all events, he escaped, apparently unobserved, and ran back to the village crying: 'Kah-hah-ton-wan! Kah-hah-ton-wan!' (Chippewa! Chippewa!) The news reached the mission station as soon as it came to the village and the Pond brothers were at the side of the murdered warrior as soon as the Indians.[9]

Samuel Pond tells us: "I was there a few minutes after he was killed and saw in the tall grass the trail of the Chippewas, leading to a small cluster of young poplars. There were no tracks leading from the grove, and all knew that they were there. We afterwards learned that they remained there till dark. I urged the Indians to try to kill them, but though there were as many as fifty armed Dakotas, they refused to go near them."¹⁰

A later reference indicates how the two Pillagers survived:

> It is now known that after they had shot the Badger and taken his scalp, they fled eastward and made their way to the "Little Falls" now the Falls of Minnehaha.
> Behind the sheet of water they crawled and hid themselves. Here they remained for two days and a night. All about the falls there were brambles and brushwood and the big white blanket of the cataract completely shielded them from view.
> On the second night, they stepped out and made their way back to their village.¹¹

Dr. Blegen also has added a historical footnote: "The Lake Calhoun band sent Rev. Stevens to tell Taliaferro of the attack and to ask his advice, but as they later told the agent, when the people 'looked a moment on their friend's bleeding body—their feelings could not be stopped, and the young men rushed on for revenge.' They did not wait to hear Taliaferro's counsel, but said later that even if he had told them to stop, 'they would still have done as they did'."¹²

It seemed that it took but a moment for all the bands of the area to hear of this murder; and the braves assembled, determined to pursue the main bodies of Chippewa who had left the fort the day before. It was decided that Little Crow and his warriors should pursue the St. Croix Chippewa, who had the previous evening stopped at Kaposia and spent some hours in a friendly visit there.

Little Crow's contingent struck across the country to intercept their quarry as they came up the St. Croix in their canoes.

The Sioux route was through the present site of St. Paul and across the prairie to Stillwater, and the distance was compassed in a day. That night they found the Ojibways encamped in the big ravine where the penitentiary now stands. The old trader, William A. Aitkin, was in the camp and the Sioux did nothing to hurt him, for he was a white man and had a good name among all Indians.

Just at dawn the Sioux made known their presence. They had crept up within easy gun shot and bow shot of the Chippewa camp and from the commanding bluffs poured in a sudden plunging fire upon its occupants. The first volleys were followed by a wild charge. The Chippewas retreated towards the shore of Lake St. Croix, the women and children in front, the warriors protecting the rear, fighting bravely. In a little time, the Sioux attack was checked. Then after half an hour's fierce fighting, they retreated, and the Chippewa did not follow them.[13]

The other Dakota bands under Red Bird, the war chief and head medicine man of the Lake Calhoun band, pursued the Chippewa up the Mississippi as they returned to the Mille Lacs region.

Seven or eight miles north of St. Anthony Falls, the Chippewa had separated — Hole-in-the-Day's band continued up the Mississippi, but the Mille Lacs band struck out in a diagonal direction toward the Rum River "with a view of procuring game, as they were nearly destitute of provisions."

The Dakota came upon the Mille Lacs Chippewa early in the morning,

> as they were making a portage from Red Cedar or Rice Lake across to Rum River, encumbered with canoes, children and luggage, where they had made their encampment the night previous. Most of the warriors had left in

pursuit of game; and the old men were nearly half a mile from those in the rear with the canoes, and the women and children following with the infants and lighter luggage. The slaughter was indiscriminate, and principally with the knife and tomahawk. It appears that the whole line was attacked almost simultaneously, and that there was one continuous shriek for the space of half an hour.[14]

The Dakota later told Samuel Pond that the Chippewa "did not at first realize their danger; they stood awhile with their burdens on their backs gazing on their pursuers as though they did not know what to think of them."[15]

Heavy loss was suffered by the Chippewa in this engagement: "About seventy of the Chippewa were killed. The slain were most of them women and children. The few men who were present defended the women and children bravely, and sold their lives dearly. After discharging their pieces, they would retreat far enough to reload, and then stand again on the defensive, and continued to do so till they were killed." Rev. Gear tells us that the loss of the Chippewa "is variously estimated, some putting the number as high as a hundred and thirty-three, and others admitting only sixty or seventy, but all, that it consisted principally of women and children. The Sioux, in order to swell the amount, are charged with dividing the scalps, and this is supposed to be true."[16]

Jane DeBow and others at the Mission observed the strange happenings back at the Lake Calhoun Village.

> The sun went down and all was still. The village of the Sioux seemed silent as if deserted. Gideon Pond went to care for the cattle and his calmness helped to allay the fears of the little group in the Mission House.
>
> Next morning, wailing cries came from the tepees. Cornelia (Rev. Steven's niece) came in and said, "Dread-

ful! the squaws are . . . " and she lowered her voice as she hurried to her room. Janie tried to see what was "dreadful", but Gideon closed the door and drew her near him.

"I'll tell you a story, Janie, and for a while you and I are not going to look toward the village. Let me tell you of a little girl called Red Riding Hood."

"But the squaws?" she questioned him.

"They are mourning because Badger was killed yesterday," answered Mr. Pond.

"I want to hear your story now," said Janie and the doors remained closed. But the days were long—afternoon gave way to evening, Janie and the boys went out to talk to their dusky playmates.

There was a sudden shout of "Nush-ka-mush-ka." All the children took up the word, for in the distance appeared a Sioux—a runner, who stopped to cup his hands and call words that were known to mean: "I bear good news"—"Ninety scalps! Now Badger is avenged!"—"The braves are returning!" and the children from the mission felt elated because of the joy of their companions. But for the people of the tented city there was sorrow too. Red Bird was numbered among those slain in battle.

On the sandy shore of Lake Harriet, the Scalp Dance continued for a month. Janie and the boys, Dwight and Evert, learned the chant. A wild chant repeated over and over, as the warriors circled around the tall poles, where the wind waved the black hair—called the scalplock, that had been snatched from the head of some dying Chippewa —man, woman, or child, it mattered not.

"Yaw-hi-hi-hi-yaw-yaw-hi-hi-hi-yaw-yaw-hoo-hoo-how-ow." (Some of the chant Mrs. Gibbs rendered:)

"You Ojibway, you are mean!
We will use you like a mouse!
You are wicked and bad!

> We have got you,
> And we will strike you down!
> My dog is very hungry—
> I will give him this Ojibway scalp."[17]

The scene was one of the wildest and fiercest which that generation of the Mdewakanton had ever known. "It seemed as if hell had emptied itself here."[18]

Rev. Gear has also described the occurrences after the return of the Mdewakanton bands from the massacre.

> But the most disgusting part of the story remains to be told. The two war paries (Red Bird's and Little Crow's) to the number of three or four hundred, returned in triumph, accompanied by the women and children from the villages, leaving the scalps of their victims stretched upon ozier hoops or branches, and elevated upon poles, and commenced the horrid dance peculiar on these occasions. And it seemed as if all the spirits of darkness had been let down upon us. Nothing can be conceived more horrid and disgusting than this exhibition, and it is with pleasure I turn from it, to mention that many of the old men, heathen though they are, possess the feelings of humanity, and lament with the deepest sorrow such a sacrifice of human life and have been seen weeping over the bloody trophies of war.[19]

Among those lamenting undoubtedly was Cloudman, who for twenty years had been denouncing war and bloodshed and all the barbaric and inhumane practices connected with it. His dream was at stake, but he was engaged in a losing battle. The youth of the villages were captured by the romance and glory, the empty honor and the color of war.

When Taliaferro remonstrated with the chiefs of the Sioux villages after the massacres he met with the same reply from all. They were sorry for the slaughter of so many women and children, but, "we did not begin it. We had smoked, eaten, and made peace together but the day before. We did this that we might be at peace and hunt quietly on our lands, but it was all spoiled by the bad conduct of the Pillager Chippewas." Chief Shakopee said that they did this of their own free will and nothing could have stopped us. We thought of the many insults offered our people and the murder in cold blood of three lodges of our women and children last year by Hole-in-the-Day. Chief Good Road hoped that Taliaferro would give a fair account of the matter to the president, whose words the Indians recollected. The president had told them to go back to your people and keep the peace with all nations— go to war against none, but if struck upon by your enemies, then you may revenge it. We have been struck upon, and we have revenged it (Taliaferro's Journal, July 5, 6, 1839).[20]

Though they had accomplished a great victory over their age old enemies at Rum River, the Mdewakanton on the banks of Lake Calhoun no longer felt secure there. The Inland Village was most easily accessible to the Chippewa and it would most certainly be descended upon when the Chippewa decided to avenge the deaths of so many of their number. Taliaferro emphatically warned them that "attacked they would be sooner or later, on that fact they may rely." (Journal, July 14, 1839). "The belief generally prevails among those who are best acquainted with the character of the Chippewas that they will rally before winter and make a descent upon the Sioux in some unguarded hour and take ample vengeance, and that nothing else can make an atonement."[21]

In preparation for this expected attack the Calhoun Band fortified their village as best they could, for they felt they had to remain there, at least until the corn ripening in the fields was gathered. The Pond brothers' little cabin was torn down to obtain material for breast works, and, in general, Cloudman's people "walked in fear and trembling" the rest of the summer and early fall of 1839.

During the summer of 1837 Major Joseph Plympton had taken command of Fort Snelling. He was not in favor of white settlers dwelling on the government land around the fort, and it appears he felt the same about the Indians. In July, 1838, he forbade "all persons not attached to the military from erecting any building or buildings, fence or fences, or cutting timber for any but public use within the line which has been surveyed and forwarded to the War Department." The reason the military authorities gave for desiring to banish the white settlers was that some of them were engaged in an illicit liquor traffic with the Indians and with the soldiers of the garrison.

Whether or not this was the real reason for Major Plympton's orders, the removal of the Indians from the Lake Calhoun area fit well into his plans of clearing the reservation about the fort of all but the military personnel and their families. He and Colonel Bruce, who had been appointed Indian agent in Major Taliaferro's place upon his resignation late in 1839, decided to locate this band on the Credit River, near the site of the present city of Savage, on the south side of the Minnesota River.

In October of 1838 Major Taliaferro paid the following sums of money to the local Dakota, to Big Thunder's Band, $850, to Black Dog's, $600, to Penasha's, $700, to the Lake Calhoun Band, $800. These payments, together with $1,050 to Shakopee constituted the final payment for the land around the fort which had originally been purchased almost twenty years earlier. The Indians had understood that "they only gave Pike a mile around the present site of Fort Snelling, or as they say, just as far as can be seen around the Fort without elevating the eyes, which would be at the rate of two miles in some places, one mile in others."[22]

The soldiers at the fort, however, were cutting timber from the entire "nine mile square" area. Earlier that year one of the chiefs had demanded payment for timber which had been cut near his village, and though Taliaferro maintained the correctness of the nine mile square area, he nevertheless prevailed upon the government for the additional four thousand dollars. After making the last of the payments to the Indian bands on October 15 Taliaferro entered into his journal: "This sum settles all difficulties in future to the land and the use of fire wood and timber destroyed by the troops and even the traders."

Major Taliaferro submitted his formal resignation July 15 due to "enfeebled health after twenty-seven years in the public service in a high latitude,"[23] but he continued in office until the close of 1839. On August 25, 1839, the harassed public servant, who for so long had acted as agent at the fort, wrote in his journal: "I leave the whole nest this fall—Indians and traders. I am disgusted with the life of an agent among such discordant materials and bad management on the part of Congress, the Indian Office, etc."

His successor was Col. Amos J. Bruce, who worked out with Major Plympton the relocation plans for the village at Lake Calhoun. The Indians were not unwilling to relocate after the great slaughter of the Chippewa mentioned earlier. But they were apparently unhappy with the new location at the mouth of the Credit River where it joined the Minnesota River.

So 1839 saw the end of Taliaferro's dream, Eatonville,

as well as the end of Cloudman's large village on the shore of Lake of the Loons, or Lake Calhoun as the white men had named it. When Mr. D. E. Dow came to the area in 1850, he found no trace of Indian habitations on his claim, but only the ruins of the old Mission. The fields which had held such great promise to Cloudman and Taliaferro had returned to nature.

The Indians left the area around Lake Calhoun in the fall of 1839 directly after harvesting their corn crop. The Pond brothers remained at the Mission House on Lake Harriet all winter because preparations had already been made for wintering the cattle belonging to the Indians and in Gideon's charge as the government farmer for the Calhoun band. However, in spring Major Plympton ordered Gideon Pond to plow for the Indians at the new Credit River location.

> Our Indians were very unwilling to go to Credit River and other Indians were opposed to their going there, but we had a Colonel and a Major to deal with and their orders were imperative, so having pulled down our house and taken away the lumber from Lake Harriet, we started for Credit River with three or four yoke of oxen and a load of lumber, swimming our oxen across the river at Mendota and drawing our cart across it by a strong cord of rawhide long enough to reach across the river. Our cart disappeared as it went into the river, and spectators said we should never see it again, but it reappeared as it ascended the opposite bank. When we reached the Credit River we were not at all pleased with the location, and were unwilling to build there, but we hardly knew what to do, for Major Plympton and Col. Bruce, had, after personal inspection, pronounced it a good one.[24]

As the brothers expected, when the Indians returned in

the spring, they were unwilling to set up their summer village at the mouth of the Credit River, but encamped in two bands on the Minnesota River between the fort and Nine Mile Creek.

Leaving Gideon at Credit River to begin building a cabin, Samuel returned to the fort to see Major Plympton. He describes his interview with the Major: "I did not venture to complain of the location but I told him that our band had selected a place at Bloomington, and as the Indians above were opposed to their going to Credit River (referring, no doubt, to the band of lower Wapeton living near present Carver), I did not believe they would go there that season. After a long talk with him, he reluctantly gave us permission to plow for them that spring at Bloomington but declared he would compel them to go to Credit River the next year. Colonel Bruce was indifferent about the matter."

Meanwhile, Gideon had almost completed a cabin at the new location since he had little hope of Samuel's success in changing Major Plympton's mind. However, Indians living upstream had ordered him away, and upon Samuel's return with the news, the brothers willingly abandoned their cabin and moved to where their band was encamped.

By the spring of 1840, the rivalry which existed between Karboka or the Drifter and Cloudman had reached the point where the band actually divided into two groups —the "missionary" and the "anti-missionary" as Gideon Pond calls them. Karboka's Band encamped nearer the fort, and Cloudman's Band encamped nearer Nine Mile Creek in Bloomington close to Good Road's. "During the two years, 1840 and 1841, the Pond families resided in the 'Stone House' at Camp Coldwater, but Samuel was absent for the latter year supplying at Lac qui Parle for one of the missionaries there. In the summer of 1843, they all moved into the large house which Gideon Pond had built near the Indian camp on the Minnesota, in the south part of what is now the township of Bloomington, Hennepin County.* Gideon Pond lived in it or in the better one which replaced it till the end of his life in 1878."[25] This later house, built in 1855, is still standing at 401 East 104th Street, in Bloomington.

> While Gideon was plowing for Cloudman's band, a large number of Karboka's followers went up and drove away his oxen, but when he perceived what their intentions were, he slipped off the yoke, and they got nothing but the oxen. When Major Plympton heard of it, he told Campbell (the interpreter at the fort) to tell Karboka that if the men who brought away the oxen did not take them back immediately, the soldiers would be after them, and if any man attempted to plow for them with Gideon's team, he would find himself in the guard house. They hurried back with the oxen and Gideon went up and finished the plowing.[26]

In order to teach Karboka and his men a lesson then, Gideon refused to plow for them as he had originally intended. Samuel reports: "It did them good, and they caused less trouble afterwards."

Samuel wrote later that he had intended to plow for Karboka's party, but "when Indians attempted to drive us, we always found it best to be a little obstinate." The result was that Drifter's band did not get any land plowed that spring and the women had to prepare their corn ground as best they could with hoes, probably no small task, as it

---

*It is possible that the site which the Drifter chose was where Long had found Penasha's village in 1823 "five and a half miles from the mouth of the St. Peter's, situated on the right bank."

Medicine Bottle's Village by Henry Lewis.
Minnesota Historical Society.

was the first year in that vicinity and the ground had probably not been previously worked.

Thus by 1840 the Drifter, Cloudman, and Good Road* (the son of Penasha III) were all residing with their bands on the north side of the Minnesota River five or six, eight and nine miles, respectively, from its mouth. Mazaroto or Grey Iron resided on the south side of the river three or four miles upstream from its mouth, his village called Tetankatane or Magayutashmee. Probably these bands remained more or less stationary, returning each spring to the village sites, until they were all removed by the Treaty of 1851.

Little Crow's Kaposia at South St. Paul had been unaffected by the Treaty of 1837. As previously mentioned, Medicine Bottle's band had been compelled by the Treaty to move across the Mississippi River to the west bank at the place now called Pine Bend.

> The situation of the village was a fine one for the Indians. The marshes and heavy timber on the bottomlands were full of small game such as geese, ducks, muskrats, and mink; and on the high land were found the prairie chicken, foxes, partridges, and quail, and pigeons by the thousands that sometimes nested and roosted in the heavy timber. The timber consisted of soft maple, cottonwood, elm, hackberry, and ash.
>
> Spring Lake, southeast of this village a short distance, was alive with large fish, among which were catfish, buffalo, pike, and pickerel, also sunfish and other small kinds.
>
> The old Indian trail from Wabasha's village on the site of Winona, to Little Crow's village at Kaposia, or a

---
*Sometime in those years Good Road's village, Long Avenue, received the name Hayzatoton or Bad People.

branch of this trail, ran into Medicine Bottle's village and out again. Also a branch of this trail went to Fort Snelling.[27]

Medicine Bottle and his band lived at Pine Bend fifteen years, leaving there finally in 1852 to take up residence on the reservation on the upper Minnesota River. After Medicine Bottle was accidentally killed, Dr. Asa W. Daniels, the government physician at the Redwood Agency, wrote of him:

> We looked upon Medicine Bottle as a civilized Indian. He lived in a frame house, cultivated a plot of ground, did not believe in conjuration nor practice it, but possessed considerable knowledge in bleeding, cupping, and the hot steam bath, and kept medicinal barks, roots, and herbs, which he used in cases of sickness. He was an Indian of much ability, honest, truthful, and bore the duties of life faithfully, and always gave good advice and worthy example to the others of his people.

Kaposia and Neighboring St. Paul
1846-1851

IN THE FALL of 1845 Big Thunder lay on his deathbed and directed that one of his sons should succeed him as chief. Though His Red Nation did in fact succeed his father and become Little Crow V,* it is not clear whether Big Thunder intended that this should happen. There are three different versions of this historic incident, each of interest; and thus all three have been included. Which one is correct is a matter of conjecture at this late date.

Dr. Thomas S. Williamson who was acquainted with His Red Nation at Lac qui Parle recalled the following:

> The father of Little Crow had four sons, two of whom were killed while leading a war party against the Ojibways. Little Crow was the elder of the surviving sons and the heir apparent to the chieftainship. This honor he felt assured of, but he was ambitious to be chief of a western

---
*Perhaps Little Crow V, being somewhat theatrical by nature, wore the skin of the crow on his back below the right shoulder as mentioned in Chapter 4. Possibly significant in this respect is the fact that Little Crow V, when he signed the Treaty of 1858, used neither Little Crow, nor his personal name, His Red Nation, but his grandfather's personal name, Chetanwakamini, Walks Pursuing a Hawk; and it also seems that he was using that name in 1851 when his portrait was painted by F. B. Mayer.

band as well. While he was away, his father was accidently killed, and before his death, had placed his medals upon his younger son and proclaimed him his legitimate successor.

News of this occurrence soon reached Little Crow, when he immediately set about securing a party of followers. This done, he left for Kaposia, determined to assert his right to the chieftainship. The brother learned of this hostile movement and organized a considerable party of warriors for his support. When Little Crow reached Kaposia he was met by his brother and an engagement followed in which this brother was killed and Little Crow had the bones of both wrists shattered by a musket ball passing through them. The right to the chieftainship was duly acknowledged, but his wounds were of such serious nature as to render him totally helpless.

It was decided to take him to Fort Snelling for the advice and aid of the army surgeon. When they reached the fort with their wounded chief and the examination was made, the surgeon pronounced that to save his life both arms should be amputated. A council of the headmen followed, who determined that a chief without hands would be helpless, and that they would return with him and treat him as best they could; that if the Great Spirit looked with favor upon him and desired that he should be chief, he would recover, and if not, another could be selected. After months of careful nursing, he recovered with two useful hands, though a marked deformity remained during life.[28]

Henry Sibley, the trader who was intimately acquainted with Big Thunder, has recorded that His Red Nation was actually present at his father's deathbed. It may be that Sibley was not well acquainted with the several sons of Big Thunder and therefore did not correctly distinguish among them.

Big Thunder, directed the lodge to be cleared of all but ourselves and sent for his son Taoyateduta, the Little Crow who led the savages in the murderous outbreak of 1862. When he entered, the father told him to seat himself and listen attentively to his words. Addressing him, he told his son frankly that it had not been his intention to make him chief; that, although he was his eldest born, he had very little good sense, and moreover he was addicted to drinking and other vicious habits.

"But," said he, "my second son, on whom I intended to bestow the chieftainship at my death has been killed in battle with the Chippewas, and I can now do no better than to name you as my successor."

He proceeded to give him counsel as to his future course in the responsible position he was about to assume as the leader of the band which would have reflected no discredit upon a civilized man similarly situated, except that he did not suggest a change of religious faith to that of the whites. On that topic he remained silent. After referring to the differences existing between the two races, he told his son that the Dakotas must accomodate themselves to the new state of things which was coming upon them. The whites wanted their land and it was useless to contend against their superior forces. The Dakotas could only hope to be saved from the fate of other tribes by making themselves useful to the whites, by honest labor, and frank and friendly dealing in their intercourse with them.[29]

This report of Sibley induced the historian Holcombe to make a very careful investigation of the facts surrounding the death of Big Thunder as remembered by members of the Kaposia band who were still living at the time he wrote the second volume of *Minnesota in Three Centuries*. Holcombe's conclusion was that Sibley erred since his account was written twenty-seven years after Big Thunder's death.

Little Crow V (His Red Nation), photograph by Joel E. Whitney.

Minneapolis Public Library Bromley Collection.

Holcombe's version, on the basis of personal reminiscenses of the Kaposia Indians, reads as follows:

> At the time of, and some years before his father's death, Taoyateduta (His Red Nation) was at Lac qui Parle and had been living on the Upper Minnesota among the Wapetons of Eshnmanne's band. He had married three daughters of the chief, lived with and was practically a member of the band. At rare intervals he had made a brief visit to Kaposia. He was in bad repute and ill favor with his father's band because he was a Lothario in morals, a debauchee in habits, and yet was of a haughty and overbearing disposition, especially towards his half-brothers. He had been forced to leave Kaposia because of threats against him by certain husbands whom he had wronged.
>
> At Lac qui Parle the young prince had been well received by Chief Eshnmanne, became an inmate of his household, and finally, his threefold son-in-law. After his marriage he seems to have abandoned his bad habits, except that he was lazy and did not like to hunt and never went out with but one war party against the Chippewas. He had many admirers among the Wapetons and Sissetons because of his smooth speech, agreeable manners, and rare good judgment. When the news of the death of his father reached him, Taoyateduta began preparations for assuming the chieftainship held, and the titular name borne by him. The death message had been accompanied by a stern warning that the assumption would be resisted to the death point by his half brothers and other members of the band who regarded him as wholly unfit to be their chief.[30]

Almost immediately after taking over the Kaposia band, His Red Nation invited Dr. Thomas S. Williamson, whom he had known at Lac qui Parle, to come to Kaposia and open a school. Dr. Williamson had worked at Lac qui

Parle for a number of years under the Presbyterian Board of Missions. After the death of his benefactor, Joseph Renville, Dr. Williamson apparently became discouraged at Lac qui Parle. At any rate in the fall of 1846 he decided to accept Little Crow's invitation to come to Kaposia on the Mississippi River and open a Mission there. Dr. Williamson's Kaposia mission lasted five or six years and was about as successful as other Dakota missions were—the children attended the schools if sufficiently bribed; a few women were usually converted; and the men, with a few exceptions, ignored the missionaries or opposed them more openly if encouraged to do so by their medicine men.

In the case of the Kaposia mission a number of Indian boys and girls did attend the school and learned some English. In fact a visitor to the school in 1849 was quite impressed.

> I went to Crow's village, but it was at a time when very few children were in attendance at Mr. Cook's school (the government school). Such as were present showed that they were learning to read, and one was writing. I found many girls in attendance at the American Board of Foreign Mission's school, instructed by Jane Williamson and was much pleased by the ability displayed by the instructress, and interested by the conduct of the children.
>
> They were all asked to read in their Indian books, and produced specimens of their work that would do credit to any girls of their age. Miss Williamson certainly deserves great praise for the toil and skill she has bestowed on these children; to them, her kindness and tenderness equal that of the most affectionate.[31]

As at other Missions in this period, there were attached to Dr. Williamson's mission farmer-missionaries—namely,

Louis Martin, a Frenchman, and Hazen Mooers, the trader. As a result, the Indian men learned to plow and even to do rudimentary carpentry.

Dr. Williamson also organized a small Dakota church. However, the membership consisted principally of young women, for the majority of the men of the band shunned the religion of the white men and resented the new customs which they tried to introduce.

Even the Pond brothers—in fact, all the missionaries—experienced the same difficulty with respect to the Dakota men during this period. At the mission stations farther away from the fort there seems to have been much actual persecution of the missionaries in the form of theft, killing of oxen, etc. Fortunately for Dr. Williamson, at Kaposia Little Crow V had effective control over his people and forbade any unkind conduct toward the missionaries, who had come by his invitation. However, he himself never embraced Christianity.

There are a number of instances on record to indicate the animosity of the Indian men toward any of their number who adopted the religion and the manners of the whites. Joseph Napayshneeduta (Red Man Who Fears Nothing), the first full-blooded Dakota baptized, according to Dr. Williamson, certainly experienced the ostracism which went along with adoption of the new religion.

> He took his family to reside at Little Crow's village, a few miles below Fort Snelling, on the Mississippi, where many of his kindred lived. In this region game was more abundant and goods much cheaper than at Lac qui Parle. He was taken down with a fever soon after he arrived among them. Some of his relatives, principal men of the village, called to see him. They inquired of him if it was true, as they heard, that he had abandoned the religion

and customs of their fathers, and embraced the religion of the white men? He replied that it was. They then told him if he would return to their customs and worship as they did, they would attend to him in his sickness as they did to each other, and furnish him with food and medicine. If he would not do this, he must look to his new friends for help, for they could do nothing for him. Knowing that for the cure of disease they relied chiefly on the aid of the spirits they worshipped, and that God forbids such worship, he told them he would be pleased if they would furnish his family with food till he got well, but he did not believe in any of their gods, nor wish any of their incantations about him. If it was the will of the great God he worshipped that he should recover, He would restore him to health, if not he was willing to die. Hearing this they left him to get along as he could. He and his family suffered much for food and the fever continued for weeks. One day one of his acquaintances, a man he had not seen for a long time, brought them some food, and asked if there was anything more he could do for him. He requested him to go to Fort Snelling, tell the surgeon there how he was, and ask for medicine for him. The medicine was obtained, broke the fever, and he soon got well.

A year or two after this, having obtained a horse, he bought a harness, made a small sled and hauled his fire wood, instead of having his wife carry it, as was the custom. When the sleighing became good, he took his wife and youngest child on the sled and gave them a ride to Fort Snelling, where Major R. G. Murphy, the agent, commended him for his industry and ingenuity. His comrades viewed the matter differently; said his wife was no better than theirs; such innovations must not be allowed, and killed his dog. He nevertheless persevered in drawing his wood. Soon after they killed his horse. Being unable to buy another, his harness and sled were useless. Major Murphy would have been pleased to remunerate him for his losses, by taking the money from the annuities of those who had injured him, but the laws of our country do not allow such interference with Indian customs.[32]

At Kaposia, Dr. Williamson became convinced of the need for a school in the white village located across the river, earlier called Pig's Eye, but now rechristened St. Paul's Landing or St. Paul. Accordingly, he wrote to ex-Governor Slade of Vermont, president of the National Popular Education Society. He lamented the condition of the white man's town—"This village has five groceries, as they call them, at all of which intoxicating drinks constitute a part, and I suppose, the principal part, of what they sell"—and requested that a teacher be sent to the vicinity.

In response to this letter, Miss Harriet E. Bishop came to St. Paul as the first regular school teacher in the white settlements of Minnesota. Miss Bishop recorded her arrival at the village of Kaposia.

> Slowly and surely progressed the (steamboat) "Lynx" and rapidly the hours sped on. All nature had conspired too, for a glorious day when we first looked on Little Crow's village at Kaposia, where we landed on the morning of July 16, 1847. The ringing of the bell occasioned a grand rush, and with telegraphic speed, every man, woman and child flew to the landing.
>
> To an unsophisticated eye like mine, the scene on shore was novel and grotesque, not to say repulsive; blankets and hair streaming in the wild, limbs uncovered, children nearly naked, the smaller ones entirely so, while a papoose was ludicrously peeping over the shoulder of nearly every squaw.
>
> In the midst of the waiting throng appeared the missionary and his sister.
>
> It was a moment of no ordinary interest, of calm,

Dakotah Village by Seth Eastman, Kaposia in 1850.
James Jerome Hill Reference Library, St. Paul.

undefinable joy when I entered the mission house. The day succeeding my arrival was the sabbath. To the poor Indians all days are alike. Only a few assembled at the house of worship; a messenger being sent to invite others to come in, the room was soon full. Some listened with profound attention, others remained in listless indifference, and others dozed quietly in their seats. A few were inclined to laugh, some left, but most remained until the services closed.

The Indians commenced their favorite game of ball, arrangements for the same having been going on all morning, which continued for several successive days. The competitors for the prize place their most valued possessions on a pole, which was carried around by two girls to receive the stakes, and when the last was entered the game commenced.

The ball is thrown and caught by a small circle with leather bands on each side attached to a lever two or three feet long. When uncaught, the women fly off in its pursuit, and though they have no other interest in the game, they seem equally engaged with the men. In this game, the wives of the chief are most active.

Towards evening, two Frenchmen were seen approaching the village, suspicion was immediately rife with the villagers that they were bringing with them "fire-water" and some of them came in breathless haste entreating Dr. Williamson to prevent it, for too well they knew its disastrous consequences.[33]

Recalling her stay at Kaposia Miss Bishop wrote: "It must be borne in mind that St. Paul (in 1847) was a small trading post giving yet no sign of its unprecedented growth. The council fires were but just extinguished on the east side and were still brightly blazing on the west of the river. Our village was almost daily thronged with Indians, where they frequently encamped in larger numbers than the entire adult male population of the Territory. Tragic scenes were often enacted upon them by unprincipled whiskey-sellers."

Whiskey appears to have been St. Paul's chief attraction to the dwellers of the nearby Kaposia as well as more distant villages.

> Under the influence of a vile class of whiskey sellers that infested the neighborhood of what is now the capital of Minnesota, the Dakotas were a nation of drunkards. Men would travel hundreds of miles to "The place where they sell Minnewakan" as they designated St. Paul, to traffic for a keg of whiskey.[34]

Gideon Pond wrote that the Indians "would have whiskey. They would give guns, blankets, pork, lard, flour, corn, coffee, sugar, horses, furs, traps, anything for whiskey." Mr. James McMullen, who came to St. Paul in 1849, said, "If you had half a pint of whiskey in those days and were willing to trade with the Indians, you could get almost anything they had."

In this connection reference is made to what undoubtedly was Governor Ramsey's most famous temperance speech. This was delivered at a council held on March 14, 1850 in St. Paul, where he warned the Indians of the dangers of over-indulgence in spirit water, and urged them to quit drinking. "The white men," he said, "have quit drinking." The interpreter then translated precisely what the governor said, but the Indians looked a little astonished and incredulous at this statement on the governor's part. So he qualified it by adding, "in a great measure." The interpreter then translated this phrase literally: in a large sized vessel. To this one of the old chiefs exclaimed, "Perhaps they have quit using a *large,* but most of them still use a *small* measure."

On the other hand, the Indians contributed much to the trade of St. Paul.

> They used to supply the local market with fish, wild fowls, venison, bear meat, cranberries, furs and products of the forest generally; besides moccasins, bead-work and trinkets of that class. They would always demand gold and silver for their products, which they would reinvest in ammunition, blankets, flour, cutlery or anything they fancied. They were pretty sharp at a bargain too, be it known, and scarcely ever got overreached.[35]

Observers of the period have also made innumerable references to Indians "begging."

> In these early days it was common for the Indians to pounce into the kitchen of the lady of the house, and clean out her larder of all that was in it. I do not mean to say that they would steal, but they begged so hard and so audaciously that it was equivalent to it. Of course, the whites gave cheerfully because it was for their interests to do so, besides, they desired to keep on the good side of the red men so if possible to avoid an outbreak.
>
> One day while Mrs. Stees was scrubbing her floor, several Indians pushed into her kitchen and seeing a large dish of chicken and pig feed, the latter composed somewhat of dish water, and supposing it was for them, seized it, sat down upon the wet floor and before the good woman could make any protestation, had swallowed the whole, and then, smacking their lips and grunting, left the premises.
>
> That night the chickens went to roost without supper and the pigs squealed until morning for something to eat.
>
> The next day, about the same hour, the same Indians made their appearance, but the rooster crowed, the hens cackled, and the pigs grunted, for their mistress had cir-

St. Paul, Minnesota, by Jean Baptist Wengler, 1851.
Oberoesterreichisches Landesmuseum, Linz, Austria.

cumvented the Indians by giving her dumb family an early meal. Once again the Indians gathered at the hospitable kitchen and this time Mrs. Stees had thoughtlessly left her dish water in a huge pot on the stove, and it was lukewarm. The Indians seized and drank it before the presiding genius of the kitchen knew they were present.

They soon left and were heard to exclaim: "Me heap sick" and the general contortions of their features clearly showed that they were telling the truth. They threw up this kind of fare and never visited the family again.[36]

Although Folsom would not "say that they steal," there is sufficient evidence that although they probably did not come to St. Paul with that express purpose in mind, many of her red visitors succumbed to this prevalent vice. Witness this short article from the *Pioneer* in 1850, headed "Substitution of a Thief":

The other day an Indian came into the jewelry shop of Mr. Spicer on Robert Street and while there, stole a watch. Mr. Spicer followed him up the street, to Mr. Fuller's store, and collared him, and seeing no one to assist, left the Indian standing by the side of Mr. Fuller's store while he went inside to get someone to help him search the Indian.

Returning in two or three minutes, he found an Indian standing in the same spot in the same attitude he had left the thief in, his blanket philosophically folded around him, but he was another Indian, who had taken the place of the thief during Spicer's absence, while the thief himself slipped around the house and fled.

But not all the Indians who came to St. Paul had business to attend to—whether it were trading or begging. Many of them undoubtedly came out of simple curiosity. They could be observed at almost any time of the year, just standing on the street and looking at the new and strange sights the settlement had to offer.

In April, 1849, James M. Goodhue came to St. Paul and established his newspaper, the *Pioneer*. One of his first articles relates an instance of this curiosity.

> A tall dark Sioux Indian, led by curiosity into our office while we were working off the outside of the *Pioneer*, after looking on for a moment in wonder, with his right hand placed over his mantle and his head slowly waving forward and backward, gave utterance to something like the following:
>
> "Hay har hais! Wasejon taku wowawe kau raph roy u kee: wahkon per do! Now pag day on kaug rah-shnee!"
>
> All this we understand means in plain English: "How ingeniously they work! They are wizards! This writing is not done with the hand."
>
> He proceeded by saying to the interpreter: "This beats the fire-canoe (steamboat). By looking at those little marks, he can understand one's thoughts. But so it is. The Great Spirit has not made his children alike. To the white man he has given the power of making with his hands what he pleases; but to us Indians, he has given the talent for speaking in council—the power to run down the deer and to follow our enemy to his wigwam. See! This is not work for women."

The August 30, 1849, issue of the *Pioneer* reads: "We called on friend Brawley the other day at his brickyard. He is now in a most successful state of operations. He employs two mills, ten men, and has now on hand some 400,000 brick. The quality is better than can be shown north of St. Louis." This was the first brick burned in Minnesota, and it was used to construct the first brick building, a residence for Rev. E. D. Neill, Minnesota's first historian, on Fourth

Street near Washington Street. Neill himself records that the Indians watched the erection of the building

> with wonder, as they had not before seen bricks. They seemed to them to be as well adapted for pipes as the sacred red pipe stone, and coveted them. Some even took a few without leave, and hid them under their blankets and carried them to their village, but when they began to scrape them, were disappointed in finding that like "apples of Sodom," they turned to dust.[37]

In the same year a young man by the name of C. D. Bevans arrived and set up a tin shop—a frame building located at Rice and Irvine's addition on Third Street between Washington and Franklin.

> For the first few weeks after its erection it was the most attractive spot on earth to some of the Sioux of the Kaposia village. They stood near its window in eager expectancy, and as the tinner would throw out the thin scraps, the refuse of his shears, there was a scramble for their possession. At night they could be seen in their village with long tin pendants attached to their leaden earrings, and pleased as if possessed of the "wealth of Ormus and of Ind."[38]

The young Indians also came into St. Paul to sing and dance for the settlers, expecting of course to be shown appreciation in the tangible form of handouts. One reporter recorded, "Our citizens were visited on Tuesday last by a company of twenty or thirty more juvenile Sioux from Little Crow's band, who danced the 'beggar dance' in different parts of town. The young redskins, from five to eighteen years of age, presented a grotesque appearance. They were naked and painted."[39]

The "grotesque appearance" here referred to is aptly described by one of early St. Paul's more famous visitors, Miss Fredrika Bremer, a distinguished novelist from Sweden. She devoted considerable space of her entertaining book *Homes of the New World,* to facts about this "eighteen month old town of two thousand persons" and her impressions of life there.

Visiting in October, 1850, she found St. Paul "thronged with Indians. The men for the most part go about gaudily ornamented," she wrote. "They paint themselves so utterly without any taste that it is incredible. Here comes an Indian who has painted a great spot in the middle of his nose; here another who has painted the whole of his forehead in lines of black and yellow. The women are less painted, with better taste than the men generally, with merely one deep red little spot in the middle of the cheek and the parting of the hair is dyed purple."

What seemed to the whites grotesque and fantastic in the Indians' manner of self-decoration was not a haphazard or careless application of color, but a definite effort on their part to attract admiration or inspire fear.

As long as Kaposia remained in the region of the Mississippi River, there appear to have been forays annually against the nearby Chippewa. As a young man His Red Nation had probably earned his eagle feather in such a foray, and in later years he was remembered by Medicine Bottle as the war chief who had led the band in battles against the Chippewa. However, there seems to be no evidence that His Red Nation led any war parties after he took over the Kaposia band and became Little Crow V.

The hostilities between the Chippewa and Dakota which occurred in April of 1850 involved braves from Kaposia though reports make no mention of Little Crow V. On this occasion the band of Chippewa under Hole-in-the-Day was collecting sap and making maple sugar on the Apple River, a tributary of the St. Croix River in Wisconsin, an area that had been ceded to the United States.

The Last Years on the Lower Minnesota
1847-1851

AFTER THE MOVE from Lake Calhoun, Samuel Pond went to Lac qui Parle for a year, then returned to join his brother at Oak Grove on the Minnesota River. In the fall of 1847 Chief Shakopee, residing near where the town with the same name now stands, invited Samuel to build a mission near his village. Samuel accepted the invitation, constructed the mission—the first framed house on the Minnesota above Mendota—and named it Prairieville. At about this time his family acquired as foster daughter a granddaughter of Cloudman, who was given the name Jane. Her mother, Cloudman's daughter Hushes the Night, had been married to the trader Daniel Lamont. She gave her small daughter, who knew only the Dakota language, to the Samuel Ponds to be raised as a white child. Jane grew up with the Ponds and married their nephew Star Titus. Their family eventually included three sons and two daughters and in later years two of these sons became prominent bankers in North Dakota while the third son farmed near Tracy, Minnesota.

The Samuel Ponds seem to have had a strong influence on the Indian children in their midst.

Among the many children taught by my wife were

two little boys, brothers. They were both bright boys and the younger, though a wild, head-strong boy, was very much attached to his books, and notwithstanding the ridicule of the Indians, persisted in carrying them with him wherever he went. He sometimes called on me at Shakopee (in later years) and commonly had a portion of the Scriptures along with him, but he was very eccentric and we did not consider his case a very hopeful one. He was in the prison at Mankato with the men who were condemned, and some who were confined with him told me that it was through his influence, more than anything else that they were first led to call on God. He died at Rock Island, but his brother* is one of the best known and influential men at Flandreau, South Dakota.[40]

Though his brother had joined Shakopee's village, Gideon Pond continued to serve the Cloudman and Drifter bands further downstream on the Minnesota River. He diligently applied himself to the study of theology during these years and by 1848 was sufficiently prepared to be ordained as a minister. He lamented the changes in the living habits of the Indians which the advent of white "civilization" had wrought.

Most of the Indians have returned from their winter hunt (tuka okiran hdi) but starving because the young men must needs hunt Chippewa instead of deer. They will now receive their annuity money and will then be able to get more whiskey probably than they have ever had before. They had a happy new year yesterday, crying, singing, and fighting.[41]

It appears that Travelling Hail,** a member of Black

---

*This brother took the name of Joseph Blacksmith and was active in mission work at Flandreau. There a number of Christian Dakota, who had left their reservation, settled on farms of their own.
**Also known as Wassonweechastishnee or Bad Hail.

Dog's band, joined Cloudman's band soon after it had moved to the Minnesota. As Cloudman was the exponent for adaption to the white man's religion and ways, so Travelling Hail became the spokesman for those who resisted this trend.

Although the area west of the Mississippi had not yet been opened to settlement, Colonel John H. Stevens, who arrived in 1849, built a house on the west bank at St. Anthony Falls. He became well acquainted with the Indians on the lower Minnesota in these last years and left extensive writings.

> Frequently on Sundays in 1849, after the morning service in the little chapel at Fort Snelling, Colonel Loomis would suggest that we go, as soon as we had lunched, to the Oak Grove Mission and listen to the excellent afternoon sermon by Rev. G. H. Pond. In the forenoon, Mr. Pond usually preached to the Indians in their own language and in the afternoon to the whites who besides his own family were mostly employed in the interest of the Indians.[42]

Gideon Pond himself was less optimistic.

> Last week the Indians renewed their threats against those who come to our religious meetings; the fact that two or three women who have never before attended have been attracted to us a few Sabbaths of late, is the occasion for it. The great men appear to fear that if they let them alone all the common people will go away and believe on Jesus. It is reported that Red Boy said that whereas the missionaries were getting away with all the money, the clothes should be torn from all who came to our meetings on the Sabbath.[43]

At a later time Samuel Pond looked back with compassion on his brother's trials in these years.

Gideon had more than his share of hardships, and at times, I cannot think of the trials that he went through without feelings of sadness, for they wore out his strong constitution and I believe, shortened his life.[44]

The close neighbor to Cloudman and Drifter at Oak Grove was Long Avenue, the village of Penasha, which had had a long history on the Minnesota River. At this time Long Avenue was under the leadership of Good Road, the son of Penasha III.

There is evidence that Good Road and at least part of his band dwelled with Cloudman on Lake Calhoun during the last summer there—1839. In that year the population of the Inland Village numbered five hundred people, more than the combined totals for both Penasha's and Black Dog's villages just a few years before.

Though Good Road may not have inspired the affection of the missionaries, there is no doubt that he was worthy of their respect. Samuel Pond recorded an anecdote which illustrates Good Road's sharp tongue as well as his considerable physical endurance.

In the summer of 1844, some young men of the Penasha band or village insulted a half-breed woman, the wife of the government blacksmith, and Captain Backus who was in charge of the fort ordered Good Road to bring in the offenders to Fort Snelling, but Good Road said something to the messengers which offended the captain, and he at once dispatched a company of infantry to arrest the chief.

The officer in charge of the expedition had orders to march the men to Penasha and back in the shortest time possible. No one supposed it was necessary to send a military force to arrest Good Road. An invitation from the commander would doubtless have brought him at once to

Fort Snelling, but Captain Backus said he wished to let the Dakotas know that the United States infantry could march as well as they.

They, however, were more amused than alarmed by that forced march and it is to be feared that the lesson which he was so anxious to teach the Dakotas has not been learned to this day.

The march was rapid enough and the eighteen miles were passed over quickly, but several of the strongest soldiers fell out by the way, and were left lying on the ground. The writer passed over the prairie with the troops on their return to the fort, and saw Good Road, who was then probably fifty or sixty years of age walking in advance of his captors, a little faster than his ordinary pace, but apparently with no great exertion while his guard, both officers and men, were all panting like over driven oxen.* The offense for which he was arrested was not a very aggravated one and he was discharged from custody soon after reaching the fort.[45]

History is greatly indebted to Mary Eastman, the wife of Captain Seth Eastman whom he brought back to Fort Snelling when he returned for a second assignment there in the 1840's. Mary Eastman wrote a book entitled *Dakotah, Life and Legends of the Sioux*,[46] based on her own experiences and observation. Mrs. Eastman's appealing and heart-warming manner tempts this author to quote whole pages from her work.

The scenery about Fort Snelling is rich in beauty. The falls of St. Anthony are familiar to travellers, and to readers of Indian sketches. Between the fort and these falls are the "Little Falls," forty feet in height, that emp-

---

*Perhaps it was such escapades as this that earned for Good Road and his band the name of "The Bad People."

ties into the Mississippi. The Indians call them Minne-ha-ha, or laughing waters. In sight of Fort Snelling is a beautiful hill called Morgan's Bluff; the Indians call it "God's House." They have a tradition that it is the residence of their god of the waters, whom they call Unk-ta-he. Nothing can be more lovely than the situation and appearance of this hill; it commands on every side a magnificent view, and during the summer, it is carpeted with long grass and prairie flowers. Opposite the fort is Pilot Knob, a high peak, used as a burial place by the Indians; just below it is the village of Mendota, or the "Meeting of the Waters."

Undoubtedly, most of the Dakota who pitched their tepees within sight of Fort Snelling, especially looking south, across Pike Island and the Minnesota River were of Grey Iron's band. Mrs. Eastman observed that "Tepees could be seen in every direction."

The first impression created by the Sioux was the common one, fear. In their looks, they were so different from the Indians I had occasionally seen. There was nothing in their aspect to indicate the success of efforts made to civilize them. Their tall, unbending forms, their savage hauteur, the piercing black eye, the quiet indifference of manner, the slow stealthy step—how different were they from the eastern Indians, whose association with the white people seems to have deprived them of all native dignity of bearing and of character.

The yells heard outside the high wall of the fort at first filled me with alarm, but I soon became accustomed to them, and to all other occasional Indian excitements that served to vary the monotony of garrison life.

Before I felt much interest in the Sioux, they seemed to have great regard for me. My husband, before his marriage had been stationed at Fort Snelling and at Prairie

Black Dog's Village by Seth Eastman
Harper's Weekly, July, 1853.

du Chien. He was fond of hunting and roaming about the prairies, and left many friends* among the Indians when he obeyed the order to return to an eastern station. On going back to the Indian country, he met with a warm welcome from his old acquaintances, who were eager to shake hands with "Eastman's squaw."

The old men laid their bony hands upon the heads of my little boys, admired their light hair, said their skins were very white; and although I could not understand their language, they told me many things, accompanied with earnest gesticulation. They brought their wives and young children to see me. I had been told that Indian women gossipped and stole, that they were filthy and troublesome. Yet I could not despise them; they were wives and mothers—God had implanted the same feelings in their hearts as in mine.

Some Indians visited us every day and we frequently saw them at their villages. Captain Eastman spoke their language well, and without taking any pains to acquire it, I soon understood it so as to talk with them.

The women of the Sioux exhibit many striking peculiarities of character—the love of the marvelous, and a profound veneration for any and everything connected with their religious faith, a willingness to labor and to learn, patience in submitting to insults from servants who consider them intruders in families; the evident recognition of the fact that they are a doomed race and must submit to iniquities that they dare not resent. They seem, too, so unused to sympathy, often comparing their lives of suffering and hardship with the ease and comfort enjoyed by the white woman. It must be a hard heart that could withhold sympathy from such poor creatures.

Their home was mine—and such a home! The very

---

*During his first stay at Fort Snelling Seth Eastman had taken as his wife the daughter of Cloudman.

sunsets, more bright and glorious than I have ever seen, seemed to love to linger over the scenes amongst which we lived; the high bluffs of the "father of many waters," and the quiet shores of the "Minnesota"; the fairy rings on the prairie, and the "spirit lakes" that reposed beside them; the bold peak, Pilot Knob, on whose top the Indians bury their dead, with the small hills rising gradually around it—all were dear to the Sioux and me. They believed that the rocks and hills and waters were peopled with fairies and spirits, whose power and anger they had ever been taught to fear. I knew that God, whose presence fills all nature was there. In fancy, they beheld their deities in the blackened cloud and fearful storm, I saw mine in the brightness of nature, the type of the unchanging light of heaven.

Mrs. Eastman mentions Grey Iron, who was then nearing fifty years of age, commenting that "his age seemed to have brought him wisdom," but although she writes of quite a few individuals of his band, none of her stories or tales are specifically about him.

The son of Major John Bliss, commander of the fort in 1833, says, "With so many Indians around us, we were soon familiar with their different dances, feasts, and games, and when tourists visited us, something of the sort was gotten up for their amusement just outside of the fort, but on such occasions the big gate was always closed if they were in large numbers. They were unmitigated barbarians."[47] Yet Mrs. Eastman found her neighbors "the greatest objects of interest and curiosity" and has few harsh words to say of them though she honestly describes their uncivilized barbarism.

One could soon know all that was to be known about Pilot Knob, or St. Anthony's Falls, but one is puzzled completely to comprehend the character of an Indian man, woman, or child. At one moment, you see an Indian chief raise himself to his full height, and say that the ground on which he stands is his own; at the next, beg bread and pork from the enemy. An Indian woman will scornfully refuse to wash an article that might be needed by a white family, and the next moment, declare that she had not washed her face in fifteen years! An Indian child of three years old will cling to his mother under the walls of the fort and then plunge into the Mississippi and swim half way across in hopes of finding an apple that has been thrown in. We may well feel much curiosity to look into the habits, manners, and motives of a race exhibiting such contradictions.[48]

In this connection, we might note Wm. Joseph Snelling's Preface to *Tales of the Northwest:* "The key to much that appears strange in the character of the aborigines may be found in one word: Inconsistency. No certain judgment of an Indian's future conduct can be determined by the past. His behavior in all probability will not be the same in the same circumstances. He is the child of nature, and her caprice will dictate his course." And perhaps inconsistency is also the by-word for Mary Eastman's detailed description of Good Road's village at this time.

Good Road's village, like other Indian villages, abounds in variety more than anything else. In the tepee farthest from us, right on the edge of the shore, there are three young men carousing. One is inclined to go to sleep, but the other two will not let him; their spirits are raised and excited by what has made him stupid. Who would suppose they are human beings? See their bloodshot eyes; hear their fiendish laugh and horrid yells; probably before the revel is closed, one of the friends will have buried his knife in the other's heart.

We will pass on to the next tepee. Here we witness a scene almost as appalling. "Iron Arms," one of the most violent warriors of the band is stretched in the agonies of death. "Old Spirit Killer," the medicine man is gesticulating by his side, and accompanying his motions with the most horrid noises. But all in vain, the spirit of "Iron Arms," the man of strength, is gone. The doctor says that his medicine was good, but that a prairie dog had entered into the body of the Dakota and he thought it had been a mud-hen. Magnanimous doctor! All honor, that you can allow yourself an error.

While his friends of the dead warrior are rending the air with their cries, we will find out what is going on in the next wigwam. What a contrast!

"The Whirlpool" is seated on the ground smoking; gazing as earnestly at the bright coals as if in them he could read the future or recall the past; and his young wife, whose face, now merry, now sad, bright with smiles at one moment and lost in thought the next, gained for her the name of "Changing Countenance" is hushing her child to sleep, but the expression of features does not change now—as she looks on her child, a mother's deep and loving devotion is pictured on her face.

In another tepee, "Dancing Woman" is wrapped in her blanket pretending to go to sleep. In vain does "Flying Cloud" play that monotonous courting tune on the flute. The maiden would not be his wife if he gave her all the trinkets in the world. She loves and is going to marry "Iron Lightening" who has gone to bring her—what? a brooch?—a new blanket? no, a Chippewa's scalp, that she may be the most graceful of those who dance around it. Her mother is mending the moccasins of the old man who sleeps before the fire.

And we might go around the village and find every family differently employed. They have no regular hours for eating or sleeping. In front of the tepees, young men are lying on the ground, lazily playing checkers, while their wives and sisters are engaged in laborious household duties.[49]

From Col. Stevens we learn more of the country and the activities of the Indians of Good Road's and Cloudman's Bands during the years from 1849 until their removal.

Game was plenty in those early times in Minnesota. Indians were plenty too; but some way, the more Indians, the more game. At the proper season of the year, deer-, buffalo-, and bear-steaks could be obtained at very reasonables rates, while there seemed no end of wild geese and ducks in the fall and spring. Prairie chickens were abundant.

Partridges were found in great abundance in the wooded and brush lands. The wild pigeons were the most numerous of all birds. The sky would for days at certain hours, be almost obscured by them. For several days they were taken in great numbers in nets.

Fish then were caught in great numbers. The New England speckled trout sported in many of the clear streams in southern Minnesota.

Most of the large game disappeared with the departure of the Indians. It was by no means a difficult task in the early fifties to obtain all the meat necessary for one's household from the fruits of the chase. Wild bees, too, were abundant, but with the disappearance of the shadow of the tall oak, the wild busy bee is a thing of the past.

Most of the valuable fur-bearing animals, the great staple of earlier days is done, too. A family of otter had a real nice home in what is now (1890) known as Bassett's Creek where Fourth Street crosses it in this city when I lived alone on the bank of the river where the Union depot is built. In fact, they were resident there some years afterwards. The cowardly wolves, but in greatly reduced numbers, still remain. They appear to be too mean to follow the Indian. The bear is still found, but not one where there were ten, forty years ago.

There are many more birds here now than there were in those days—all the desirable birds are fond of frequenting the haunts of civilized man.[50]

On his first visit to St. Anthony Falls, Stevens found "a few Indians belonging to Good Road's Band who had their tepees up and were living temporarily in them, in the oak openings on the hill."

"The Indians were never so numerous in the neighborhood of the Falls as in 1850. The different bands of Sioux remained in camp on the high-lands just above the falls. They did not interfere with my stock, but made sad havoc with my garden. As a general rule, the Indians respected the private property of the whites residing outside of their own lands."[51]

After he had built his frame house,* across the street where the Great Northern Depot is now located, Stevens tells us that many of the local Indians visited him.

Little Crow, Good Road, Grey Eagle, Shakopee and other Dakota chiefs held consultations with the government agents, Major R. Murphy and Major McLean in that house. Hole-in-the-Day and his Chippewa braves frequently dropped in. The nearer the dinner hour the better it suited them to make their call.

A barrel or two of crackers and a good supply of salt pork was a special delight to the red brothers. It was thought advisable that these Indian luxuries should always be on hand, and ready for any emergency. They prevented depredations on the garden, growing crops, and stock.

---

*In 1896 the house was moved to Minnehaha Park where it still stands.

The winter of 1851-1852 was the last season that Good Road's and Cloudman's bands on the lower Minnesota appear to have spent there as a unit. Col. Stevens tells us of Cloudman's last visit to his house.

> The Indian chieftain, Man of the Clouds, with several of his tribe came down from Oak Grove on Christmas seeking alms. He said he could not expect to see his white friends in this neighborhood in the future, as his band would soon move for the winter into the hunting grounds of the big woods, and when spring came, should follow the Dakotas to their reservation on the upper Minnesota River.
>
> He was desirous of accepting such gifts with the compliments of the season as his white friends should see proper to give him, which he should cherish as tokens of friendship in his new home. As the wily chieftain mostly solicited perishable gifts such as bread, meat, sugar, coffee, and the like, it was evident that the immediate wants of the stomach were the tokens by which his former friends were to be remembered.
>
> We made the old Man of the Clouds and his wives and children happy. If I remember correctly, the old man was right in saying that he was visiting the Falls for the last time.
>
> Not so, however, with Good Road, chief of the other band of the lake Dakotas. He remembered us with visits after the removal to the Redwood country, but the close of the year 1851, in a measure ended the protracted visits of the Dakotas to the Falls. It is true they would occasionally swarm down on us by the hundreds, but in after years their sojourn was of short duration.[52]

The Great Treaty
1851-1852

NEITHER THE treaty signed at Prairie du Chien in 1830 nor the Treaties of 1837 were of much benefit to the Indians. Not unmindful of this and hoping "to acquire from the Sioux an extent of country large enough to furnish reservations for all other Indian tribes and remnants of tribes east of the Mississippi," the governor of the Wisconsin Territory, James D. Doty, negotiated an unusual treaty with the Dakota at Traverse des Sioux in July of 1841. The Mdewakanton chiefs and principal warriors signed this treaty at Mendota on August 11, 1841, the other bands of the Santee Dakota having already signed it at Traverse des Sioux on July 31. History will never know what the effects of the treaty might have been, for the United States Senate failed to ratify it. Nevertheless, the treaty is worthy of our attention.

This treaty embodied the utopian dream of an Indian Territory where the red men would reside on farms and in villages, living their lives after the style of the whites, having a constitutional form of government with a legislature of their own people elected by themselves, the governor to be appointed, however, by the president of the United

States. They would be "hemmed in" thus, "by the laws of the United States and guarded by virtuous agents, where abstinence from vice, and the practice of good morals should find fit abodes in comfortable dwellings and cleared farms."[53] The Indians were to be taught the arts of peace, to be paid annuities and to be protected from their Indian enemies on the west as well as from their white exploiters on the east.

"By the terms of the treaty, the Sioux, as the recognized rightful owners of the country," Holcombe reports, "sold all their lands in what is now Minnesota, the Dakotas, and Northwestern Iowa, except small designated portions thereof reserved for their homes." But, he continues, "the object of the Doty treaty was not to open the country purchased to white settlement; on the contrary, it devoted and destined all the vast expanse of territory acquired to Indian occupancy forever."[54]

Human nature being what it is, this plan would probably not have been at all practicable considering the desirability of the land involved; nevertheless a similar system has been in practice in the desert states of our country and has proven workable. However, this abortive treaty does demonstrate that responsible men were duly concerned about the situation which the westward flow of civilization had created for the red man as well as the white, and that efforts to find workable solutions to the problems involved were being made. Whether the government failed to ratify this treaty on political grounds, or whether on more practical grounds—greed—white men of influence prevailed in keeping this fertile field of exploitation open to them. The Doty treaty of 1841 was never ratified and never put into action. Agitation for the opening of the area west of the Mississippi, moreover, increased as each year passed.

Mendota from Fort Snelling by Edward Thomas, about 1850.
Gilcrease Institute of American History and Art, Tulsa.

On March 3, 1849, the act creating Minnesota Territory went into effect, and on April second Alexander Ramsey, a former Congressman from Pennsylvania, was appointed governor of the new Territory. From the time of his arrival in May of 1849,

> there was not a day in which, whether in season or out of season, Ramsey was not reminded that the one predominant and absorbing interest of the white people of the territory was the acquisition of the lands occupied by the Sioux Indians, lying west of the Mississippi River.[55]

Already in October of that year, efforts were made to assemble the Mdewakanton at Mendota for the purpose of acquiring their land, but this attempt failed because of disinterest on the part of the chiefs and principal warriors to cede at this time, a disinterest probably instigated by the traders among them, who, we are told, did not feel that they were being adequately repaid for the many goods they had advanced the Indians over the years.

Because of delays in Washington during the 1850 session of Congress, it was not until the spring of 1851 that President Fillmore appointed Governor Ramsey and the Honorable Luke Lea of Mississippi, commissioner of Indian affairs of this area, to serve as treaty makers with the Dakota. It was decided that it would be advantageous to treat first with the bands of Dakota located on the upper Minnesota, because they were not so opposed to giving up their lands as were the lower bands. After these upper bands had sold their land, it was reasoned, it would be easier to convince the others to follow suit.

Accordingly, in July of 1851 the Upper Bands, the Sisseton and Wapeton, were assembled at Traverse des Sioux. Many of the Mdewakanton were present at these negotiations and became thoroughly acquainted with the objectives of the treaty and the cessions made therein by the Upper Bands. This treaty was signed July 22, 1851, and provided that the Sisseton and Wapeton should cede to the United States government "all their land in Iowa, as well as their lands east of the line from the Red River to Lake Traverse and thence to the northwestern corner of Iowa," reserving for their use and occupation a tract stretching from Lake Traverse down the Minnesota to the Yellow Medicine River and extending ten miles on each side of the former stream.

From July 29 to August 5, 1851, Mendota was the scene of the conference which opened the land west of the Mississippi including the entire greater Twin Cities area, to white settlement, excluding of course the fort reservation. Within the few years following the Treaty of Mendota, Little Crow V of Kaposia, Grey Iron of Black Dog's village, Good Road of Penasha's village, Cloudman, of Oak Grove (Bloomington), and their bands left forever their beloved village sites and took up a ten year residence on the reservation established for them on the Minnesota River just south of the Upper Band's reserve delineated in the preceding paragraph.

As stated earlier, the chiefs and head men of the lower bands, the Mdewakanton and the Wapekute, were thoroughly familiar with the proceedings at Traverse des Sioux the weeks before.

The first session of the Mendota negotiations was held in the warehouse of the American Fur Company, but the Indians "found the atmosphere stifling, and not in accord with their usual method of outdoor councils, so the consideration of the treaty was taken up under a large brush arbor erected on an elevated plain near the high prominence known as Pilot Knob."[56] Holcombe[57] very fully reported the Treaty at Mendota and from this report the following condensation has been made, limiting the discussion as much as possible to speeches and action of the chiefs and principal warriors of the local bands present.

Before the Mdewakanton were willing even to talk about a new treaty, they felt that they should be heard concerning certain grievances they held with regard to the Treaty of 1837. Wabasha, the appointed speaker for the lower bands, said on the first day of the conference: "I have but one thing to say to you, fathers, and then we will separate for the day. I was among those who went to Washington and brought home the words of our Great Father. According to what he then said we have some funds lying back in his hands. We spoke of these funds to the commissioners who were here fall before last. These men you see around you are anxious to get that which is due them before they can do anything."

These funds which Wabasha had reference to and which were causing discontent were the education funds that had been set up by the Treaty of 1837. Most of this money had not been used for the red man's good as had been intended, but lay idle in the treasury, probably because no practical method could be determined for dividing the fund among the various missionary societies working in the region during this period.

The second day the Indians requested more time to discuss the draft of the treaty which they had received, but on the third day of negotiations, July 31, Wabasha told the commissioners that "these other chiefs around me may have something to say, too. I will sit and listen to what is said."

"Then ensued another long, constrained and uncomfortable silence which was finally broken by the deliberate and graceful rising of Little Crow, chief of the Kaposia band, the brainiest, shrewdest, and most influential Indian then west of the Mississippi," who next addressed the council. Little Crow V, His Red Nation, had not been the chief of the Kaposia band at the time of the signing of the Treaty of 1837, but had become chief upon the death of his father Big Thunder in the middle forties. In 1851 he was comparatively young, thirty years of age or thereabouts. He alludes to this fact in the opening words of his speech on this occasion: "There are chiefs here who are older than myself, and I would rather they had spoken, but they have put it upon me to speak, although I feel as if my mouth was tied."

Little Crow was dressed elaborately for the occasion and "was indeed, a striking and attractive figure." Attired in "a white shirt and collar, a gaudy neckerchief, his tastefully embroidered medicine bag suspended from his neck, a red belt with a silver buckle about his waist and wearing a pair of elaborately beaded trousers and moccasins, his long black, curling hair, soft and almost as silken as a white woman's flowing over his shoulders and with his keen black eyes alight," one can picture him in his mind's eye, elaborating on the grievances which the other chiefs and head men had appointed him to make known.

"These chiefs went to Washington long ago and brought back a good report concerning the settlement of our affairs in the treaty made there and they and we were glad. But things that were promised in that treaty have not taken place. This is why these men sit still and say nothing. You perhaps are ashamed (or disgraced, ishtenya in Sioux) of us; but you, fathers, are the cause of its being so. They speak of some money that is due them, it was mentioned the other day to Governor Ramsey and we spoke about it last fall, but we have not yet seen the money. We deserve to have it laid down to us. It is money due on the old treaty, and I think it should be paid, we do not want to talk about a new treaty until it is all paid."

For the next five days, formal negotiations were at a seeming stand-still, but much bickering was carried on informally, the time being "spent by the whites in privately preparing a treaty which would be acceptable to the Indians."

In the end, most of the chiefs were placated. The head speaker of the Mdewakanton, Wabasha, was still opposed to any treaty, and he expressed his feeling when formal negotiations were reopened on Monday, August the fifth: "When I went to Washington to see our Great Father, he asked us for our land and we gave it to him, and he agreed to furnish us with goods and provisions for twenty years. I wish to remain in this country until that time expires."

But Little Crow and other sub-chiefs were in favor of a treaty if the terms were fairly liberal and the assent of their bands could be obtained. Little Crow especially, realizing that his band would eventually be compelled to leave the area anyway, felt it would be most sensible to get as good a deal as possible in the process and move westward as the whites wished.

Of course he disliked the thought of abandoning his old Kaposia home.

"Here were the graves of his father and mother and other kinspeople, here was the site of his birthplace and his boyhood, and here he had been chief of the old and noted band of his ancestors."

He, with the others, repeatedly requested in the Monday

session of the proceedings that the new reservation be extended so as to include more woodland. He said he had been raised in country where there were extensive woods in which wild game could readily be found. The land provided by the treaty as their new reserve, was "too much prairie."

Realizing that the chiefs were divided and uncertain regarding the region considered best by them for a reservation, the commissioners adroitly turned attention upon the younger braves, the greater number of whom were in favor of selling the land, though some had expressed the determination to shoot the first man of their tribe "who put his hand to the goose quill preparatory to subscribing to the hated contract." The younger warriors felt, as one of them stated, that the land west of the Mississippi belonged "to the people who did not go to Washington and make the first treaty." Ramsey knew this and therefore placed it before the assembly that the soldiers "tell us what chief shall sign first."

In due fairness to the commissioners, Lea and Ramsey, it must be stated that they considered the reservation proposed by the treaty—that is, the ten mile strip on each side of the Minnesota extending from the mouth of the Yellow Medicine River southeastward to the mouth of Rock Creek encompassing about forty-five miles of river land bordered by timber—to be a good place for the Dakota to set up their permanent villages. There would be plenty of wood and water and it was understood that the Indians could continue to hunt in the Big Woods and other parts of their former possessions until the whites should come in and settle upon the land. Few realized that this would occur as quickly as it did.

To turn the principal warriors against the chiefs in

open council was perhaps not a very ethical procedure, but the commissioners doubtless did it in good faith, and it did accomplish the purpose which they were after—the signing of the treaty. When asked by Ramsey which chief should sign first, Medicine Bottle the head soldier of Little Crow's band replied: "There is one chief among us who did not go to Washington at that time (1837), and the soldiers want him to sign first. He has been a great war chief and has been our leader against the Chippewas. We want him to sign first."

Holcombe describes the memorable scene:

> Little Crow rose promptly. Without a tremor he faced the scowling warriors who were opposing the treaty, and in his well known clarion voice keyed to a high pitch thus addressed them:
>
> "Soldiers, it has been said by some of you that the first that signs this treaty you will kill. Now, I am willing to be the first but I am not afraid that you will kill me. If you do, it will be all right. A man has to die sometime and he can die but once. It matters little to me when my time comes, nor do I care much how it comes, although I would rather die fighting our enemies. I believe this treaty will be best for the Dakotas, and I will sign it, even if a dog kills me before I lay down the goose quill."
>
> Then, turning to the commissioners, he said, "Fathers, I hope you will be willing to let our new reservation come down to Traverse des Sioux, so that our people can be comfortable and not crowded, and have plenty of good hunting and fishing grounds. The Swan Lake and other lakes have plenty of fish and wild rice and there is plenty of wood. Rock Creek is not down far enough for us. I am glad we can hunt in the Big Woods as heretofore, but I hope you will bring our new home down to Traverse des Sioux."

If Little Crow's request had been granted, the eastern boundary of the new reservation would have extended about forty miles below Rock Creek, or two miles east of St. Peter and would have included the present sites of that city and New Ulm and Mankato.

The commissioners declined the request. Colonel Lea said, "The reservation is all right as it is." Governor Ramsey said, "We have marked out a large piece of land for your home, the soldiers asked us for more and we gave it. It is all that we can do." Colonel Lea added: "No man puts any food in his mouth by much talk, but often gets hungry if he talks too long. Let the Little Crow and other chiefs step forward and sign."

Finding that the commissioners were firm, Little Crow now stepped to the table and being handed a chair, sat down and "wrote his own name" to each of the duplicate copies. This is the account given by Le Duc, in his "yearbook" for 1852. Another account says that Little Crow had been taught to write, in Sioux of course, by Reverend Riggs, at Lac qui Parle. It is probable, however, that he was taught by Reverend Doctor Williamson at Kaposia. To the treaty he signed his original name, Tah-o-ya-te Duta, meaning His Red Nation.

It may be possible too that Little Crow V was taught to write his name by Rev. Gideon Pond at Lac qui Parle, for we read in his diary under date of August 2, 1837, "Taoyateduta (Little Crow) came here this afternoon to read. I have some hope that he will apply himself; if so, I shall endeavor to assist him while he stays."

Wabasha then made his mark, and the other chiefs and principal warriors followed suit. In all there were sixty-five Indian marks or signatures. Eleven head men signed with Little Crow V of Kaposia, one of whom was Medicine Bottle who had previously separated from Kaposia and moved his village to the west bank of the Mississippi about nine miles below Kaposia. Another of Little Crow's soldiers who signed this treaty with him and who established a separate village later on the reservation was Rattling Runner, or Rattling Moccasin. Three soldiers signed with Good Road whose band had become very small, and five with Grey Iron, one of whom was Bad Hail or Traveling Hail, whose father or possibly grandfather signed the treaty of peace and friendship made in 1816 following the War of 1812. The Traveling Hail of 1851 came into prominence later when he was elected head speaker of the Lower Bands after Little Crow V came into disrepute among the majority of the Mdewakanton bands for selling the eastern half of the reservation to the whites in 1858. When the members of Cloudman's band moved to the reservation, Traveling Hail was their chief as Cloudman had turned the chieftainship of most of the band over to him.[58]

In the final session of the treaty negotiations no mention was made of the monies yet due the Indians under the Treaty of 1837 which had not run out yet, nor of the "education fund," as it was called. This omission was taken care of, however, by inserting an article in the Treaty of 1851 providing that the whole annuity guaranteed by the Treaty of 1837 should be continued and the education fund be paid in cash directly to the Indians. Thirty thousand dollars was due immediately, and "it was probably no accident that the American Fur Company had that amount of specie on hand and at once advanced it to the Indian agent, who paid it out the next day."[59]

Generally speaking, the Indians wasted this money on whiskey and horses and had little to show for it when the horses died, as most of them did, before the winter was over. "Although greatly in need of provisions, the Indians would not buy any considerable quantities and in three weeks they were begging for food."[60]

In time, most of the provisions of the Treaties of 1851 were ratified by the Senate, but only after long delay and much political maneuvering which need not be gone into here. Finally, in the fall of 1852, on September 4, the chiefs of the lower bands assembled at Governor Ramsey's residence in St. Paul and signed the amended treaty.

The Indians were allowed to remain in their old villages or, if they preferred, to occupy their reservations as originally designated in the Treaty of 1851. However, one of the amendments provided that this land was to be bought by the government at the rate of ten cents an acre and the Indians were to be permanently established in an area to be chosen by the President, presumably farther west. The selection of this new reservation was never made, and in 1853 Governor Willis A. Gorman, who had succeeded Ramsey on May 15th of that year as governor of Minnesota Territory, was ordered by the government to remove the local Indian bands, or such as had not already left, to the tract of land provided by the Treaty of Mendota. Even at this time, we learn not all the Indians went up, for we find Little Crow taking up his "last division" in June of 1854. This division, we are told by Dr. Daniels "consisted of the old men, women, and children of the band."[61]

The great migration, which included not only the bands of the lower Minnesota and Kaposia, but other Dakota bands as well, was a major undertaking and, according to the report of one of the white participants, met with little enthusiasm on the part of the Indians.

As there were upwards of six thousand Indians upon

the Mississippi and the Minnesota rivers, and among them the celebrated chiefs, Little Crow and Wabasha, this undertaking was considered a difficult and extremely delicate task. The governor, however, after taking counsel with such men as Gov. Sibley, Philander Prescott, Franklin Steele, H. M. Rice, George Culver, John Farrington, N. Myrick, Alexis Bailly, Alex. Faribault, and W. H. Forbes to all and to each of whom he ever expressed the greatest obligations, commenced the removal of the Indians, only aided by two or three interpreters and Joseph R. Brown, and a few other old traders. He accompanied the Indians on their long and tedious march and although he had with him $250,000 in gold for the tribes, he took no force or guard but permitted the Indians to guard the money themselves.

The journey was accomplished in safety with but one slight incident. When the Indians arrived at the "Big Woods" at a point near where Belle Plaine is at present, they demanded a "big talk" or council, with "the man with the eagle's eye," as they styled the governor. Their request was granted. The council ring was formed and the chiefs centered about the governor.

The chief Wabasha first addressed the governor, speaking about as follows: "You have given us plenty of flour and plenty of beef and white man's meat. But Indians love venison. Our young men want to hunt. The fall hunt is now approaching. When you leave us, your beef will soon be gone. We will have no fresh meat or dried beef for winter. When we reach our new home, the buffalo will run away. Unless our great father permits us to kill game in the Big Woods our squaws and our papooses will starve next winter."

When this speech was finished, Eagle (Big Eagle?) and Red Iron followed, insisting that they be permitted to make their fall hunt in the Big Woods. The governor appreciated the situation, but was determined not to yield

Big Eagle II, son of Grey Iron, photograph by Simons and Shepherd.

Minnesota Historical Society.

to a demand inconvenient to all concerned. He replied that he would like to please them, but they had made a treaty; had sold their lands and were to be paid in regular yearly installments within twenty years. The government would not see them starve, but would help them adopt some part of the white man's habits, and for this purpose would give them implements and furnish farmers to instruct them. They could not remain there longer than three days.

As he finished, one of the warriors of the Lake Calhoun band arose and said that the traders would get all their money, and they must stay there till the "next moon," anyway.

Little Crow in the meantime had been silent but he now arose, and in a loud voice said: "If we stay down here and get our money the traders will be sure to get it, and all our blankets. We have agreed to go, and we must do as our great father asks us. But we would like some better cattle than you have along."

He sat down and the young Calhoun Lake warrior again arose, and said determinedly that the chiefs and women might go on but the young men would stay, they wouldn't go. At this, the governor, in wrath, told the interpreter to tell that young man he should go to Redwood if he had to send to Fort Snelling for troops.

The council then broke up and the Indians retired to a private consultation. That night the governor secretly sent a messenger to the fort, asking for a force, and by nine o'clock the next day, one hundred dragoons, under Captain McGruder, with a battery of artillery, drew up before the astonished Indians.

After a while, Little Crow made the soldiers a speech advising them to go on, and the Indians all gathered about the governor to shake hands with him, assuring him of their willingness to start. No further trouble was experienced.[62]

Neither Gideon or Samuel Pond elected to follow the Indians to the reserve; rather the brothers stayed to minister to the whites who were settling their areas. "After the Treaty of 1851 was made," Samuel reports, "we were not long in deciding what to do. We had witnessed the effects of the Treaty of 1837, and believed that the results of the (new) treaty would be evil, and only evil."

However, Dr. Williamson, who operated the mission at Kaposia, did join his villagers in their move to the reservation, reestablishing his mission at Yellow Medicine.

Holcombe recorded in detail the areas of settlement of the various bands after their arrival at the new reservation.

> Of the Mdewakanton, the sub-band farthest to the westward was that whose leader was the Jug or Medicine Bottle. It was a very small band whose tepees were a few miles below the Yellow Medicine.
>
> (The sub-band of Shakopee was a mile or more west of the mouth of the Redwood River.)
>
> All about the Lower or Redwood Agency were the other Mdewakanton sub-bands. The old Kaposia village of Little Crow was on the south side of the Minnesota, a little west of the small stream called Crow's Creek. Near Little Crow's village was the band of the Great War Eagle, commonly called Big Eagle, and this had been the band of Grey Iron, of Fort Snelling.
>
> (Below the Agency was the sub-band of Wabasha. Near him was the village of Wacouta, chief of the old Red Wing Band.)
>
> In the vicinity was the band of Traveling Hail, sometimes called Passing Hail. Old Cloudman was alive, but was old and feeble, and had turned over the chieftainship to Traveling Hail, formerly of Cloudman's band of Lake Calhoun; and farther down the Minnesota, but along the crest of the high bluff was the band of Mankato, who

had succeeded his father, the historic old Good Road, in chieftainship of one of the old Fort Snelling bands.[63]

John H. Stevens in his reminiscences states: "The close of the year 1851 in a measure ended the protracted visits of the Dakotas to the Falls of St. Anthony. It is true they would occasionally swarm down on us by the hundreds, but in after years their sojourn was of short duration." In another place, he tells us: "It is well known that after their removal to the new reservations they would on any occasion possible, visit their old haunts." Mrs. Heman (Jane DeBow) Gibbs told of visits made by the Indians of the old Lake Calhoun band to her farm home in Rose Township as late as the year of the Great Outbreak.

However, eventually "by the offer of cabins to live in, or other substantial inducements, nearly all of them were induced to settle on the Redwood Reserve, so that in 1862, at the time of the outbreak, less than twenty families of the Mdewakantons and Wapekutes were living off their reservation."[64]

New Cities and New Settlers
1852 On

FOLLOWING THE RATIFICATION of the Treaty of 1851, white settlers poured into the village of St. Anthony and the new town of Minneapolis in ever greater numbers. Though most of the red men left, nevertheless there continued to be contact between whites and Indians in the infant cities. *Old Rail Fence Corners* contains some interesting reminiscences concerning Indian activity here in the first half of the fifties:

> Mr. D. E. Dow (Hopkins): I was supposed to live alone in my cabin but hardly ever spent a night without the companionship of some of the Sioux Indians who were hunting around here. I gladly received them, as they were friendly, and their company was much better than none.
>
> One winter they came in such numbers that at night the floor was entirely covered by their sleeping forms. Early in the morning they would go out, and all day hunt the deer, with which the woods abounded. It was very cold and the slain deer froze immediately. They stacked them up, making a huge pile. Suddenly, all the Indians left.
>
> One morning shortly after, I was working in the clear-

ing around my cabin, when I saw a line of squaws which I think was a block long, coming over the trail which led from Shakopee to Hopkins. The squaws went to the pile of deer. Each took one on her back and silently trudged away over the trail toward Shakopee. Some of the squaws were so small that the frozen carcass had to be adjusted by another squaw, or it would drag on the ground. They were two weeks removing the pile of deer and had to walk twenty-eight miles with each one before they got home with it.

Mr. Irving A. Dunsmoor (Richfield): During our first winter, a party of about fifty Sioux Indians came and camped in our woods just west of where the Washburn Park water tower now stands. They put up about twenty tepees made partly of skins and partly of canvas. We boys would often go in the evenings to visit them and watch them making moccasins.

They would often come to our house to beg for food, but in all the time they remained there, nearly the whole winter, they committed no depradations, except that they cut down a great deal of our fine timber, and killed a great quantity of game, so that when they wanted to come back the next winter, father would not allow it.

Once after they had gone away, they came back through the farm and went off somewhere north of us where they had a battle with the Chippewas. When they returned, they brought two scalps and held a "pow-wow" on the side of our hill.

Colonel Levi Longfellow (Brooklyn Center): In the spring of 1853, our family moved from St. Anthony to a farm in Brooklyn Center, about nine miles out of town. Roving bands of Indians often used to camp near our home. We never enjoyed these visits, but neither did we wish them to think we were afraid, so we never locked our doors or refused them anything they demanded in the way of food.

Teepees at Bridge Square in Minneapolis, 1855. Note John H. Stevens' house in background.

Minneapolis Public Library Bromley Collection.

Mr. Chester L. Hopkins (Hopkins): When I was a little boy we had a grindstone in our yard which was used by us and our few scattered neighbors. One night we were awakened by hearing the grindstone going, and father went to the door to see who was using it. A party of forty Sioux braves on their ponies were standing around while some of the braves ground their knives which each in his turn put in his belt. It was a bright moonlight night and we could see them as plainly as if it was day.

The Indians were in full war paint and feathers and after their task was accomplished, rode one after the other over the hill where they stood out like black silhouettes, and finally disappeared.

Mr. Charles Bohanon (Minneapolis): While my father was in the woods, the Indians used to come and sleep in the dooryard. Sometimes it would be full of painted Sioux. They never stole anything or begged, but would gratefully accept anything offered them. They were very friendly and kind and full of curiosity, as their looking in the windows at all times showed.

Mrs. Carrie Stratton (Minneapolis): We children were very much entertained by the novel sight of the Indians in their gay blankets and feathered head-dress. They were frequent visitors, but always peaceable ones, never committing any misdemeanor.

Mrs. C. H. Pettit (Minneapolis): I had never seen Indians as we had just moved to town. I was walking along through the woods on what is now Fourth Street when I was surrounded by yelling, painted Indians on ponies. Seeing that I was frightened nearly to death they continued these antics, circling round and round me, whooping and yelling, until I reached my home. Then they rode rapidly away, undoubtedly taking great pleasure in the fright they had given the Paleface.

Miss Florinda Hopkins (Hopkins): When I was a little girl, a number of Indians came in on a rainy day and tired

St. Anthony and Minneapolis in 1857.
Minneapolis Public Library Bromley Collection.

from a long tramp, lay asleep on the floor of the kitchen. The party consisted of a chief and seven braves. My mother was making dried apple pies.

When she finished, she cut two of them into six pieces each, and gave each Indian a piece, which he ate with the greatest relish. All of them kept a watchful eye on the remaining pieces which they regarded wistfully.

The chief with a noble gesture, motioned them all to leave the house and remained himself. As soon as they were outside he motioned for the rest of the pie and ate it all with the greatest relish while the rest of the band looked enviously through the window.

Were these not, indeed, children?

I remember a Sioux war party of ten or more going by our house. They were doing their war song business as they trotted along and swinging one pitiful scalp on a pole. Their battles were generally like this. Ten was a small number to kill one Chippewa. When the Chippewa retaliated, they would go in the same proportion.

One morning a party stopped here. They were very tired. They had probably trotted a long, long way for their endurance was wonderful. They just said: "Chippewa?" and as soon as they knew we had seen none, were flying on again.

We often traded food with the Indians, as well as giving it to them, allowing them to make their own terms. They would bring a pair of fancy beaded moccasins and trade them for six doughnuts.

As late as 1856, Chippewa war parties were seen in present Minneapolis,

On the twelfth of June, several Ojibways entered the farm house of Mr. Whallon, who resided in Hennepin county on the banks of the Minnesota a mile below the Bloomington ferry. The wife of a farmer, a friend, and three children besides a little Dakota girl who had been brought up in the mission-house at Kaposia, and was so changed in manners that her origin was scarcely perceptible, were sitting in the room when the Indians came in. Instantly seizing the little Indian maiden, they threw her out of the door, killed and scalped her and fled before the men who were nearby in the field could reach the house.[65]

Mrs. John Brown, of Bloomington, remembered this incident and included it in her reminiscences, pages 260 and 261 of *Old Rail Fence Corners*:

> The Sioux Indians did not often give a child to be brought up by white people, but Jane Williamson, "Aunt Jane" took little Susan and David, two very young Dakota children, to see what environment would do for the Indian. Later they were placed in other families.
>
> Little Susan, though a Sioux Indian, was dreadfully afraid of Indians, having always lived with the white people. One day, when all the men about the two places were busy plowing the field back of our house, Mrs. Whallon with whom Susan lived, felt nervous as a number of Indians had been seen about, so she took little Susan and came to spend the day with me, her nearest neighbor. The house was just a small temporary board one.
>
> Little Susan asked for a piece of bread and butter and went out and sat on the Indian mound by the house to eat it. Here the Indians must have seen her, for soon after she went back into the house, twenty Indians came into the yard, and up to the open doorway, the door not yet being hung. Twelve Indians filed in and filled the room.
>
> My baby was in the cradle by the door. Little Susan, Mrs. Whallon and I were also in the room. The braves began to ask questions about little Susan:
>
> "Is she good squaw? We are Sioux and love little Sioux girl. We want to shake hands with her."

They passed her along, one handing her hand to another, till the one nearest the door pushed her out. The Indians out doors shot her through the arm and breast and she fell forward. I seized my baby from the cradle and, looking out the door saw that five or six of the Indians had their feet on little Susan's breast, scalping her.

I screamed for the men, who were hidden from view by the trees between the house and clearing. When they reached the house, the Indians, Chippewas, were gone. For months afterwards, arrow-heads and other things which they had dropped in their flight were found about the place. One large bundle was found in the yard. There is a stone in memory of little Susan in the Bloomington Cemetery.

Downstream on the Mississippi, St. Paul continued to grow and prosper. Though Little Crow V had left Kaposia with most of his band, a few continued to reside where South St. Paul now is for a number of years.

In April, 1853, the people of St. Paul saw a bit of Indian warfare at very close range. The trouble originated in the killing of a Chippewa in the neighborhood of Shakopee. In revenge for this murder, the Dakota bands sent out war parties in their usual fashion.

Warriors from the Kaposia band made an expedition up the St. Croix River valley, and near the Falls, met some Chippewa. In the ensuing battle the Dakota killed an Ojibway but lost two sons of their chief. This of course called for counter-action on the part of the Chippewa. Williams probably gives us the best description of this phase of the battle.

A party of some eighteen Ojibways started for St. Paul determined to assassinate any unlucky Sioux found hanging around the town, as plenty always were. They stealthily entered town on the night of April 26, and concealed themselves until day-break, in an unfinished building in lower town.

At daylight, they carefully scouted along the river bank to watch for Sioux coming up from Kaposia in their canoes. Ere long, one came in sight, making for the landing. It contained Old Bets, her brother Woodenlegged Jim, and her sister.

Soon as the Chippewa noted this they sprang down the bank and made tracks for the landing, designing to ambush the Sioux at that spot. (Passing around a marsh and over a small hill) at a rapid dog trot, they found to their great disappointment, as they arrived near the Merchants Hotel, that owing to the delay, the Sioux had (already) landed and were coming up Jackson Street. This street had been cut through the bluff, leaving a high bank of dirt on each side.

The Sioux advanced carelessly up the hill, fearing no danger, and turned up the steps of the "Minnesota Outfit" a large frame trading house of the American Fur Company in charge of Wm. H. Forbes. The Chippewas, fearing of losing their prey, rushed forward and stood on the road bank opposite the store, and on a level with it.

The Sioux had just entered the store, when they drew up their guns and fired a volley at them. The sister of Old Bets fell mortally wounded. There were several persons in the store at the time and it is miraculous that they were not killed. The Chippewas jumped down the bank and rushed towards the store determined to finish their work. They were met at the door by two white men who happened to be present, and who peremptorily commanded them to clear out—or they would get into trouble. This brought them to a sense of their rashness, and they at once retired by the route they came.

The wounded woman proved to be dying and at her

request was put in the canoe and taken to Kaposia where she died the same morning.

Meantime, the firing and excitement attracted a number of citizens who, as soon as they learned what had taken place, pursued the retreating Chippewas, whether to arrest them, or for what purpose, no one hardly knew. They soon overtook the pagans, who turning calmly around and confronting them said:

"White man, why do you pursue us? This is none of your affair! Do you mean to interfere in our fights?"

No one knew what reply to make and as they were unarmed, allowed the Chippewas to pass unmolested.

But we almost overlooked Wooden-legged Jim, who in his day had been quite a famous fighter. As soon as the Chippewa's volley had been fired, he drew out an old pepper-box revolver he carried and rushing to the door tried to fire at them but not a barrel would go off. Throwing it down, he picked up a loaded gun standing in the store and pursued them a short distance, getting a shot at them and, it is said, wounding their chief. The latter returned the salute, knocking a splinter out of Jim's wooden leg, after which the latter stumped back, defiantly yelling the war whoop.

Governor Ramsey at once dispatched a courier to Fort Snelling for troops to pursue and punish the Chippewas. A Sioux guide was procured and off they went on a gallop. The guide tracked the Chippewas to Saint Croix Falls where they were overtaken at noon next day. Seeing they were pursued, the Chippewas retreated to the bush where they fired on the dragoons. The latter charged them and the lieutenant in command of the dragoons shot one with his revolver. His scalp was brought back as a trophy, and thus ended this singular chapter of early scenes in St. Paul.[66]

Among those who could not be induced to accompany

Sioux on Marshall Avenue in St. Paul.
Minneapolis Public Library Bromley Collection.

their relatives to Redwood was Old Bets, the Kaposia woman who was one of the principals in the "battle" of 1853 in St. Paul. Her name was Azayamankawan, Berry Picker, but she was called Old Bets by the settlers, and her dependence upon the sociability and, of course, the hand-outs she received here, was cut off only by her death which occurred in early May of 1873.

She was born near Mendota in 1788, married "Iron Sword," had several children, among them Taopi, a convert to Christianity who was the government farmer on the Reservation at the time of the Outbreak, and had at least two brothers—Heindakoo, a famous warrior and medicine man, and Peg-leg Jim.

Old Bets was such an institution in early St. Paul that it seems quite appropriate to include this rather lengthy recollection of her:

> The familiar face of Old Bets, an Indian squaw, peered in upon my vision for about twenty years, when all of a sudden, it disappeared, and the news came that she was dead! Very few who met her wrinkled face, her laughing eyes, her grotesque figure, or heard her whining voice asking for "kosh-poppy," or money, knew of the romantic history attached to that old squaw, as she almost daily paraded the streets of our frontier city and sold her moccasins or begged for aid.
>
> Old Bets was once young and handsome. Young Bets was greatly loved, not only for her beauty, but for her kind disposition as well as for her bravery; so it came to pass that a young man who had won great renown in the tribe sought the hand of the young girl in marriage, and in turn she looked upon his attention with favor. Her brother however, being himself a warrior and a medicine man, objected to the match.
>
> The merry laugh of the maiden gradually died away.

Her joyous nature turned to soberness, as she thought of the young heart which beat only for her. She besought her brother to consent, but the stoical face and hardened heart would not relax.

Turning away in great sorrow she entered the forest nearby; and unexpectedly she met her suitor. The interview terminated with a solemn resolve that on the morrow they were to bid goodbye to old associations and mounted on ponies flee the village as man and wife.

With the rising of the sun, the young and lovely Berry Picker had fled, accompanied by her beloved. Her brother, mounted on one of his fleetest ponies, and well armed, started in pursuit as soon as he was aware of what had occurred.

At noon he overtook the flying couple, who conscious of his desperate hatred, redoubled their speed. Soon the horses were neck and neck, speeding rapidly over the plain together. Young Bets' brother then rode in front, and drawing his horse's head across the path of the lover, sought to cut him down with his tomahawk.

His sister pleaded for his life, but seeing that her pleadings were all in vain, she reigned in her pony, brought him close to the side of her lover and with one spring from her animal landed in his lap. With one arm about the waist of his love, the young man fought bravely for his life but encumbered with the maiden, he fought to great disadvantage; when all of a sudden, his antagonist struck him with his tomahawk on the head from behind and the young man sank to the earth, and in the arms of his sweetheart breathed out his last farewell.

The maiden was carried back into camp, and though she subsequently married a man of note in her tribe, yet the great sorrow of her early love never left her, and traces of that sorrow could be seen upon her face, even in her old age.

For many years this inoffensive old woman traveled the

streets of the white man's city and, became a marked character both to the citizens and to strangers. I remember her as the possessor of a wrinkled face, peculiar eyes, disheveled hair, large mouth, uncovered neck, uncouth form, but always with her cheerful "ho-ho's" as she plodded along under the weight of years and her great unknown sorrow. She was a kind and devoted friend of the whites; was the means of saving several lives during the massacre in Minnesota and before her death became quite poor, but it is a credit to humanity to be able to state that she was aided by pecuniary help during her sickness and finally died in the Christian belief and was accorded a Christian burial. Good-bye, Old Bets.[67]

Writing in 1888, W. H. C. Folsom observed, "No history of the early days would be complete without mention of the celebrated and picturesquely homely squaw known as Old Bets and the tribe to which she belonged. The camp of the latter may still be seen at South St. Paul to the number of three or four tepees. The Indians are the descendants of the warriors of Little Crow. They live in canvas tepees of primitive style, but with the exception of moccasins and a few Indian trinkets have conformed somewhat to the costumes of the civilized people around them."[68]

"The Indians living in this vicinity," wrote A. L. Larpenteur later in the *Pioneer Press,* "represent a remnant of the Minnesota Sioux who were not taken to the reservation after the massacre. There may be nearly a score of families in all, including the inhabitants of the little Indian village at South St. Paul, the aboriginal residents at Mendota and some red men living near Newport. These are mostly descendants of the members of Little Crow's band. Three or four families have descended from the famous old squaw known as Old Bets."

For a marvelous account of the activities and lives of the Dakota who filtered back into the state after the Outbreak and of those who remained in Minnesota through these hectic years the reader may wish to refer to the *History of the Santee Sioux by* Roy W. Meyer.

Epilogue

IT IS NOT strange that so many of the Dakota spent little time on the Reservation established for them after the treaties of 1851. "No people are more attached to the land of their birth and to the graves of their kindred than are these Indians."[1]

In the early years of the decade between their removal from the Twin Cities area and 1862, the year of the Great Uprising, little was done to alleviate the hardships in the new environment. The Indians did not receive what had been promised them, or even that which they had enjoyed in their former location. The annuities which they received in 1853 and 1854 were paid so late and in such small amounts that starvation in the winter certainly faced them if they remained on the Reservation. Little plowing had been done for them in these years, and for lack of passable roads, transportation of supplies to them was practically impossible most of the time. "Even Agent Murphy himself did not see fit to reside at the agency, but bought a house at Shakopee."[2]

Most of the missionaries also did not see fit to accompany their charges to this inhospitable environment. Dr. Williamson, we have seen, elected to move out to the Reservation, but when he did, he established his new station a few miles above the mouth of the Yellow Medicine River and worked among the Upper Dakota. Many of the Christian Indians who had lived in the Twin Cities area then chose to live among the Upper bands.

Cloudman lived not far from Running Walker's Wapeton band. Since there were probably related members in the two bands, it was not unnatural that Cloudman and those who remained with him probably affiliated themselves with Running Walker. The majority of Cloudman's band followed Traveling Hail, a soldier from the old Black Dog band who had joined Cloudman's band and who, after Red Bird's death, seems to have become head soldier. However, it does appear that a few of Old Cloudman's friends and relatives remained with him. As late as 1868 Cloudman's band was still a separate entity and represented by his son.[3]

But the Pond brothers had decided to remain at their old grounds—Gideon in Bloomington and Samuel in Shakopee. Lest they be judged too harshly for this considered action, it is well to detail the results of their early years of missionary activity as prosecuted by them and the other devoted men and women who labored here.

To begin with, it must be borne in mind that, in the words of Dr. Riggs, "From the time that the chief men came to understand that the religion of Christ was an exclusive religion, that it would require the giving up of their ancestral faith, they set themselves in opposition to it." Thus the new religion required the complete rejection of the Indian's ancestral faith and way of life. This is well illustrated by a quotation from Cloudman's brother, Little

Paul Mazakootamane. He was converted to the Christian faith at Lac qui Parle and this quotation appears in an article he wrote in the Dakota language concerning the activities of the Christian members of his nation during the Great Uprising. It was translated by Dr. Riggs.

I was born an Indian, and consequently I did not know to distinguish between the good and the bad. I followed the Dakota customs alone—and this I did until I was twenty-nine years old. Then the American sacred men came among my people and commenced to teach them. But I did not understand, and I thought if I should give my attention to it for ten years, I should still not understand it.

But when I had learned to put two or three letters together, I began to comprehend the writing, from which I progressed until I was able to read a little. Then I began to read the sacred writing, but I did not still know that the great God would have mercy on me.

By and by I came to know this, and then the sacred writing showed me that for all my past evil deeds I must die. Afterwards came the conviction that I was even now dead, but the great God was merciful and had given His Son only Begotten to die for us; and He had died for sin, that through His death we might live. So the question came up, "What shall I do to be saved?" and morning and night I sought by prayer to know how I could be saved.

After a while, the great God my Father wrought in me great thanksgiving, and made me a member and an office bearer in His church. Thus the Good God brought to us wild men the way of life, and now the Gospel has taken root and will grow among the Indians. For this we give great thanks.

Then the sacred men who came to us counseled me and told me to put off my Dakota clothes and be like a white man, to cut off my hair and put on white man's clothes. This I thought was good advice and I acted in accordance therewith.[4]

Samuel Pond gives us an insight into the manner in which he and his brother endeavored to bring their religion to the Calhoun Dakota.

> When we first began to speak their language, we strove to make them understand that we came here to promote their religious interests, and though we were willing to aid them in things pertaining to this life, we considered things spiritual and eternal of paramount importance. But such language was new and strange to them and they were slow to understand how men could be activated by such motives.
>
> The Dakotas had a general belief in the immortality of the soul, and a vague apprehension that men would be punished in another world for crimes committed in this. They also held that theft, lying, adultery, murder, etc. were crimes that deserved punishment so they had little to say against the doctrine of future retribution, but when we made known to them the peculiar doctrines of Christianity, they maintained that though it was a good religion for us, it was not for them. They, however, were most of them very reserved in regard to their views of religious subjects, and when we set before them the claims of the Gospel, they either listened in silence, or simply remarked that it was all very good, so that it was difficult to ascertain whether they understood us, but in the summer of 1837, I entered a tent where there were some visitors from the upper country, and the man of the house who was a brother of the chief (Little Paul?), told them who I was and what I said to them about religion. I was surprised to learn that he had a clear understanding of the most important doctrines of Christianity and could state them in plainer language than I could have done at that time in Dakota.

We talked with the Dakotas, or rather talked to them on religious subjects in season and out of season, whether they would hear or whether they would forebear so that there were few within our reach who were not compelled to hear how much they needed salvation and what they must do to be saved. A few of them we believed were converted, but not many.[5]

A multitude of complex causes finally erupted in what has become known as the Outbreak or the Great Sioux Uprising of 1862. Recently much has been written concerning this catastrophe upon the occasion of its centenary anniversary. Robinson tells us that the situation on the Reservation "was tense . . . Only the lighting of the first spark was required to set off the conflagration."[6]

Big Eagle II who became chief of the old Black Dog band after Grey Iron's death in 1853, dictated in his reminiscences of the events of this era:

> The whites were always trying to make the Indians give up their life and live like white men—go to farming, work hard and do as they did—and the Indians did not know how to do that, and did not want to anyway. It seemed too sudden a change. If the Indians had tried to make the whites live like them, the whites would have resisted, and it was the same way with many Indians.[7]

Roy Meyer divides the military history of the Uprising "into two phases: a short period of about a week when the Indians were on the offensive, and a longer period when they were gradually driven back by growing military forces."[8]

Little Crow V, of course, has become the symbol of the "Bad Indian" who was responsible for the deaths of some five hundred settlers and whose final defeat required the

Camp of the Friendlies at Fort Snelling, 1862, photograph by B. R. Upton.

Minnesota Historical Society.

services of thousands of troops at the cost of hundreds of thousands of dollars.

The whole story of the Sioux Uprising is too long to tell here, but as it is well known, it resulted in the eventual expulsion of the majority of the Dakota from the borders of Minnesota. Nearly four hundred Sioux were tried for their crimes in the Uprising by a military commission set up by General Sibley. Three hundred and six were condemned to death, and finally on December 26, 1862, thirty eight were hanged in Mankato, the rest having been given reprieve by President Lincoln.

Nearly two thousand Dakota had surrendered to Sibley's forces, and most of these were moved down the Minnesota to Fort Snelling. They "spent a wretched winter in a stockaded camp on the flat ground below the bluffs."[9] Cloudman, among others died there toward the end of the winter of 1862-63.

"In May, 1863," those of the Dakota who had managed to survive the hard winter "were herded into river steamboats and transported to the Missouri River and far into Dakota Territory. The men who had been condemned, but not sentenced to hang, were taken from the prison in Mankato to a government prison in Davenport, Iowa. Later they were permitted to rejoin the other Sioux on the Western reservations."[10]

In the prison at Mankato a great religious revival took place. On February 3, 1863, 274 of the Sioux captives were baptized, and the total number of baptisms eventually exceeded three hundred. Gideon Pond writes of this memorable event.

> There are over three hundred Indians in prison, the most of whom are in chains. There is a degree of religious interest manifested by them which is incredible. They

huddle themselves together every morning and evening in the prison and read the Scriptures, sing hymns, confess one to another, exhort one another, and pray together. They say that their whole lives have been wicked—that they have adhered to the superstitions of their ancestors until they have reduced themselves to their present state of wretchedness and ruin.

They declare that they have left it all and will leave all forever, that they do and will embrace the religion of Jesus Christ, and adhere to it as long as they live; and that this is their only hope, both in this world and the next. They say that before they came to this state of mind—this determination—their hearts failed them with fear, but now they have much mental ease and comfort.

About fifty men of the Lake Calhoun band expressed a wish to be baptized by me, rather than by anyone else, on the ground that my brother and myself had been their first and chief instructors in religion. After consultation with Rev. Marcus Hicks of Mankato, Dr. Williamson and I decided to grant their request, and administer to them the Christian ordinance of baptism. We made the conditions as plain as we could, and we proclaimed there, in the prison, that we would baptize such as felt readily, heartily to comply with the conditions—commanding that none should come forward to receive the rite who did not do it heartily to the God of heaven, whose eye penetrated each of their hearts. All by a hearty—apparently hearty—response signified their desire to receive the rite on the conditions offered.

(As soon as preparations were completed,) they came forward one by one as their names were called, and were baptized into the name of the Father, the Son, and the Holy Ghost—three hundred in a day.[11]

Samuel, in his characteristic humility and conscientious manner, adds this summary to the missionaries' activities among the Dakota during the years preceding the Great Outbreak: "The sudden awakening of the men in prison at Mankato was not among an ignorant people who had never heard the Gospel, for it had been pressed upon their attention almost daily for a long series of years. So one soweth and another reapeth. But the labor of sowing was often painfully discouraging and seemed wasted. What troubled me most was the apprehension that the mission money that I was spending might be more profitably applied in some other field, and I endeavored to get along with as little of that money as possible."[12]

As we have seen in the case of Old Bets, some of the Dakota who had lived in the Twin Cities area never left, either to take up residence on the Reservation on the Minnesota in the fifties, or after the Sioux Uprising. In June, 1866, a census of these "Scattered Sioux" as they came to be called, was made. At that time there were 374 Dakota in Minnesota. In July of the next year, as many of these as wanted to go, were removed at government expense to the Santee Reservation in Dakota Territory. Some were allowed to remain behind. The removal was put in charge of Samuel D. Hinman.

> Hinman found seventy-five Sioux at Faribault, two at Mendota, four at Wabasha, and one lodge above Fort Snelling. All those at Faribault seemed willing to go except Taopi and his relatives and another man who had bought land in the vicinity. Those at Mendota and near Fort Snelling were cultivating large fields under the protection of their friends and relatives who were citizens, and they had no wish to leave.
>
> Two of the four at Wabasha seemed willing to leave but were deterred by the others, including one who lived across the river in Wisconsin. Hinman also learned that

John Bluestone had bought a farm near Shakopee and was doing well at farming. All of these people he left behind. Those he took with him to Santee numbered five lodges, or thirty-nine individuals.[13]

The fifty or so remaining in the the state when Hinman removed the rest were joined in later years by a good many who preferred the risks of independence in their old homeland to the security of reservation life.

The 1870 census showed 175 Indians, nearly all of whom were presumably Sioux, scattered through the southern counties. Aside from 34 in Chippewa County, the largest concentrations were at Faribault and Traverse des Sioux, with smaller groups at Bloomington (the residence of Gideon Pond), in the Shakopee-Prior Lake area, and on Grey Cloud Island in Washington County. The number continued to increase in subsequent years, until in 1883 a special census revealed 237 Sioux in Minnesota.

None of the fourteen localities in which they had settled accounted for many families. The largest, Shakopee, had eleven families, or forty-seven individuals; the second largest, near Wabasha, had nine families, or forty individuals. Thirty-three were camped on Grey Cloud Island, twenty-four at Mendota, and twenty at Bloomington. The other groups were even smaller: six families at Faribault, three at Hastings and Redwood, two at Red Wing, one each at Prior Lake, Kapozha, West St. Paul, and St. Peter, and four families at Maiden Rock, Wisconsin.

Most of them lived in tepees, set up on the lands of white men who did not object to the Indian's presence.[14]

Through the latter quarter of the nineteenth century land purchases were made and houses were built for the Sioux of Minnesota at Birch Coulee, Shakopee and Prairie Island, but much local opposition accompanied the establishment of these Sioux communities. By 1900 the settlements near the Twin Cities—Mendota, Grey Cloud Island and Bloomington—had dwindled to the point of virtual abandonment.

Major Chiefs of the Area

	Chieftainship
Kaposia (Light-foot)	
Little Crow I	? - ?
Little Crow II	? - c.1795
Little Crow III, Chetanwakamani (Walks Pursuing A Hawk)	c.1795 - 1833
Little Crow IV, Wakinyantanka (Big Thunder)	1833 - 1845
Little Crow V, Taoyateduta (His Red Nation)	1845 - 1863
Oanoska (Long Avenue) later: **Hayzatoton** (Bad People)	
Penasha I (Penneshaw, the French trader)	
Penasha II, Whygenage (Sees Standing Up)	c.1780 - 1815
Penasha III, Takopepeshene (Fears Nothing)	1815 - 1833
Tucanwashtay (Good Road)	1833 - 1854
Mahkato (Blue Earth)	1854 - 1862
Tetankatane (Old Village) later: **Magayutashnee** (Eat Not Geese)	
Black Dog, Wamditanka (Big Eagle I)	c.1800 - 1838
Mazarota (Grey Iron) or Pamayza (My Head Aches)	1838 - 1853
Wamditanka (Big Eagle II) (died in 1906)	1853 - 1863
Reyataotonwe (Inland Village)	
Mapiyawichasta (Cloudman)	c.1829 - 1854
Wasuwichastani (Bad Hail)	1854 - 1863

Chronology

1642 - First notice of the Dakota — "Nadoussis."
1660 - Groseilliers and Radisson visit Dakota of Mille Lacs.
1670 - Founding of Hudson's Bay Company.
1679 - Du Luth visits Dakota of Mille Lacs.
1680 - Hennepin passes through Twin Cities area on way to Mille Lacs in Spring; returns in the Fall and names Falls of St. Anthony.
1686 - Perrot builds temporary post on Lake Pepin.
1689 - Perrot takes formal possession of this area for France.

1692 - Large numbers of Chippewa concentrate around La Pointe (Wisconsin).
1695 - Le Sueur builds temporary post on Prairie Island. Takes Tioscaté, Mantanton Dakota Chief to Montreal.
1698 - Battle of Point Prescott (approximate).
1700 - Le Sueur builds Ft. L'Huillier on the Blue Earth River; Mantanton Dakota under Chief Wakentape, visit him there.
1702 - Fort L'Huillier abandoned.
1720 - Birth of Wabasha I (approximate).
1723 - Charlevoix recommends establishment of permanent French post near this area.
1727 - Fort Beauharnois established on Lake Pepin.
1730 - Birth of Little Crow II (approximate).
1740 - Wabasha I involved in murder of two Ottawa.
1744 - Battle of Kathio, Mille Lacs (approximate).
1750 - Wabasha establishes himself as head of band in this area (approximate).
1759 - Ixatape, of Wabasha's Band, murders Mallard Duck, trader at Mendota (approximate).
1760 - French posts turned over to British.
1760 - Wabasha goes to Quebec to give himself up as hostage for Mallard Duck's murder.
1760 - Penneshaw, the French trader is permitted to trade with Wabasha's band.
1760 - Penasha II, son of the trader and a woman of Wabasha's band, is born (approximate).
1763 - Dakota braves visit Lt. Gorell at Green Bay (Wisconsin).
1766 - Jonathan Carver visits area, winters with Prairie Dakota (probably near present New Ulm, Minnesota).
1767 - Spring: Carver visits cave at present St. Paul.
1768 - Battle of Crow Wing.
1770 - Birth of Little Crow III, Chetanwakamani, Walks Pursuing A Hawk (approximate).
1772 - First Battle of Elk River.
1773 - Second Battle of Elk River.
1773 - Peter Pond establishes himself at Prairie du Chien.
1773 - Black Dog, Wamditanka, Big Eagle I, is born.
1774 - Quebec Act: Northwest could be settled.
1775 - End of great Dakota battles, according to Robinson.
1777 - Gautier approaches Wabasha and his braves to serve as "frontier raiders" in war with colonies.
1778 - French enter Revolutionary War on American side.

Appendices 245

1778 - Penasha III, Takopepeshene, Fears Nothing, grandson of Penneshaw, the trader, is born (approximate).
1779 - Wabasha and his braves at Prairie du Chien, awaiting orders from British.
1780 - Wabasha aids in attempting to capture Spanish Ste. Genevieve and American Kaskaskia.
1781 - Little Crow II, Penasha II, and other local Dakota won over to the Spanish (French) at St. Louis.
1783 - War over; Wabasha promises to "be quiet" with regard to Americans, and wait.
1783 - Northwest Fur Company formed.
1783 - Battle of St. Croix Falls.
1784 - Wabasha and most of his band leave Twin Cities area permanently, taking up residence nearer Prairie du Chien.
1788 - Robert Dickson begins trading with the Dakota.
1790 - Birth of Little Crow IV, Wakinyatanka, Big Thunder (approximate).
1794 - Jay's Treaty sets time limit, June 1, 1796, for removal of British soliders.
1794 - Dickson is made American justice of the peace at Prairie du Chien, although not renouncing British allegiance.
1795 - Birth of Tucanwashtay, Good Road (approximate).
1795 - Birth of Mapiyawichasta, Cloudman (approximate).
1795 - Little Crow II dies — Little Crow III becomes chief of Kaposia (approximate).
1800 - Spain returns the Louisiana Territory to France.
1800 - Mazarota, Grey Iron, is born (approximate).
1803 - United States buys Louisiana Territory.
1804 - Louisiana Territory officially becomes American soil.
1805 - Pike visits area; buys land at mouth of St. Croix and mouth of St. Peters (Minnesota) River to Falls of St. Anthony.
1805 - Faribault establishes trading post at Little Rapids of the Minnesota (near Carver, Minn.).
1806 - On return trip from up north among the Chippewa, Pike holds peace conference with Dakota.
1806 - Michilimackinac Fur Company established.
1808 - American Fur Company beginnings.
1811 - Southwest Fur Company formed.
1812 - War with Great Britain; Dickson hires Dakota to fight against the Americans.
1813 - Dakota at Siege of Ft. Meigs (near present Fremont, Ohio); Little Crow III and sixteen of his warriors remain with

Dickson after siege is lifted, and he wants to attack Fort Stephenson.

1814 - Spring, Little Crow III at Mackinac awaiting orders, then spends fall and early winter at Prairie du Chien, after it was abandoned by the Americans.

1815 - Little Crow III and Wabasha at Drummond Island, getting paid for services in War of 1812.

1816 - Revival of American Fur Company.

1817 - Major Stephen H. Long visits Twin Cities area.

1819 - Major Thomas Forsyth arrives to pay Dakota for land sold to Pike in 1805.

1819 - Colonel Leavenworth arrives with troops.

1820 - Birth of Little Crow V, Taoyateduta, His Red Nation.

1820 - Cass visits area, Schoolcraft accompanying the party. Taliaferro arrives.

1820 - Fall, Colonel Snelling succeeds Leavenworth, lays cornerstone of the Fort.

1822 - Columbia Fur Company Established.

1822 - Birth of Mahkato, Blue Earth, son of Chief Good Road.

1823 - Arrival of the first steamboat, the Virginia.

1823 - Major Stephen H. Long passes through area, up the Minnesota River to explore northern regions.

1824 - Fort St. Anthony completed and name changed to Fort Snelling.

1824 - Taliaferro takes Dakota chiefs to Washington to visit President Monroe.

1825 - First Treaty of Prairie du Chien — "Dakota-Chippewa Boundry Line" established.

1826 - Dakotas murder a Chippewa near Fort Snelling.

1827 - Flat Mouth's party of Chippewa attacked near Fort; Fort Dakota turned over to the Chippewa, compelled to "run the gauntlet."

1827 - Birth of Wamditanka, Big Eagle II, son of Chief Grey Iron of Black Dog Village.

1828 - Earliest beginnings of agricultural experiment on shores of Lake Calhoun by Prescott and Taliaferro.

1829 - Rev. Alvin Coe and Rev. J. D. Stevens make survey of area to consider establishment of mission among Dakota.

1830 - Second Treaty at Prairie du Chien — "Neutral Strip" established.

1833 - Death of Little Crow III; his son, Big Thunder, becomes chief of Kaposia.

1833 - Death of Penasha III, Fears Nothing; his son, Good Road, becomes chief of Oanoska.
1834 - Samuel W. and Gideon H. Pond arrive at Fort to begin mission work among Dakota.
1834 - Henry H. Sibley arrives at Mendota as agent of the American Fur Company.
1835 - Dr. T. S. Williamson and Rev. J. D. Stevens parties arrive —Stevens chooses to work at Lake Harriet.
1837 - Rev. S. R. Riggs joins Lake Harriet Mission for few months to start learning Dakota language.
1837 - Methodist Mission established at Kaposia.
1837 - Dakota sign treaty at Washington giving up their claim on land east of the Mississippi River.
1838 - April, Hole-in-the-Day attacks Dakota hunting party near Lac qui Parle; G. Pond helps bury the dead.
1838 - Death of Black Dog, Big Eagle I; his son, Grey Iron, becomes chief.
1838 - August, Dakota murder companion of Hole-in-the-Day near Fort.
1839 - May, Rev. E. G. Gear arrives to begin his work as chaplain at Fort Snelling.
1839 - July, murder of Badger, brave of Lake Calhoun Band; leads to Rum River Massacre and the Battle of Lake St. Croix.
1839 - Fall, Rev. Stevens leaves Lake Harriet Mission to become government farmer for Wabasha's Band; Taliaferro resigns as agent at Ft. Snelling.
1839 - The last growing season that the Lake Calhoun Band spends at that location. In spring of 1840, they set up village at present Bloomington.
1840 - Four Chippewa kill and scalp a Dakota man and woman.
1841 - April, Karboka, old chief under Cloudman at Lake Calhoun, killed by Chippewa.
1841 - April, Little Crow's two sons killed by Chippewa at Falls of St. Croix.
1841 - April, Dakota of Lake Calhoun Band attack Chippewa at Lake Pokegama.
1842 - Battle of Kaposia.
1843 - Gideon Pond builds at Bloomington near Good Road's and Cloudman's Villages.
1845 - Little Crow IV, Big Thunder, accidentally shoots himself and His Red Nation becomes chief of Kaposia.

1846 - Dr. Williamson moves from Lac qui Parle to Kaposia and establishes school for Little Crow's people.
1847 - Rev. S. W. Pond leaves Bloomington to establish mission among Shakopee's people.
1849 - Minnesota Territory created; Governor Ramsey arrives at St. Paul.
1850 - June, Ramsey holds Indian Council at Fort Snelling.
1850 - *Dakota Friend,* Indian newspaper, established by Rev. Gideon Pond.
1851 - Treaties of Traverse des Sioux and Mendota.
1853 - April, Sioux and Chippewa fight in the streets of St. Paul.
1853 - Governor Gorman leads most of the Dakota to their reservation at Redwood.
1854 - Last main division of Dakota remove to reservation under Little Crow; attacked by Chippewa near Fort Ridgely; Dakota parties often revisit old village sites for short periods until the summer of 1862; a few families remain, even after the Great Outbreak, living at Kaposia, Mendota, and Red Rock.

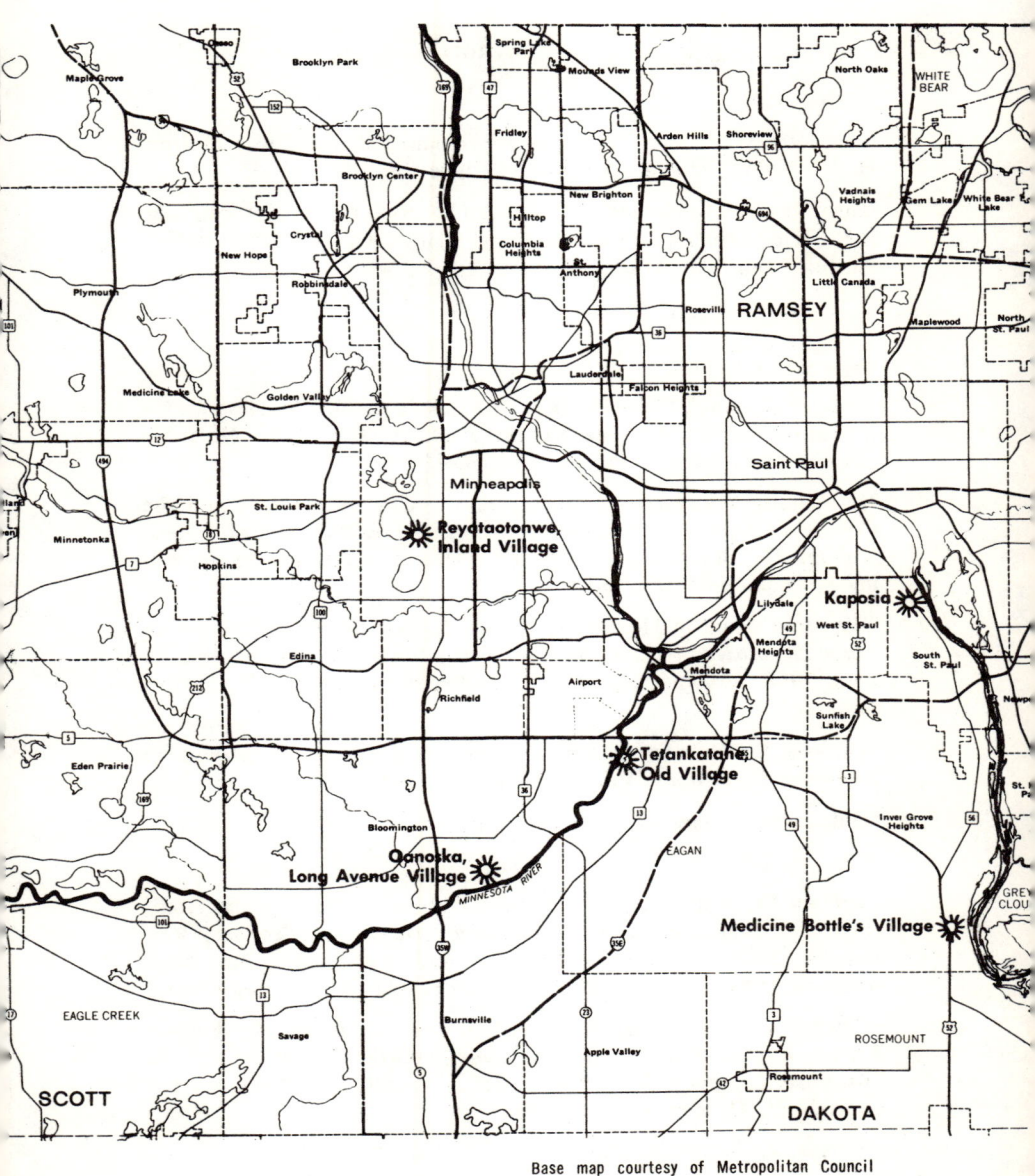

Base map courtesy of Metropolitan Council

Footnotes

PROLOGUE

[1] Charlotte Whitcomb, "A Pioneer Woman, Reminiscences of Mrs. H. R. Gibbs." *Minneapolis Journal,* June 26, 1897.

[2] Lucy L. W. Morris and others, ed. *Old Rail Fence Corners, The A B C's of Minnesota History,* The F. H. McCulloch Printing Co., Austin, Minn. 1882, p. 109.

THE WHOLE LOG

[1] Samuel W. Pond, "The Dakotas or Sioux in 1834," *Minnesota Historical Collections,* Volume XII, St. Paul, 1908, p. 492. (Hereafter referred to as Pond. *"Dakotas . . . 1834."*)

[2] J. Fletcher Williams, "A History of the City of St. Paul and the County of Ramsey, Minnesota," *Minnesota Historical Collections,* Volume IV, St. Paul, 1876, p. 13. (Hereafter referred to as Williams, *History of St. Paul.*)

[3] Warren Upham in Holcombe, Return I., and others, *Minnesota in Three Centuries, 1655-1908,* Publishing Society of Minnesota, St. Paul, 1908, Volume I, p. 86. (Hereafter referred to as Holcombe, *Minnesota . . .*)

[4] Thomas S. Williamson, "Who Were the First Men," *Minnesota Historical Collections,* Volume I, 1902, p. 243.

[5] Holcombe, *Minnesota . . .,* Vol. I, p. 248.

[6] Ibid., p. 257.

[7] William W. Warren, "History of the Ojibways, Based Upon Traditions and Oral Statements," *Minnesota Historical Collections,* Volume IV, St. Paul, 1885. Reprinted by Ross and Haines, Inc., Minneapolis, 1957, p. 164. (Hereafter referred to as Warren, *Ojibways.*)

[8] Edward D. Neill, *The History of Minnesota, From the Earliest French Explorers to the Present Time,* Fourth Edition, Minnesota Historical Company, Minneapolis, 1882, p. 149. (Hereafter referred to as Neill, *History of Minnesota.*)

[9] Warren, *Ojibways,* p. 165.

¹⁰Ibid., p. 167.

¹¹Ibid., p. 169.

¹²Holcombe, *Minnesota* . . ., Vol. I, p. 259.

¹³Neill, *History of Minnesota,* p. 179.

¹⁴Warren, *Ojibways,* p. 161.

¹⁵Jacob V. Brower, *Kathio* in Volume IV of *Memoirs of Explorations in the Basin of the Mississippi,* H. L. Collins Co., St. Paul, 1901. This quote is from p. 92.

¹⁶Pond, *"Dakotas . . . 1834",* p. 489.

¹⁷Newton H. Winchell, *The Aborigines of Minnesota,* Pioneer Company for Minnesota Historical Society, St. Paul, 1911, p. 540, quoting Henry R. Schoolcraft, *The American Indian, History, Conditions and Prospects,* 1851, p. 137.

¹⁸Doane Robinson, *A History of the Dakota or Sioux Indians,* South Dakota Department of History, 1904. Reprinted by Ross & Haines, Inc., Minneapolis, 1956, p. 57, note. (Hereafter referred to as Robinson, *Dakota.)*

¹⁹Ibid., p. 57, note.

²⁰Winchell, *Aborigines,* p. 541.

²¹"Lieut. James Gorrell's Journal," *Wisconsin Historical Collections,* Madison, Wisconsin, 1903, Volume I, p. 36 and 41.

²²William J. Snelling, *Tales of the Northwest,* Introduction by J. T. Flanagan, University of Minnesota Press, Minneapolis, 1936, p. 191-223. (Hereafter referred to as Snelling, *Tales.)*

²³Edward D. Neill in Andrews, C. C., ed., *History of St. Paul, Minnesota,* D. Mason and Co., Syracuse, New York, 1890, p. 19. (Hereafter referred to as Andrews, *St. Paul.)*

²⁴Ibid., p. 19.

²⁵Winchell, *Aborigines,* p. 545.

²⁶Holcombe, *Minnesota* . . ., Volume I, p. 283.

²⁷Ibid., p. 283.

²⁸William W. Folwell, *A History of Minnesota,* Minnesota Historical

Society, St. Paul, 1921, reprinted 1956, Volume I, p. 56, note. (Hereafter referred to as Folwell, *Minnesota*.)

[29] Johnathan Carver, *Three Years Travels Through the Interior Parts of North America,* Key and Simpson, Philadelphia, 1796. Reprinted by Ross & Haines, Inc., Minneapolis, 1956, pp. 63-65.

[30] Ibid., p. 84.

[31] Theodore C. Blegen, *Minnesota, A History of the State,* University of Minnesota Press, Minneapolis, 1966, p. 70.

[32] Holcombe, *Minnesota . . .,* Volume II, p. 272.

[33] Warren, *Ojibways,* pp. 227 and 228.

[34] Ibid., p. 230.

[35] Robinson, *Dakota,* p. 62.

[36] Ibid., pp. 61-64.

[37] C. M. Gates, editor, *Five Fur Traders of the Northwest,* Minnesota Historical Society, St. Paul, 1965, p. 59.

[38] Louise P. Kellogg, *The British Regime in Wisconsin and the Northwest,* State Historical Society of Wisconsin, Madison, 1935, p. 136. (Hereafter referred to as Kellogg, *British.*)

[39] Ibid., p. 147.

[40] Ibid., p. 167.

[41] Ibid., p. 165.

[42] Ibid., p. 168.

[43] Neill, *History of Minnesota,* p. 230.

[44] Winchell, *Aborigines,* p. 542.

[45] Kellogg, *British,* p. 200.

[46] Asa W. Daniels, "Reminiscences of Little Crow" *Minnesota Historical Collections,* Volume XII, p. 516.

[47] Edward D. Neill, "Dakota Land and Dakota Life," *Minnesota Historical Collections,* Volume I, St. Paul, 1902, p. 211.

[48] Elliot Coues, *The Expeditions of Zebulon Montgomery Pike,* Ross & Haines, Minneapolis, 1965, Volume I, p. 83.

⁴⁹Thomas Foster, *St. Paul Democrat,* May 4, 1854.

⁵⁰Coues, *Pike's Expeditions,* Volume I, p. 231.

⁵¹Ibid., p. 197.

⁵²Robinson, *Dakota,* p. 80.

⁵³Kellogg, *British,* p. 284.

⁵⁴Neill, *History of Minnesota,* p. 281.

⁵⁵Kellogg, *British,* p. 296.

⁵⁶Ibid., p. 312.

⁵⁷Ibid., p. 316.

⁵⁸Ibid., p. 317.

⁵⁹Robinson, *Dakota,* p. 99.

⁶⁰Ibid., p. 100.

⁶¹Ibid., p. 100.

⁶²Andrews, *St. Paul,* p. 40.

⁶³Holcombe, *Minnesota . . .,* Volume I, p. 348.

⁶⁴Robinson, *Dakota,* p. 95.

THE SHARED LOG

¹Folwell, *Minnesota,* Volume I, p. 133.

²Lyman C. Draper, ed., "Major Forsyth's Narrative," *Minnesota Historical Collections,* Volume III, St. Paul, 1880, pp. 139-167.

³Holcombe, *Minnesota . . .,* Volume II, p. 39.

⁴Warren Upham, "Minnesota Geographic Names," *Minnesota Historical Collections,* Volume XVII, St. Paul, 1920, p. 442.

⁵Henry R. Schoolcraft, as quoted in Neill, *History of Minnesota,* p. 326.

⁶Neill, *History of Minnesota,* p. 325.

⁷"Major Forsyth's Narrative," p. 161.

[8] William H. Keating's narrative of the 1823 Long expedition as quoted in Holcombe, *Minnesota* . . ., Volume I, p. 366.

[9] Holcombe, *Minnesota* . . ., Volume I, p. 367.

[10] Folwell, *Minnesota,* Volume I, p. 145.

[11] Neill, *History of Minnesota,* p. 339.

[12] Holcombe, *Minnesota* . . ., Volume II, p. 271.

[13] Folwell, *Minnesota,* Volume I, p. 146.

[14] Robinson, *Dakota,* p. 143.

[15] Marcus L. Hansen, *Old Fort Snelling, 1818-1858,* State Historical Society, Iowa City, Iowa, 1918. Reprinted by Ross & Haines, Inc., Minneapolis, 1958, p. 141. (Hereafter referred to as Hansen, *Ft. Snelling.*)

[16] Edward D. Neill, in Andrews, *St. Paul,* p. 49.

[17] Pond, *"Dakotas . . . 1834,"* p. 491.

[18] Snelling, *Tales,* p. 222.

[19] Ibid., p. 223.

[20] Ibid., p. 223.

[21] Theodore C. Blegen, ed., Henry H. Sibley, *Iron Face, The Adventures of Jack Frazer,* The Caxton Club, Chicago, 1950, p. 52, note.

[22] Pond, *"Dakotas . . . 1834,"* p. 326.

[23] Edward D. Neill, "Explorers and Pioneers of Minnesota," as found in Warner and Foote, *History of the Minnesota Valley,* North Star Printing Company, Minneapolis, 1882, p. 105.

[24] Neill, *History of Minnesota,* p. 411.

[25] Taliaferro's diary, May 7, 1831.

[26] Philander Prescott, "Autobiography and Reminiscences," *Minnesota Historical Collections,* Volume VI, St. Paul, 1894, p. 482. See also note, p. 49 of Roy W. Meyer, *History of the Santee Sioux,* University of Nebraska Press, Lincoln, Nebraska, 1967.

[27] Folwell, *Minnesota,* Volume I, p. 185.

[28] Samuel W. Pond, Jr., *Two Volunteer Missionaries Among the*

Dakotas, Congregational Sunday School and Publishing Society, Boston, Mass., and Chicago, Ill., 1893, p. 47.

[29]William H. Keating, as quoted in Neill, "Dakota Land and Dakota Life," *Minnesota Historical Collections,* Volume I, p. 213.

[30]Lawrence Taliaferro, *Report, 1834. Indian Office Files 1834, No. 203,* as quoted in Hansen, *Ft. Snelling,* p. 83.

[31]Thomas Hughes, *Indian Chiefs of Southern Minnesota,* Free Press Company, Mankato, Minnesota, 1927, p. 19. (Hereafter referred to as Hughes, *Indian Chiefs.*)

[32]"Dakota Portraits" from *Minnesota History* November, 1918, p. 547, reprinted from an article entitled "Etawawenehan, or Fearful Face" by S. R. Riggs, published for the Minnesota Free Press, June 23, 1858.

[33]Gideon Pond's *Diary,* as quoted in Pond, S. W. Jr., *Two Volunteer Missionaries,* p. 137.

[34]Philander Prescott, *Minnesota Historical Collections,* Volume VI, p. 482.

[35]Pond, *"Dakotas . . . 1834,"* p. 326.

[36]Hughes, *Indian Chiefs,* p. 24.

[37]Pond, *"Dakotas . . . 1834,"* p. 327.

[38]Ibid., p. 406.

[39]Gideon Pond's *Diary,* July 12, 1845, as quoted by John H. Stevens in *Personal Recollections of Minnesota and Its People and Early History of Minneapolis,* M. Robinson, Minneapolis, 1890, p. 390. (Hereafter referred to as Stevens, *Minnesota and Its People.*)

[40]Hughes, *Indian Chiefs,* pp. 26 and 27.

[41]Neill, *History of Minnesota,* p. 399.

[42]Samuel W. Pond, "Two Missionaries in the Sioux Country — the Pond Narrative," Theodore C. Blegen, editor, *Minnesota History,* Vol. 21, 1940, p. 28. (Hereafter referred to as Pond, *Narrative.*)

[43]Folwell, *Minnesota,* Volume I, p. 195.

[44]Stephen R. Riggs, *Mary and I, Forty Years With the Sioux,* Congregational Sunday School and Publishing Society, Boston, Mass.

and Chicago, Illinois, 1880, p. 42. (Hereafter referred to as Riggs, *Mary and I.*)

[45] Letter dated June 22, 1837, to Mary Riggs' grandfather. Ibid., p. 43.

[46] Letter dated July 8, 1837, to Mary Riggs' mother. Ibid., p. 45.

[47] Jane DeBow Gibbs' reminiscences, *Minneapolis Journal,* June 26, 1897.

[48] Neill, *History of Minnesota,* p. 447.

[49] Pond, *Narrative,* p. 161.

[50] Ibid., p. 163.

[51] Gideon Pond, Letter to Edward D. Neill quoted in Neill, *History of Minnesota,* p. 771.

[52] Letter written by Gideon Pond in 1856, Neill, *History of Minnesota,* p. 770.

[53] Letter written by Samuel Pond dated May 25, 1834.

[54] Ibid.

[55] Henry H. Sibley, "Reminiscences of the Early Days of Minnesota," *Minnesota Historical Collections,* Volume III, St. Paul, 1874, p. 251.

[56] Pond, *"Dakotas . . . 1834,"* p. 324.

[57] Holcombe, *Minnesota . . .,* Volume II, p. 263.

[58] Sibley, "Reminiscences," *Minnesota Historical Collections,* Volume III, pp. 252, 253.

[59] Neill, *History of Minnesota,* p. 466.

[60] Ibid., p. 467.

[61] Holcombe, *Minnesota . . .,* Volume II, p. 176.

[62] Ibid., p. 178.

[63] Ibid., p. 180.

NO LOG AT ALL

[1] Pond, *"Dakotas . . . 1834,"* p. 378.

[2] Folwell, *Minnesota,* Volume I, p. 209.

[3] Henry H. Sibley, "Reminiscences, Historical and Personal," *Minnesota Historical Collections,* Volume I, St. Paul, 1902, p. 378.

[4] Samuel W. Pond, "Indian Warfare in Minnesota," *Minnesota Historical Collections,* Volume III, St. Paul, 1880, p. 130.

[5] Ibid., p. 130.

[6] Theodore C. Blegen, ed., "Armistice and War on the Minnesota Frontier — Ezekiel G. Gear's Account," *Minnesota History,* Volume 24, No. 1, 1943, p. 18, note. (Hereafter referred to as Gear's *Account.)*

[7] Ibid., p. 19.

[8] Ibid., p. 20.

[9] Holcombe, *Minnesota,* Volume II, p. 164.

[10] Pond, "Indian Warfare," p. 136.

[11] Holcombe, *Minnesota . . .,* Volume II, p. 169.

[12] Gear's *Account,* p. 21, note.

[13] Holcombe, *Minnesota . . .,* Volume II, p. 168.

[14] Gear's *Account,* p. 23.

[15] Pond, "Indian Warfare," p. 130.

[16] Gear's *Account,* p. 24.

[17] Lillie Gibbs LeVesconte, *Little Bird That Was Caught, the Story of the Early Years of Jane DeBow Gibbs,* Ramsey County Historical Society, St. Paul, 1968, p. 33.

[18] Gideon Pond speech recorded in Stevens, *Minnesota and Its People,* p. 396.

[19] Gear's *Account,* p. 25.

[20] Dr. Blegen in *Minnesota History,* Vol. 24, p. 24, note.

[21] Gear's *Account,* p. 25.

[22] Taliaferro's Diary, Sept. 7, 1830, as quoted in Folwell, *Minnesota,* Volume 1, p. 447, note.

[23] Ibid., p. 142, note.

[24] Pond, *Narrative,* p. 167.

25Folwell, *Minnesota,* Volume I, p. 197.

26Pond, *Narrative,* p. 169.

27John H. Case, "Historical Notes of Grey Cloud Island and Its Vicinity," *Minnesota Historical Collections,* Volume XV, St. Paul, 1915, pp. 373 and 374.

28Asa Daniels, "Reminiscences of Little Crow," *Minnesota Historical Collections,* Volume XII, p. 515.

29Henry H. Sibley, "Early Days of Minnesota," *Minnesota Historical Collections,* Volume III, p. 251.

30Holcombe, *Minnesota . . .,* Volume II, p. 180.

31Frank B. Mayer, *With Pen and Pencil on the Frontier,* Bertha L. Heilbron, ed., Minnesota Historical Society, St. Paul, 1932, pp. 130 and 131.

32Rev. T. S. Williamson, Memoir of Napehshneedoota, *Minnesota Historical Collections,* Volume III, pp. 189-190.

33Harriet E. Bishop, *Floral Home or First Years of Minnesota,* Sheldon, Blakeman and Co., New York, 1857, p. 93.

34Neill, *History of Minnesota,* p. 509.

35Williams, *History of St. Paul,* p. 274.

36T. M. Newson, *Pen Pictures of St. Paul, Minnesota and Biographical Sketches of Old Settlers,* Volume I, St. Paul, 1886, p. 211.

37Andrews, *St. Paul,* p. 59.

38Ibid., p. 59.

39*Democrat,* May 27, 1851.

40Samuel W. Pond, Jr., *Two Volunteer Missionaries,* p. 235. See also Hughes, *Indian Chiefs,* p. 25.

41Letter dated January 2, 1843.

42Stevens, *Minnesota and Its People,* p. 51.

43From Gideon's diary dated May 13, 1850.

44Pond, *Narrative,* p. 175.

45Pond, *"Dakotas . . . 1834,"* p. 327.

[46] The volume was almost unobtainable until 1962 when it was photographically reproduced and republished by Ross & Haines.

[47] John H. Bliss, "Reminiscences of Fort Snelling," *Minnesota Historical Collections,* Volume VI, St. Paul, p. 347.

[48] Mary Eastman, *Dakota, or Life and Legends of the Sioux Around Fort Snelling,* New York, 1849. Reprinted by Ross & Haines, Inc., Minneapolis, 1962, pp. i-v.

[49] Ibid., pp. 40-41.

[50] Stevens, *Minnesota and Its People,* p. 49.

[51] Ibid., p. 87.

[52] Ibid., p. 162

[53] Folwell, *Minnesota,* Volume I, p. 458.

[54] Holcombe, *Minnesota . . .,* Volume II, p. 286.

[55] Folwell, *Minnesota,* Volume I, p. 266.

[56] Holcombe, *Minnesota . . .,* Volume II, p. 305.

[57] Ibid., pp. 305-324.

[58] Hughes, *Indian Chiefs,* p. 23.

[59] Folwell, *Minnesota,* Volume I, p. 287.

[60] Ibid., p. 287.

[61] "Reminiscences of Little Crow," *Minnesota Historical Collections,* Volume 12, p. 520.

[62] The Life and Services of Hon. Willis A. Gorman," *Minnesota Historical Society Collections,* Volume III, pp. 318-320.

[63] Holcombe, *Minnesota in Three Centuries,* Volume III, p. 273. Those portions of the quotation enclosed in parentheses do not apply to the former Twin Cities bands.

[64] Holcombe, *Minnesota . . .,* Volume II, p. 326.

[65] Neill, *History of Minnesota,* p. 618.

[66] J. Fletcher Williams, *History of the City of St. Paul,* pp. 336-338.

[67] T. M. Newson, *Thrilling Scenes Among the Indians,* S. A. Maxwell & Co., Chicago, Ill., 1888.

[68] W. H. C. Folsom, *Fifty Years in the Northwest,* Pioneer Press Co., St. Paul, 1888, pp. 757-759.

EPILOGUE

[1] Robinson, *Dakota,* p. 14.

[2] Roy W. Meyer, *History of the Santee Sioux, United States Indian Policy on Trial,* University of Nebraska Press, Lincoln, Nebraska, 1967, p. 91. (Hereafter referred to as Mayer, *Santee.*)

[3] Hughes, *Indian Chiefs,* p. 25.

[4] Steven R. Riggs, "Narrative of Paul Mazakootamane," *Minnesota Historical Collections,* Volume III, p. 82.

[5] Pond, *Narrative,* p. 273.

[6] Robinson, *Dakota,* p. 268.

[7] Return I. Holcombe, ed., "A Sioux Story of the War," *Minnesota Historical Collections,* Volume VI, p. 384.

[8] Meyer, *Santee,* p. 118.

[9] Willoughby M. Babcock, "The Sioux Uprising of 1862," *Gopher Historian,* Minnesota Historical Society, St. Paul, Volume 17, No. 1, Fall, 1962, p. 13.

[10] Ibid., p. 13.

[11] Gideon Pond in Riggs, *Mary and I,* p. 368.

[12] Pond, *Narrative,* p. 274.

[13] Meyer, *Santee,* p. 268.

[14] Ibid., pp. 270 and 274.

Bibliography

Adams, A. T., ed. *The Explorations of Pierre Esprit Radisson.* Loren Kallsen, modernizer. Ross and Haines, Inc., Minneapolis, Minnesota, 1961.

Andreas, A. T., *Illustrated Historical Atlas of the State of Minnesota.* Andreas, Chicago, Illinois, 1874.

Andrews, C. C., ed., *History of St. Paul, Minnesota.* D. Mason & Co., Syracuse, N. Y., 1890.

Atwater, I., and J. H. Stevens, *History of Minneapolis and Hennepin County.* (2 Volumes) Munsell Publishing Co., New York, 1895.

Bishop, H. E., *Floral Home, or First Years in Minnesota.* Sheldon, Blakeman & Co., New York, 1857.

Blegen, T. C., *Building Minnesota.* D. C. Heath and Co., New York, 1938.

────── *Grass Roots History.* University of Minnesota Press, Minneapolis, Minnesota, 1947.

────── *The Land Lies Open.* University of Minnesota Press, Minneapolis, Minnesota, 1949.

────── *Minnesota, a History of the State.* University of Minnesota Press, Minneapolis, Minnesota, 1963.

────── "The Pond Brothers." *Minnesota History.* Vol. 15, No. 3. St. Paul, 1934.

────── and P. D. Jordon, ed., *With Various Voices, Recordings of North Star Life.* Webb Publishing Co., St. Paul, Minnesota, 1949.

Brandon, W., *The American Heritage Book of Indians.* American Heritage Publishing Co. Inc., 1961.

Brings, L. M., ed. *Minneapolis, City of Opportunity.* T. S. Denison and Co., Minneapolis, Minnesota, 1956.

Brower, J. V., *Kathio.* Volume IV of *Memoirs* . . . H. L. Collins Co., St. Paul, Minnesota, 1901.

Brower and D I. Bushnell, Jr. *Mille Lac.* Volume III of *Memoirs* . . . H. L. Collins Co., St. Paul, Minnesota, 1900.

Bryant, C. S., and A. B. Murch, *History of the Great Massacre by the Sioux Indians of Minnesota.* Rickey and Carroll, Cincinnati, Ohio, 1864.

Callender, John M., *New Light on Old Fort Snelling, an Archeological Exploration, 1957 and 1958.* Minnesota Historical Society, St. Paul, 1959.

Campbell, M. W., *The North West Company.* St. Martin's Press, New York, 1957.

Carney, M. V., *Minnesota, The Star of the North.* D. C. Heath Co., New York, 1918.

Carter, E. R., *The Gift is Rich.* The Friendship Press, New York, 1956.

Carver, Jonathan, *Travels Through the Interior Parts of North America.* Ross and Haines, Inc., Minneapolis, Minnesota, 1956.

Castle, H. A., *History of St. Paul and Vicinity.* Lewis Publishing Co., Chicago and New York, 1912.

Coleman, Frogner, and Eich, *Ojibway Myths and Legends.* Ross and Haines, Inc., Minneapolis, Minnesota, 1962.

Coues, Elliot, *The Expeditions of Zebulon Montgomery Pike.* Vol. I. Reprinted by Ross and Haines, Inc., Minneapolis, Minnesota, 1965.

Curtiss-Wedge, F., *History of Dakota and Goodhue Counties.* Volume I. H. C. Cooper, Jr. and Co., Chicago, 1910.

Delanglez, J., *Hennepin's "Description of Louisiana."* Institute of Jesuit History, Chicago, 1941.

Drake, S. G., *The Aboriginal Races of America* . . . Charles De Silver and Sons, Philadelphia, Pennsylvania, 1859.

Eastman, Charles A., *Indian Boyhood.* McClure, Phillips, and Co., New York, 1902.

——————— *Indian Heroes and Great Chieftains.* Boston, Massachusetts, 1923.

Eastman, *The Indian Today.* Doubleday, Page, and Co., New York, 1915.

——— *From the Deep Woods to Civilization.* Little, Brown, and Co., Boston, Mass., 1920.

——— and E. G. Eastman, *Wigwam Evenings; Sioux Folk Tales Retold.* Boston, 1909.

Eastman, Mary, *Dahkota, or Life and Legends of the Sioux Around Fort Snelling.* (Originally printed in 1849.) Reprinted by Ross and Haines, Inc., Minneapolis, 1962.

Folsom, W. H. C., *Fifty Years in the Northwest.* Pioneer Press Co., St. Paul, 1888.

Folwell, W. W., *A History of Minnesota.* Volumes I and II. Minnesota Historical Society, St. Paul, Minnesota, 1921 and 1924.

Fremont, J. C., *Narratives of Exploration and Adventure.* Longmans, Green and Co., New York, 1956.

Fridley, R. W., "Fort Snelling, From Military Post to Historic Site." *Minnesota History,* Volume 35, No. 4, St. Paul, 1956.

Gear, E. G., Letters in "Armistice and War on the Minnesota Frontier." Edited by T. C. Blegen. *Minnesota History,* Volume 24, No. 1, St. Paul, 1943.

Gilfillan, J. A., "The Ojibways in Minnesota." *Minnesota Historical Collections, Volume IX,* St. Paul, 1901.

Gray, J., *Pine, Stream, and Prairie: Wisconsin and Minnesota in Profile.* Alfred A. Knopf, New York, 1945.

Greenbie, S., *Frontiers and Fur Trade.* The John Day Co., New York, 1929.

Hamilton, Charles, *Cry of the Thunderbird, the American Indian's Own Story.* The Macmillan Company, New York, 1950.

Hans, F. M., *The Great Sioux Nation.* M. A. Donohue and Co., Chicago, 1950.

Hansen, Marcus L., *Old Fort Snelling, 1818-1858.* State Historical Society, Iowa City, Iowa, 1918. Reprinted by Ross and Haines, Inc., Minneapolis, Minnesota, 1958.

Havighurst, W., *Upper Mississippi, a Wilderness Saga.* Ferrar and Rinehart, New York, 1944.

Heilbron, B. L., *The Thirty-Second State, a Pictorial History of Minnesota.* Minnesota Historical Society, St. Paul, 1958.

————— ed., *With Pen and Pencil on the Frontier in 1851, Diary and Sketches of Frank B. Mayer.* Narratives and Documents, Volume I. Minnesota Historical Society, St. Paul, 1932.

Hennessey, W. B., *Past and Present of St. Paul, Minnesota.* S. J. Clarke Pub. Co., Chicago, 1906.

Hodge, F. W., ed., *Handbook of the American Indians North of Mexico.* 2 Volumes. Government Printing Office, Washington, D. C., 1912.

Holcombe, R. I., Hubbard, and Upham, *Minnesota in Three Centuries.* Volumes I, II, and III. Publishing Society of Minnesota, St. Paul, 1908.

Holmquist, J. D. and J. A. Brookins, *Minnesota's Major Historical Sites, A Guide.* Minnesota Historical Society, St. Paul, 1963.

Hudson, H. B., *A Half Century of Minneapolis.* The Hudson Co., Minneapolis, Minn., 1908.

Hughes, Thomas, *Indian Chiefs of Southern Minnesota.* Free Press Company, Mankato, Minnesota, 1927.

————— *Old Traverse des Sioux.* Herald Publishing Co., St. Peter, Minnesota, 1929.

Jones, Evan, *The Minnesota, Forgotten River.* Holt, Rinehart, and Winston, New York, New York, 1962.

Keating, W. H., *Narrative . . . 1823.* Introduction by R. P. Johnson. Ross and Haines, Inc., Minneapolis, Minnesota, 1959.

Kellogg, Louise Phelps, *The British Regime in Wisconsin and the Northwest.* State Historical Society of Wisconsin, Madison, Wisconsin, 1935.

————— "Fort Beauharnois." *Minnesota History.* Volume 8, No. 3. Minnesota Historical Society, St. Paul, 1919.

Kunz, V. B., *Muskets to Missiles, a Military History of Minnesota*. Minnesota Statehood Centennial Committee, St. Paul, Minnesota, 1958.

Laut, A. C., *Pathfinders of the West*. Grosset and Dunlap, New York, 1904.

Lawshe, Fred E., "Kaposia." *Over the Years*. Volume III, No. 2, Dakota County Historical Society Bulletin, South St. Paul, Minnesota, 1963.

────── "Little Crow, Chief of Kaposia." *Minnesota County Officer*. September-October Issue, St. Paul, Minnesota, 1956.

Le Vesconte, L. B., *Little Bird That Was Caught*. Ramsey County Historical Society, St. Paul, Minnesota, 1968.

Lynd, James W., "History of the Dakota." *Minnesota Historical Collections, Volume II,* St. Paul, Minnesota, 1867.

Longfellow, H. W., *The Song of Hiawatha, and Other Poems*. Sowerby, Halifax, 1863.

Lindquist, M. L., and J. W. Clark, *Early Days and Ways in the Old Northwest*. Charles Scribner's Sons, New York, 1937.

Meyer, Roy W., *History of the Santee Sioux*. University of Nebraska Press, Lincoln, 1967.

Miller, F. C., *St. Paul, Location, Development, Opportunities*. Webb Publishing Co., St. Paul, Minnesota, 1928.

Minnesota in the Civil and Indian Wars, 1861-1865. The Pioneer Press, St. Paul, 1890.

Morris, L. W., and others, ed., *Old Rail Fence Corners, The A B C's of Minnesota History*. The F. H. McCulloch Printing Co., Austin, Minnesota, 1914.

Neill, E. D., "Explorers and Pioneers of Minnesota." *History of the Minnesota Valley*. North Star Publishing Co., St. Paul, Minnesota, 1882.

────── *The History of Minnesota, From the Earliest French Explorers to the Present Time*. Fourth Edition, Minnesota Historical Company, Minneapolis, Minnesota, 1882.

────── *History of St. Paul*. In Andrews' History . . ., Chapters I-IV, St. Paul, 1890.

Newson, T. M., *Pen Pictures of St. Paul, Minnesota, and Biographical Sketches of Old Settlers.* Published by the author, St. Paul, Minnesota, 1886.

———— *Thrilling Scenes Among the Indians.* S. A. Maxwell and Co., Chicago, Illinois, 1888.

Oehler, C. M., *The Great Sioux Uprising.* Oxford University Press, New York, 1959.

Pond, Gideon H., "Dakota Superstitions." *Minnesota Historical Collections, Volume II,* St. Paul, 1867.

Pond, Samuel W., "The Dakotas or Sioux in Minnesota As They Were in 1834." *Minnesota Historical Collections, Volume XII,* St. Paul, Minnesota, 1908.

———— "Indian Warfare in Minnesota." *Minnesota Historical Collections, Volume III,* St. Paul, Minnesota, 1880.

———— "Narrative, Two Missionaries in the Sioux Country." Edited by T. C. Blegen, *Minnesota History,* Volume 21, St. Paul, Minnesota, 1940.

Pond, Samuel W., Jr., *Two Volunteer Missionaries Among the Dakotas.* Congregational Sunday School and Publishing Society, Boston, Mass., and Chicago, Illinois, 1893.

Poatgieter, A. H., and J. T. Dunn, ed., *Gopher Reader.* Minnesota Historical Society and State Centennial Committee, St. Paul, Minnesota, 1958.

Parkman, *Count Frontenac.* Little, Brown, and Company, Boston, Mass. 1910.

Parsons, Dudley E., *The Story of Minneapolis.* Privately printed, Minneapolis, Minn., 1913.

Rhoads, J. B., "The Fort Snelling Area in 1835." Taliaferro's Map. *Minnesota History,* Volume 35, No. 1, St. Paul, Minnesota, 1956.

Riggs, S. R., "The Dakota Mission." *Minnesota Historical Collections, Volume III,* St. Paul, Minnesota, 1880.

———— "Dakota Portraits." *Minnesota History,* Volume 2, No. 8, St. Paul, Minn., 1918.

———— *Mary and I, Forty Years With the Sioux.* Congregational Sunday School and Publishing Society, Boston, Mass., and Chicago, Illinois, 1880.

Robinson, Doane, *A History of the Dakota or Sioux Indians.* South Dakota Department of History, 1904. Reprinted by Ross and Haines, Inc., Minneapolis, Minnesota, 1956.

Roddis, Louis H., *The Indian Wars of Minnesota.* Torch Press, Cedar Rapids, Iowa, 1956.

Scanlon, P. L., *Prairie du Chien, French, British, American.* The Collegiate Press, George Banta Publishing Co., Menasha, Wisconsin, 1937.

Sibley, H. H., *Iron Face, the Adventures of Jack Frazer.* Edited by Blegen and Davidson, The Caxton Club, Chicago, Illinois, 1950.

Smith, C. J., and J. Callahan, *The Making of Wisconsin.* Eau Claire Book and Stationery Company, Eau Claire, Wisconsin, 1927.

Snelling, William Joseph, *Tales of the Northwest.* Introduction by J. T. Flanagan. University of Minnesota Press, Minneapolis, Minnesota, 1936.

Stevens, John H., *Personal Recollections of Minnesota and Its People and Early History of Minneapolis.* M. Robinson, Minneapolis, Minnesota, 1890.

Thayer, (Mrs.) T. C., *Indian Legends of Minnesota.* Sibley House Association, Mendota, Minnesota, (no date).

Upham, W., *Minnesota Geographic Names, Their Origin and Historic Significance.* Minnesota Historical Society Collections, Volume XVII, St. Paul, Minnesota, 1920.

Van Cleve, C. O., *Three Score Years and Ten, Life Long Memories of Fort Snelling.* Minneapolis, Minnesota, 1888.

Warner, G. E., and C. M. Foote, *History of the Minnesota Valley.* North Star Publishing Company, Minneapolis, Minnesota, 1882.

────── *History of Ramsey County and the City of St. Paul.* North Star Publishing Company, Minneapolis, Minnesota, 1881.

Warren, William W., *History of the Ojibways, Based Upon Traditions and Oral Statements.* Minnesota Historical Society Collections, Volume V, St. Paul, Minnesota, 1885. Reprinted by Ross and Haines, Inc., Minneapolis, Minnesota, 1957.

West, Nathaniel, *Ancestry, Life, and Times of Hon. Henry Hastings Sibley*. Pioneer Press Publishing Company, St. Paul, Minnesota, 1889.

Whitcomb, Charlotte, "A Pioneer Woman, Reminiscences of Mrs. H. R. Gibbs." *Minneapolis Journal,* June 26 issue, Minneapolis, Minnesota, 1897.

Williams, J. Fletcher, *A History of the City of St. Paul and the County of Ramsey, Minnesota*. Minnesota Historical Society Collections, Volume IV, St. Paul, Minnesota, 1876.

Williams, Mentor L., *Schoolcraft's Indian Legends*. Michigan State University Press, 1956.

Winchell, N. H., *The Aborigines of Minnesota*. Minnesota Historical Society, St. Paul, 1911.

Index

agents, Indian, 52, 87, 146, 157, 196
agriculture, see cultivation of land
Ainse, Joseph, fur trader, 52
Aitkin County, Minn., 140
Aitkin, William A., fur trader, 152
Algonkin-Wakashan Stock, 14, 16, Ojibway or Chippewa migration, 18
altar, ceremonial, in mounds, 11
American Board of Commissioners for Foreign Missions, first visit the Dakota, 116; Presbyterian-Congregational Missions: Lake Harriet, 116-123; Kaposia, 169-173; Lac qui Parle, 118, 119, 122; new mission considered by Pond brothers, 122; Secretary Green of Mission Board, 117
American Fur Company, 133, represented by H. H. Sibley, 125; warehouse and store at Mendota, 148, 202; store at St. Paul, 224; advance payment at Mendota Treaty of 1851, 209
Americans, Big Knives, 71
Anderson, Thomas, British captain, 70
Andreas' Atlas (1874), 80, 95
annuity system, 209, first Dakota annuities, 141; Treaty of 1837, 141; detrimental effect on Dakota Indians, 141-143; possibly increased tribal restlessness, 145; Gideon Pond castigates, 185; Treaty of 1851, 231
Anoka County, Minn., 140
Apple River, Wisconsin, 183
Arrow, Dakota chief, 81
arrowheads, found in mounds, 11
Articles of Confederation, government under, 59
artifacts, in mounds, 10, 11; scattered, 12
Astor, John J., founder of South West Company, 67
Atlantic coast, Siouan tribes on, 14
Azayamankawan, Berry Picker, Old Bets, Dakota woman, 227; see Old Bets

Backus, Captain, Fort Snelling commander, 187
Bad Hail, Wassonweechastishnee, Dakota brave and chief, 185 note; see Traveling Hail
Bad Ox River, 1830 Treaty boundary, 90
Bad People, Hayzatoton, Good Road's, 163 note, 188 note

Badger, Neekah, Dakota brave, 149, 150, 154
Bailly, Alexis, fur trader, 140, 211
baptism, 20, 110, 171; at Mankato in 1863, 237, 238
bark houses, 12, 57, 85, 124; size, 105, 119
Bassett's Creek, Minneapolis, 195
beads, in mounds, 11; as trade goods, 23, 47
beaver, fur bearer, grades of pelts, 24; robe, 19, 112
begging, from the military, 97; from early settlers, 177, 181, 217, 219; substituted for hunting and trapping, 142
Belle Plaine, Minn., 211
Beltrami, Giacomo Constantino, adventurer, 63
Benton County, Minn., 140
Berry Picker, Dakota woman, 227-229; see Old Bets
Bevans, C. D., St. Paul tin-smith, 181
Big Eagle I, Wamditanka, Dakota chief, see Black Dog
Big Eagle II, Grey Iron's son, Dakota chief, 98, 211, 214
Big Iron, Dakota brave, 125
Big Knives, Americans, 71
Big Marten, Chippewa chief, 43, 45
Big Stone Lake, Minn., 16
Big Thunder, Wakinyantanka, Dakota chief, 204; 1830 Treaty signer, 93; chief of Kaposia, 124-135; death, 135; at Washington, 140; makes son, His Red Nation, chief, 165-168; see also Little Crow IV
Big Woods, Minn., 207, 211
Birch Coulee, Minn., 240
Bishop, Harriet, St. Paul teacher, describes Kaposia, 173-175
Black Dog, Wamditanka, Big Eagle I, Dakota chief, possibly Killiew, the Eagle, mentioned by Pike, 56, 60, 72; early location, 78, 86; signed Treaty of 1830, 93; "selfe made" chief, 97; later location, 98; council with Schoolcraft, 99; death, 97
Black Dog Lake, Minn., 98
Black Dog's band, 185, 187, 232; early years, see Black Dog, Big Eagle I; go against Pokegama Chippewa, 129, 131; participate in land payment, 157; under Grey Iron, 189-193; under Big Eagle II, 98, 235
Black River, 1830 Treaty boundary, 90
Blacksmith, Joseph, Dakota brave, 185
blacksmiths, 79; government paid, 187; 1830 Treaty, 101; 1837 Treaty, 143
Black Soldier, Dakota brave, 60, 73; village, 64, 65

blankets, trade goods, 47
Blegen, Theodore C., historian, 27, 151
Bliss, John, Fort Snelling commander, 192
Bloomington Cemetery, 223
Bloomington, Minn., 221, 222, 232; site of Wabasha's band, 29, 47; site of Penasha's band, 94; site of Good Road's band, 106; site of Cloudman's and Drifter's band, 131, 160, 161, 202; home of "scattered Sioux," 240, 241
Blue Earth River, Minn., 13, 22
Bluestone, John, Dakota brave, 240
Bohanon, Charles, Minneapolis pioneer, 219
boundary of 1825, 90, 99
Brawley, St. Paul brick-maker, 180
Bremer, Fredrika, Swedish novelist, 182
brick, first in St. Paul, 180
British, 92, 139; Dakota side with, against Americans, 40; western action, Revolutionary War, 46-52; War of 1812, 67-73
Brooklyn Center, Minn., 217
Brower, Jacob, historian, 26
Brown, Joseph R., fur trader, 211
Brown, Mrs. John, Bloomington pioneer, 222
Bruce, Col. Amos J., Indian Agent, 157, 158, 159
Brunson, Rev. Alfred, missionary, 126, 127
buffalo, 15, 16, 107, 108, 211
burial, 38, 129, 146; grounds: Kaposia, 84, Lake Calhoun band, 104, Black Dog's band, 189
burial mounds, 9-11

cabin, Pond brothers', 105, 157
Cadotte, fur trader, 48
Cambridge, Minn., 131
Cameron, Duncan, fur trader, 66
Campbell, Scott, interpreter, 161
Camp Coldwater, Minn., 82, 160
Canada, 58
Canadians, 33, 35, 77; disliked by Wisconsin Indians, 24; traders at Prairie du Chien, 58, at Mackinac in 1812, 67; St. Paul settler, 133
cannon, 49
Cannon River, Minn., 60
Carolinas, 11

Caramaunee, Winnebago chief, 69
Carver, Jonathan, 9, 10, 27, 45, 85; visits Mdewakanton, 35-39; colonial plans, 46
Carver, Minn., 106, 160
Carver's Cave, 36, 37, 85
Carver's Grant, 38, 39
Cass Lake, Minn., 41
Cass, Lewis, Governor of Michigan Territory, 87; visits Leavenworth's encampment, 82; sends Schoolcraft to source of Mississippi, 99
cemetery, Indian, 84, 104, 189
Chetanwakamani, Walks Pursuing a Hawk, Dakota chief, 53, 85, 93, 165, see also Little Crow III
Cheyenne River, North Dakota, 107
Chicago, Illinois, 50
Chippewa County, Minn., 240
Chippewa River, Chippewa County, Minn., 146
Chippewa River, Wisconsin, 90, 139
Chisago County, Minn., 140
Christ, 232, 238
cists, burial, in mound, 11
Clark, Governor William, 78
classification of tribes, 14
Cloud, Dakota chief, 106
Cloudman, Marpiya wichasta, Dakota chief, 97, 149, 187, 191, 209, 214, 232; heads Lake Calhoun band, 101-103; sketch, 105-111; descendents, 111-113, 184; pacifist, 109, 155; leaves Calhoun site, 159; relocates at Bloomington, 160-163; leaves Bloomington, 202; visits Twin Cities area, 197; death, 237
Cloudman's band, 97, 99, 126, 146, 157; origin, 101-103; at Lake Calhoun, 104, 113-115, 116-123; at Pokegama battle, 128, 130-132; at massacre of Chippewa at Rum River, 152-155; locate at Bloomington, 157-163; last years in Twin Cities area, 185, 186, 195-197; at Redwood Agency, 209, 214; effect of missionary work at, 234, 238
Codah, 112
Coe, Rev. Alvin, missionary, 116
Columbia Fur Company, 98
Company of the Sioux, 24, 25
Congress, United States, 77, 201, 210
Connecticut, 103, 118

Cook, Mr., Kaposia teacher, 170
copper, 13, 20
corn, raised by Dakota, 58, 85, 96, 97, 100, 107, 109, 117, 125, 159, 161
Coues, Elliot, historian, 60
council, 166, 176; yearly, according to Carver, 38; called by British, 45, 53; Pike calls, 61, 64; Leavenworth, Cass call, 82; Prairie du Chien, 1825, 89; see also Treaties
"courers de bois," illegal fur traders, 17, 23
Credit River, Minn., 157-159
Crow's Creek, Minn., 214
Crow Wing area, 147
Crow Wing, Battle of, 41-43
Crow Wing County, Minn., 140
cultivation of land, 12, 87, 96, 100, 109, 124, 143, 171, 189, 231
Culver, George, St. Paul resident 211
curiosity of Dakota, 179

Dakota Presbytery, 123
Dakota Territory, 237, 239
Daniels, Dr. Asa W., government physician, 53, 55, 164, 210
dates, preservation of, 7
Davenport, Iowa, 237
Dayton's Bluff, St. Paul, 10, 80, 85
DeBow, Jane, pioneer, i, 116, 120, 153, 154, 215
Delap, Hiram, lay missionary, 127
Demi Douzain, Le, 61; see Shakopee, Dakota chief
De Peyster, Arent, commander at Mackinac, 48
Description de la Louisiane, Hennepin, 13
Detroit, Michigan, 45, 48
Dickson, Robert, fur trader, 58, 65; leads Dakota in War of 1812, 66-69
Dodge, Henry, Governor of Wisconsin Territory, 140
Doty, James D., Governor of Wisconsin Territory, 198
Doty Treaties, 1841, 198-199
Dow, D. E., Minneapolis pioneer, 159, 216
Drifter, Kaboka, Karboka, Dakota chief, 99, 115, 163, 185; death, 128; heads own band, 160, 161
Drummond's Island, 71
drunkenness, see liquor
Du Luth, Daniel Greysolon, Sieur, 17, 18

Dunsmoor, Irving A., Richfield pioneer, 217

Eagle, Dakota brave, or Chief Big Eagle I, 211
Eagle, Killiew, Dakota chief mentioned by Pike, 56, 60, 72; see Black Dog
Eagle Help, Dakota medicine man, 106, 110
earthen homes, prehistoric Dakota, 9, 12, 26; Siouan, 14
East Seventh Street, St. Paul, 81
Eastman, Charles A., Dakota lawyer, 113
Eastman, Mary, 188-195
Eastman, Mary Nancy, 111-113
Eastman, Captain Seth, Fort Snelling commander, 111, 189, 191
Eaton, John H., Secretary of War, 103
Eatonville, 103, 116, 158, see Cloudman's band, Lake Calhoun site
education funds, Treaty of 1837, 203, 209
Elk River, Battles of, 43-45
Elk River, Minn., 43, 45; Carver's "River St. Francis," 35, 36
English, 31, 33, 77, see British; language, 126, 170; trade goods, 24
Eshnmanne, Dakota chief, 169
European contact, early, 23
excavations, 12
exploration, 10, 14, 15, 84

Falcon Heights, Minn., ii
farmers, government, 122, 123, 127, 146, 213
Faribault, Alexander, fur trader, 140, 211
Faribault, Minn., 239, 240
Farrington, John, 211
Fears Nothing, (What is He Afraid Of), Dakota chief, 63; see Penasha III
Fillmore, President Millard, 201
Fils de Pinichon, Le, 61, Penasha II
fire-canoe, steamboat, 180
Fischer, Abbie Gibbs, pioneer, iii
Flandreau, South Dakota, 150, 185
Flat Mouth, Chippewa chief, 87
Folsom, W. H. C., historian, 179, 229
Folwell, William W., historian, 26, 36, 37, 58
Fond du Lac, Minn., 99
Forbes, W. H., fur trader, 211, 224
Forsyth, Thomas, Indian agent, 65, 78-79, 83, 95

Index   275

Fort Beauharnois, 24
Fort Detroit, 45, 48
Fort L'Huillier, 13, 22, 23
Fort Meigs, 68
Fort Ridgely, 55
Fort Shelby, 69, 70
Fort Snelling, (Fort St. Anthony), 35, 56, 96, 98, 100, 134, 139, 160, 164, 166, 171, 186-189, 239; Dakota agency, 87, 91; Treaties at, 99; missionaries arrive at, 103, 104, 116, 119, 125; Dakota prisoners at, 110, 237; Taliaferro's map, 113; Indian warfare at, 145, 147-149; clearing the reserve, 157; troops used to punish Indians, 145, 213, 225
Fort Stephenson, 68
Fourth Street, Minneapolis, 195, 219
Fourth Street, St. Paul, 180
Fox Indians, 23, 24, 33, 48, 49, 51, 52, 89, 92
Franklin Avenue, St. Paul, 181
French, 30, 50; explorers and exploration, 10, 15; fur trade and traders, 17, 18, 22, 33; power declines, 31
French and Indian War, 31, 59
Freniere, Francis, interpreter, 70
Frontenac, Louis de Baude, Comte de, 19
Fuller, Mr., St. Paul merchant, 179
fur trade and traders, 57, 141; French, 13, 14-17, 22-25, 32; Spanish, 59; British, 24, 45, 58, 59, 66, 77; American, 59, 66, 77, 87, 91, 125, 140, 211; in Revolutionary War, 49-52; in War of 1812, 67-70

Gammel, Francois, early settler, 133
Gautier, Charles, fur trader, 47, 48
Gear, Rev. E. G., Fort Snelling chaplain, 148, 155
Gens des Feuilles, Wapeton Dakota, 64
Gens du Lac, Mdewakanton Dakota, 64
Gibbs Farm Museum, Falcon Heights, Minn., ii
Gibbs, Heman Rice, early settler, ii
Gibbs, Mrs. H. R. (Jane DeBow), i, 116, 120, 153, 154, 215
God, 185, 186, 191, 192, 233
God's House, 189
Goodhue, James M., St. Paul editor, 180
Good Road, Tucanwashtay, Dakota chief, 106, 156, 163, 196, 202; lineage, 35, 187; made chief, 97; Treaty of 1837 signer, 141;

Treaty of 1851 signer, 209; location at Redwood agency, 214; visits Twin Cities area after 1852, 197
Good Road's band, 106, 193-196; goes against Pokegama Chippewa, 129, 131; location, 160; Bad People, 163 note, 188 note; at Lake Calhoun, 105; see also Penasha's band
Gorman, Willis A., Governor of Minnesota Territory, 210
Gorrell, James, British commander at Green Bay, 33
Gospel, 118, 120, 233, 239
Grand Marais, Pig's Eye Lake, Minn., 78, 80
Great Britain, 67, 71
Great Father, President, 203
Great Lakes, 22, 32
Great Northern Depot, Minneapolis, 196
Great Outbreak, 215, see Outbreak of 1862
Great Plains, 15
Great Spirit, 107, 112, 166, 180
Great Uprising, see Outbreak of 1862
Great War Eagle I, Dakota chief; see Black Dog
Great War Eagle II, Dakota chief, 98, 211, 214
Green Bay, Wisconsin, 33
Green, David, Secretary of American Board, 117
Groseilliers, Medard Chouart, Sieur des, 17, 18
Gross, William H., archeologist, 11
Grey Cloud Island, Washington County, Minn., 240, 241
Grey Eagle, Dakota chief, 196, (Grey Iron or Big Eagle II?)
Grey Iron, Mazarota, Dakota chief, 56, 98, 163, 189, 192; becomes chief, 97; 1837 Treaty signer, 141; moves to Redwood agency, 202; 1851 Treaty signer, 209
Grey Iron's band, 189-193, 214; see also Black Dog's band
Gulf of Mexico, 22
Gull Lake, Minn., 41, 146
gunpowder, 9, 26

Hastings, Minn., 240
Hayzatoton, Bad People, Good Road's, 163 note, 188 note
Heindakoo, Dakota brave, 227
Hennepin County, Minn., 161
Hennepin, Father Louis, French explorer, 13
Hesse, fur trader, 49
He Sees Standing Up, Wayagoenagee, Dakota chief, 63; see Penasha II

Index 277

He That Flies, Kee-e-hie, Dakota chief, 100, 101
Hicks, Rev. Marcus, Mankato pastor, 238
hieroglyphics, Carver's Cave, 38; Chippewa pictograph, 82
Hinman, Rev. Samuel D., missionary, 239
His Red Nation, Taoyateduta, Dakota chief, 142, 182; becomes chief of Kaposia, 135, 165-169; Treaty of 1851 signer, 208; see also Little Crow V
Hockakaduta, Red Middle Voice, Dakota sub-chief, 142
Hokan-Siouan Stock, 14
Holcombe, R. I., historian, 106, 111, 167, 214
Hole-in-the-Day, Chippewa chief, 156, 182; visits Fort Snelling, 146, 147; band massacred at Rum River, 152; visits St. Anthony, 196
Holy Light, Waukan-ojan-jan, Dakota chief, 124, see Medicine bottle
Hopkins, Chester L., Hopkins pioneer, 219
Hopkins, Minn., 217, 219
Hopkins, Miss Florinda, Hopkins pioneer, 217
Hudson Bay, 24
Hughes, Thomas, historian, 106
Hupachokanaza, Middle Iron Wing, Dakota brave, 149
Hushes the Night, Cloudman's daughter, 184

Illinois River, 31, 49
inconsistency of Dakota, 193
Indian Mounds Park, St. Paul, 9, 10, 80, 81, 85
Inland Village, i, 103, 156, 187, see Cloudman's band
intoxication, see liquor
intermarriage between Dakota and Chippewa, 20
inter-tribal trade, 24
Ite-Wahanhdi-Ota, Many Lightnings, Dakota brave, 112
Iowa, 199, 201, 237
Iowa, Indians, 9, 13, 14, 89
Iowa River, 90
Iron Sword, Dakota brave, 227
iron tools, 13, 22; see blacksmiths
Iroquois Indians, 14, 17, 18
Isanti County, Minn., 140
Isanti people, (Santee Dakota), 27
Ixatapa, Dakota brave, 33

Jackson Street, St. Paul, 224
Joseph, Story of, translated by Samuel Pond, 118
Jug, Dakota chief, 214; see Medicine Bottle

Kaboka, Dakota chief, see Drifter
Kah-hah-ton-wan, Chippewas, 150
Kanabec County, Minn., 140
Kapoja, 85, see Kaposia
Kaposia, Little Crow's band, i, 163, 208, 210, 240; at Grand Marais, 80; at downtown St. Paul, 55, 84-86, 93; at South St. Paul, 12, 124-129, 165-183; attacked by Chippewa, 1842, 132-135, 1853, 223; location at Redwood agency, 214
Kapozha, 80, 240, see Kaposia
Karboka, Dakota chief; see Drifter
Karboka's band, 160, 161
Kaskaskia, Illinois, 49
Kathio, Battle of, 27
Keating, William H., 84, 95, 98
Kee-e-hie, He That Flies, Dakota chief, 100, 101
Kellogg Boulevard, St. Paul, 81
Kellogg, Louise P., historian, 46
Keoka, Wabasha's village, (Kiyuksa), Winona, Minn., 51
Khadayah, Rattler, Dakota brave, 133
Killiew, Eagle, Dakota chief, 50, 60, 72; see Black Dog
King, David, Kaposia teacher, 127
King George III, British monarch, 46
Knife River, Minn., 131
"kosh-poppy," money, 227

Lac qui Parle, Minn., 160, 165, 171, 184; mission at, 118, 119, 122, 123, 233; Chippewa murder Dakota at, 1838, 145-147; Little Crow V at, 169, 208
la crosse, Indian game, 80, 175
Lake Calhoun, Minn., 97, 187, 213, 214; Prescott at, 101; Cloudman's village, 103-123; Pond brothers, 126; removal of Dakota, 157, 184
Lake Calhoun band, 157; see Cloudman's band
Lake Erie, 68
Lake Harriet, Minn., i, 149, 153-155; mission at, 116-123, 159
Lake of the Loons, Lake Calhoun, Minn., 159
Lake Pepin, 17, 24, 31, 35, 36, 51, 56

Lake Pokegama, 128, 131
Lake St. Croix, 21, 132, 152
Lake Superior, 18, 21, 51, 52, 83
Lake Traverse, Minn., 107, 202
Lakewood Cemetery, Minneapolis, 104
Lakota, Teton Dakota, 15
Lamont, Daniel, fur trader, 184
language, Dakota, 37; English, 126, 170
La Pointe, Wisconsin, 148
La Prairie du Francois, Shakopee, Minn., 60
Larpenteur, A. L., St. Paul pioneer, 229
Lea, Luke, treaty commissioner, 201-209
Leavenworth, Colonel Henry, 78, 81, 95, 106; concludes treaty of peace between Dakota and Chippewa, 82, 87
Le Boef-qui-Marche, Red Wing, Dakota chief, 61
Le Boucasse, Wahkantahpay, Dakota chief, 61
Le Demi Douzain, Shakopee, Dakota chief, 61
Le Duc, William G., early settler, 208
Leech Lake, Minn., 41, 147
Le Fils de Pinichon, the son of Penasha, Dakota chief, 61
Le Grande Partisan, a principal soldier, Dakota brave, 61
L'Original Leve, Tamaha, Rising Moose, Dakota brave, 61
Le Petit Corbeau, Little Crow, Dakota chief, 61, 70, 82, 84; see also Little Crow III
Le Sueur, Pierre Charles, fur trader, 13, 14, 18, 19, 22, 25, 27, 29
Lewis, Theodore H., archeologist, 11, 12
Lincoln, President Abraham, 237
liquor, 77, 91, 110, 134, 167, 209; favorite trade article, 23, 47, 66; distributed by Pike, 63, refused, 64; and Rum River, 96; and the annuity system, 142, 143; illicit traffic in, 159; in early St. Paul, 173, 176
Little Beckoning Boy, Dakota brave, ii
Little Crow I, 53
Little Crow II, 37, 43, 45, 53
Little Crow III, Chetanwakamani, Walks Pursuing a Hawk, at Washington, D.C., 1824, 39, 88, 89; lineage, 53; becomes chief, 25; residence near St. Paul, 55, 56, 124; treaties with Pike, 60, 61, 63; War of 1812, 66, 68; visited by Forsyth, 78, 79, 83; described by Schoolcraft, 82; Treaty of Prairie du Chien, 1830, 89, 93; opinion of Taliaferro, 91, 92; death, 124; name used by grandson, Little Crow V, 165

280   From Whole Log to No Log

Little Crow IV, Wakinyantanka, Big Thunder, 12, 157, 204; Treaty of 1830 signer, 93; made chief of Kaposia, 124, 126; described, 125, 126; Kaposia under, 125-135; Treaty of 1837 signer, 140, 141; Lake St. Croix Massacre, 151, 152, 155; death, 135, 165-168
Little Crow V, Taoyateduta, His Red Nation, 126, 142, 196, 202, 223, 229; lineage, 53; war record, 128, 182, 207; becomes chief of Kaposia, 165-169, invites missionary to Kaposia, 169, 170; at Treaty of 1851, 204-209, leads Dakota in Outbreak of 1862, 235
Little Falls, Minnehaha Falls, 104, 151, 188
Little Rapids, Minn., 37
Little Raven, Petit Corbeau, Little Crow III, 84
Little River, Minnehaha Creek, 104
Little Rock Creek, Minn., 55
Long Avenue Village, Oanoska, i, 97, 163, 187; significance of name, 94, 95; see also Good Road's band and Penasha's band
Longfellow, Colonel Levi, Brooklyn Center pioneer, 217
Long Lake, Bloomington, 95
Long, Major Stephen H., 53, 63; 1817 expedition, 78; 1823 expedition, 84-86, 95, 98, 161
Loomis, Major Gustavus, Fort Snelling commander, 186
Louisiana, 24, 48, 59
Lower Agency, 214, see Redwood agency
Lower bands, 201, 209
Lynd, James W., historian, 28
"Lynx," steamboat, 173

Mackinac, 34, 46; fur trade center, 65-67; peace council at, 45, 46; Revolutionary War era, 48-51; War of 1812, 67-69; Chippewa agency, 146
Magayutashnee, Black Dog's village, 98, 163
Maiden Rock, Wisconsin, 240
maize, see corn
Mallard Duck, Pagonta, fur trader, 23
Mankato, Dakota chief, 214
Mankato, Minn., 13, 22, 118, 208, 237, 238, 239
Mantanton, early Dakota division, 13, 17-22, 29, 37
Man-who-floats-on-the-water, Dakota chief, 99, see Drifter
Many Lightnings, Ite Wahanhdi-Ota, Dakota brave, 112, 113
Marpiya-wichasta, Dakota chief, 101, 109, 111; see Cloudman

Marin, Joseph, fur trader, 31
marten, fur bearer, 24
Marten, Big, Chippewa chief; see Big Marten
Martin, Louis, fur trader, 171
Matchekewis, Chippewa chief, 49
Mawtawbauntowahs, Mantanton Dakota, 36, 37
Mayer, F. B., artist, 165
Mazakutamane, Paul, Dakota brave, 106, 110, 233, 234
Mazarota, Dakota chief, 97, 163; see Grey Iron
McDonnell, Colonel, 71
McDouall, Robert, 69
McGruder, Captain, 213
McKay, William, fur trader, 69
McLean, Major Nathaniel, Indian agent, 196
McMullen, James, St. Paul settler, 176
medals, trade, 32, 60
medicine bag, 54, 55
Medicine Bottle, Waukan-ojan-jan, Dakota chief, 141, 182; Kaposia brave, 124; at Pine Bend, Minn., 163, 164; 1851 Treaty signer, 207, 208; at Redwood agency
medicine lodge, 55
medicine men, 39, 110, 115, 124, 150, 194, 227
Menchokatonx, Mdewakanton, 13
Mendota, Minn., 86, 98, 106, 123, 159, 184, 189, 227; early fur trading center, 32; American Fur Company headquarters, 133, 202; Treaty of 1851, 201-203; some Dakota remain at, 229, 239, 240, 241
Mendota, Treaty of, see Treaty of 1851
Menominee Indians, Wisconsin, 33, 49, 52, 67, 69, 89
Methodist-Episcopal Church, 126
Methodist Mission at Kaposia, 126-128
Meyer, Roy W., historian, 230, 235
Michigan Territory, 67, 82
Michilimackinac Company, 65, 67
Middle Iron Wing, Hupachokanaza, Dakota brave, 149; see Badger
migration, Chippewa, 16; Dakota, 25, 57, 210
Mille Lacs, Battle of, 25-27
Mille Lacs County, Minn., 140
Mille Lacs Lake, 9, 11, 16, 40, 131; center of Dakota life, 15, 17, 30; Dakota driven from, 25-27, 29, 57; Chippewa center, 98, 152

military posts, 60, 78, 157; see also Forts
mink, fur bearer, 24
Minnehaha Creek, Minneapolis, 104
Minnehaha Falls, Minneapolis, 151, 189
Minnehaha Park, Minneapolis, 196
Minnesota Outfit, America Fur Company, 224
Minnesota Territory, 201
Minnewakan, 176, see liquor
missionaries, i, 7, 27, 141, 231-234; Presbyterian-Congregational, see American Board of Commissioners for Foreign Missions; Methodist, see Methodist Mission at Kaposia
Mission House at Lake Harriet, i, 117, 120, 123, 149, 159
Missouri River, 15, 73, 108, 237
Mohawk Indians, 35
Monroe, President James, 39, 88
Montreal, 18, 19, 29, 31, 47, 65
Mooers, Hazen, fur trader, 171
Morgan's Bluff, Minn., 189
Mound Builders, 9
mounds, 7; burial, 9-11; habitation remains, 12
Mounds Park, St. Paul, 9, 10, 80, 85
mourning customs, 96
Mud Creek, Minn., 55
Murphy, Robert G., Indian agent, 172, 196, 231
My Head Aches, Pamayayaw, Dakota chief, 97; see Grey Iron
Myrick, Nathan, 211
Mystery Lake, Mille Lacs, 15

Nadouessioux, Dakota Indians, 13, 15
Napayshneeduta, Joseph, Dakota brave, 171-173
Napoleon, 59
National Popular Education Society, 173
Naudowessie, Dakota Indians, 10, 15, 38
Neekah, Badger, Dakota brave, 149, 150, 154
Nehogatowonas, 36, 37
Neill, Edward D., historian, 10, 31, 180
neutral belt, 92, see Treaty of 1830, Prairie du Chien
Newport, Minn., 229
New Ulm, Minn., 36, 53, 208
New York, i
Nine Mile Creek, Bloomington, Minn., 29, 56, 60, 94, 106, 160

Noka, Chippewa chief, 43
North Dakota, 184
Northwest Company, 58, 65

Oak Grove, Bloomington, Minn., 106, 110, 111, 131, 184, 186, 197, 202
Oanoska, Dakota village, i, 94; see Long Avenue Village
Ohio River, 14, 46, 88
Ohiyesa, Charles A. Eastman, 113
Old Bets, Dakota woman, 224, 227-229, 239
Old Eve, Cloudman's mother, 106
oratory, 105
Original Leve L', Tamaha, Dakota brave, 61
ornaments, 11, 119, 129, 147, 181, 182, 204
Ottowa Indians, 31, 47, 49, 89
Oto Indians, 13, 14
otter, fur bearer, 24
Ouacantapai, Wakantape, Dakota chief, 22, 29, 30
Outard Blanche, White Bustard, Dakota chief, 56, 60, 65
Outbreak of 1862, 28, 142, 215, 227, 229, 233, 235, 239
Owaw Hoska, 94, 95; see Long Avenue Village

Pacific Coast, 35
Pagonta, Mallard Duck, fur trader, 32
Pamayayaw, My Head Aches, Dakota chief, 97; see Grey Iron
Panishihowa, Dakota chief, 63; see Penasha
Parrant, Pierre, St. Paul settler, 80
Passing Hail, Dakota chief, 214; see Traveling Hail
Pavillion, steamboat, 140
peace treaties, 18, 52, 73, 82, 87, 89, 90
Peg Leg Jim, Dakota brave, 224, 227
Penasha I, French fur trader, 33, 34, 94
Penasha II, Wayagoenagee, He Sees Standing Up, 53, 56; lineage, 34, 35; treaties with Pike, 60, 61, 63; in War of 1812, 66, 72
Penasha III, Takopepeshene, Fears Nothing, 86, 87, 101, 105, 187; visited by Long in 1817, 79; by Forsyth and Leavenworth in 1819, 81; 1830 Treaty signer, 93; anecdotes of, by William J. Snelling, 95-97; death, 97
Penasha's band, 146, 157, 187
Pennsylvania, 201

Perrot, Nicolas, 13, 17, 18
Peters, Rev. Samuel, 39
Petit Corbeau, Dakota chief, 61, 70, 82, 84; see Little Crow III
Pettit, Mrs. C. H., Minneapolis pioneer, 219
Phalen Creek, Ramsey County, Minn., 60, 65, 81, 86
pictographs, Indian writing, 82
Pig's Eye Lake, Minn., 56, 60, 132, 133, 173
Pike Island, 61, 81, 189
Pike Treaty, 63, 78
Pike, Zebulon M., army officer, 35, 40, 56, 86; ascends Mississippi River, 60; treaties with local Dakota, 61-65
Pillagers, Chippewa band, 149, 151, 156
Pilot Knob, Minneapolis, 189, 192, 203
Pinchon, Dakota chief, 63, 81; see Penasha
Pine Bend, Minn., 163, 164
Pine Coulie, St. Paul, 133, 134
Pine County, Minn., 140
Pioneer, St. Paul newspaper, 179, 180
Pioneer Press, St. Paul newspaper, 229
pipestone, 181
Pittsburgh Conference, Methodist Church, 126
Pittsburgh, Pennsylvania, 88
Plympton, Major Joseph, Fort Snelling commander, 146, 147, 157, 158, 160
Point Prescott, Battle of, 20, 26
Pokegama, Battle of, 129-132
Pond, Rev. Gideon H., missionary, 57, 107, 110, 145, 153; arrives at Fort Snelling, 103; describes Cloudman's village, 104; at Lake Harriet Mission, 117; at Kaposia, 124, 125; writes Dakota spelling book, 121; at Lac qui Parle Mission, 118, 122, 208; government farmer at Lake Calhoun, 123; at Oak Grove (Bloomington), 159, 161, 184, 186, 187, 214, 232; at Mankato prison, 237
Pond, Peter, fur trader, 45
Pond, Rev. Samuel W., missionary, 7, 28, 95, 98, 108, 109, 113, 126, 142, 145, 171, 186, 187, 238; arrives at Fort Snelling, 103; at Lake Harriet Mission, 117, 122; on Indian hunt, 117; in Connecticut studying theology, 118, 121; wrote Story of Joseph, 118; at Kaposia, 124, 125; witnesses killing of Badger, 150; supplies at Lac qui Parle Mission, 160, resides at Prairieville, (Shakopee), 184, 214, 232

Pope, Rev. Thomas W., missionary, 127
population, Mdewakanton, i, 105
Portage des Sioux, Missouri, 73
pottery, 11, 13
Prairie du Chien, 60, 64, 78, 86, 88; during War of 1812, 67-70; 1786 peace council at, 52, 53; British era, 45, 48-51, 58; 1825 Treaty at, 89, 90; 1830 Treaty at, 35, 92, 93, 97, 99
Prairie Island, Minn., 18, 240
Prairie Sioux, 16, 36
Prairieville, Shakopee, Minn., 184
prehistoric Indians, 12
Presbyterian Missions, see American Board
Prescott, Philander, fur trader, 100-103, 120, 122, 211
Prior Lake, Minn., 240
Proclamation of 1763, 46
Protestant missions, see denomination
pumpkins, 57, 85, 97, 100

Quane, Jerry, soldier, 53
Quebec Act, 46
Quebec, Canada, 32, 46, 48
Quinn, Patrick, government farmer, 146, 147

Radisson, Pierre Esprit, 17, 53
Ramsey County, Minn., 140
Ramsey County Historical Society, ii
Ramsey, Governor Alexander, 176, 201-209, 225
Rattler, Khadayah, Dakota brave, 133
Rattling Moccasin, Kaposia brave, 209
Rattling Runner, Kaposia brave, 209
Red Bird, Dakota war chief, medicine man, 115, 150, 152, 155, 232
Red Boy, Dakota brave, 186
Red Cedar Lake, Minn., 152
Red Eagle, Dakota chief, 81
Red Iron, Dakota brave, 211
Red Lake, Minn., 15
Red Man Who Fears Nothing, Napayshneeduta, Dakota brave, 171-173
Red Middle Voice, Hockakaduta, Dakota sub-chief, 142
Red River, Minn., 202
Red Rock, Minn., 84

Red Wing, Dakota chief, 37, 45, 51, 53, 56, 61, 72
Red Wing, Minn., 140, 214, 240
Redwood agency 55, 164, 197, 214, 215, 227, 231, 232
Redwood, Minn., 240
Redwood River, Minn., 214
Renville, Joseph, fur trader, 70, 170
Revolutionary War, 39, 46-51, 56
Reyataotonwe, Inland Village, i, 103, 105; see Cloudman's band
rice, 58
Rice and Irvine's addition, St. Paul, 181
Rice, Henry M., St. Paul pioneer, 211
Rice Lake, Minn., 152
Richfield, Minn., 217
Riggs, Mary, missionary, 119
Riggs, Rev. Stephen R., missionary, 118, 119, 208, 232
Rising Moose, Tamaha, Dakota brave, 61
River Bands, 36, 45
"road of war," 11
Robertson, A., missionary, 127
Robert Street, St. Paul, 179
Robinson, Doane, historian, 30, 42, 55, 56, 235
Rock Creek, Minn., 55, 206, 207, 208
Rock Island, Illinois, 185
Rock Rapids, on the Mississippi, 70
Rose Township, Ramsey County, Minn., ii, 215
rum, 96, see liquor
Rum River, Minn., 25, 27, 57, 96, 152, 156
Running Walker, Dakota chief, 106 note
Rush City, Minn., 131

Sac Indians, 33, 48-50, 51, 52, 70, 89, 92
St. Anthony Falls, 11, 16, 36, 37, 42, 47. 60, 61, 63, 78, 88, 116, 152, 186, 192, 196, 215
St. Anthony, Minn., 216, 217
St. Croix Chippewa, 151
St. Croix Falls, Battle of, 51, 52
St. Croix Falls, Wisconsin, 128, 131, 223, 225
St. Croix River, 13, 20, 27, 35, 36, 47, 51, 52, 56, 61, 63, 128, 131, 132, 133, 147, 148, 151, 182, 223
St. Francis River, Elk River, Minn., 35, 36
St. Lawrence River, 18

St. Louis, Missouri, 48, 49, 50, 59, 64, 66, 70, 78, 180
St. Paul's Landing, Minn., 173
St. Peter Minn., 45, 208, 240
St. Peters River, Minnesota River, 13, 47, 60, 64, 79, 95, 161
Ste. Genevieve, 49
Sandy Lake, Minn., 51, 98
Santee Reservation, 239, 240
Santee Sioux, 15, 27
Sapir, Edward, 14
Saulteur, Chippewa, 18, 19, 64
Sault Ste. Marie, 18, 99
Sauk Indians, see Sac Indians
Savage, Minn., 157
scaffold burials, 10, 84
"Scattered Sioux," 239
schools, 118, 120, 121, 127, 131, 169, 173
Schoolcraft, Henry R., Indian agent, 29, 30, 82, 89, 99, 146
Second Company of the Sioux, 25
sepulture, burial, 10, 84
Shakopee, Dakota chief, 37, 43, 45, 53, 56, 60, 78, 79, 81, 86, 90, 95, 156, 184, 196, 214
Shakopee, Minn., 37, 43, 60, 184, 185, 217, 223, 231, 232, 240
Shashweentowahs, 36, 37
shells, in mounds, 11
Sherburne County, Minn., 140
Sibley, Henry H., fur trader, 63, 120, 125, 128, 140, 141, 143, 166, 167, 211, 237
Siouan tribes, 14, 15
Sioux of the East, 13
Sioux of the West, 13
Sioux Outbreak, 28, see Outbreak of 1862
Sisseton Dakota, 15, 64, 106, 169, 201, 202
skeletons, in mounds, 11
Slade, Governor of Vermont, 173
smallpox, 32
Snake River, Minn., 51, 131
Snelling, Colonel Josiah, Fort Snelling Commander, 96, 145
Snelling, Wiliam Joseph, author, 34, 94, 193
soldiers, 28, 88, 91, 101, 106, 157, 158, 207, 225
South St. Paul, Minn., 12, 80, 124, 141, 163, 223, 229
South Dakota, 15

South Dakota Historical Society, 71
South West Company, 67
Spanish, 47, 50, 58, 59
spelling book, Dakota, 121
Spicer, Mr., St. Paul merchant, 179
Spirit Light, Medicine Bottle, Dakota chief, 124
Spring Lake, Minn., 163
Stands Like a Spirit, Cloudman's daughter, 111, 191
starvation, 32, 67, 107, 120
Steele, Franklin, early settler, 211
Stees, Mrs., St. Paul pioneer, 177, 179
Stevens, Cornelia, teacher, 153
Stevens, Dwight, 116, 119, 154
Stevens, Evert, 116, 119, 154
Stevens, Jedediah D., missionary, i, 116, 117, 120, 122, 151
Stevens, John H., Minneapolis pioneer, 106, 186, 195, 215
Stillwater, Minn., 134, 152
Stratton, Mrs. Carrie, Minneapolis pioneer, 219
strawberries, ii, 120
Strong Ground, Chippewa chief, 148
Swan Lake, Minn., 207
Swan River, Minn., 146

Takopepeshene, Fears Nothing, Dakota chief, 63, see Penasha III
Taliaferro, Major Lawrence, 96, 120, 122, 125, 126; appointed agent, 87; diary quoted, 97, 103, 151, 156, 158; at council of 1823, 87, 88; takes Dakota to Washington, 89; Treaty of Prairie du Chien, 1825, 89, 90; Treaty of 1830, 92, 93; Treaty of 1837, 139, 140-143; promotes farming among Dakota, 100-103, Eatonville, 103, 116, 158; appoints Cloudman chief, 108; retires, 158
Tamaha, Rising Moose, Dakota brave, 61
Taopi, Dakota brave, 227, 239
Tatemine, Dakota brave, 146
Taylor, Major Zachary, 70
Tayoyateduta, His Red Nation, Dakota chief, 135, 167, 208; see Little Crow V
tepees, 119, 146, 189, 217, 240
Tetankatane, Old Village, 98, 163; see Black Dog's band
Teton Dakota, 15
theft, 179
Thin Face, Dakota brave, 140

Thompson, Jim, interpreter, 127
tin shop, St. Paul, 181
Tioscaté, Mantanton chief, 19, 29, 30
Titus, Star, Dakota brave, 184
Toledo, Ohio, 68
Tomah, Menominee chief, 69
totem, 54, 55
Tracy, Minn., 184
trade goods, 10, 16, 100, 177
trading houses, 60, 77
tradition, 27, 29
Traverse de Sioux, Minn., 106, 122, 198, 201, 202, 207, 240
Traveling Hail, Dakota brave, chief, 131, 185, 209, 214, 232
Treaty of 1783, United States-Great Britain, 59
Treaties, Mdewakanton,
   1805 at Pike Island, 63, 78
   1816 at Portage des Sioux, 73, 209
   1825 at Prairie du Chien, 35, 89, 98
   1830 at Prairie du Chien, 92, 101, 103, 139, 198
   1837 at Washington, 122, 139-143, 145, 147, 163, 198, 203
   1841 at Mendota, Doty Treaty, unratified, 198, 199
   1851 at Mendota, 106, 163, 201-209, 210, 214, 216, 231
   1858 at Washington, 165, 209
Tucanwashtay, Good Road, Dakota chief, 97; see Good Road
Turner, George F., Fort Snelling surgeon, 135
turnips, 121

Union Depot, Minneapolis, 195
United States, 58, 59, 183; British relations, 1780's, 50, 59; 1805, 59; 1812, 63-73, 77; Indian relations, see Treaties, Mdewakanton
U. S. Army, 40
U. S. Cavalry, 15
U. S. Infantry, 188
U. S. Senate, 198; see also Congress
Upham, Warren, historian, 85
Unkta-he, god of waters, 189
Upper bands, 202, 232
Upper Iowa River, 35, 51, 60
Uprising, see Outbreak of 1862

village sites, 40, 57, 206; ancient, 7, 11; Mantanton, 13, 19; Mde-

wakanton, 13, 19, 37, 56, 60, 202; Mille Lacs vacated by Dakota, 25; Wabasha I, 29; Kaposia, 55, 163; Black Dog, 98; Cloudman, 104, 160; Redwood agency, 214
Virginia, 14

Wabasha, Dakota chief, Wabasha I, 29, 45; visits Montreal, 30, Quebec, 31; resides at mouth of Nine Mile Creek, Bloomington, 34, 47; in Revolutionary War, 48-50; in War of 1812, 66, 68, 71, 72; at Upper Iowa River, 35, 56; at Winona, Minn., 51, 53; Later Wabashas, 88, 123, 140, 163, 211, 214; Treaty of 1851, 203, 208
Wabasha, Minn., 239, 240
Wacoota, Wacoute, Dakota chief, 104, 214; see also Red Wing
Wahkantahpay, Dakota chief, 61
Wahpekute Dakota, 15, 61, 202, 215
Wahpeton Dakota, 15, 25, 37, 45, 64, 106, 112, 160, 169, 201, 202, 232
Wakantape, Mantanton chief, 22, 29, 30
Wakinyatanka, Big Thunder, Dakota chief, 93, see Little Crow IV
Wakon-teebe, wakan tepee, 37; see Carver's Cave
Walker-in-the-Pines, Henry H. Sibley, 63
Wamditanka, Big Eagle, 97; see Black Dog
wampum, 33, 128
warfare necessary, 83
War of 1812, 58, 66-73, 77, 92, 209
Warren, William, historian, 20, 25, 26, 27
Washburn Park, Richfield, 217
Washington County, Minn., 140, 240
Washington, D. C., 39, 88, 140, 141, 201, 203, 207
Washington Street, St. Paul, 181
Wassonweechastishnee, Dakota brave, 185; see Traveling Hail
Watson, David, Dakota brave, 150
Waukon-ojan-jan, Dakota chief, 124; see Medicine Bottle
Wayagoenagee, He Sees Standing Up, Dakota chief, 63, see Penasha II
West St. Paul, Minn., 240
Whallon, Mr., Bloomington pioneer, 221
What is He Afraid Of, Fears Nothing, Takopepeshene, Dakota chief, 63; see Penasha III
whiskey, see liquor
White Bustard, Outard Blanche, Dakota chief, 56, 65, 72, 79, 81

White Fisher, Chippewa chief, 51
White Turkey, Dakota chief, 65; see Outard Blanche
Whitford, Rev. James G., missionary, 127
Wilkinson, General James, St. Louis commander, 59
Williams, J. Fletcher, historian, 223
Williamson, Jane, missionary, teacher, 170, 173, 222
Williamson, Dr. Thomas, missionary, 12, 165, 169-171, 208
Willmar, Minn., 16
Winchell, Newton H., historian, 37
Winnebago Indians, 33, 36, 47, 49, 67, 69, 89
Winnibigoshish Lake, Minn., 41
Winona, Minn., 51, 123, 140, 163
Wisconsin, 18, 24, 46, 47, 51, 58, 92, 116, 139, 182, 239
Wisconsin River, 31, 53
Wisconsin Territory 198
Wooden-legged Jim, Dakota brave, 224, 227
Woodland cultural era, 10
Word, 120, see Gospel

Yellow Medicine River, 55, 202, 206, 214, 232
Yankton Dakota Indians, 15
Yanktonai Dakota Indians, 15